A Collection Of
Old English Plays, Vol. IV.

Editor: A.H. Bullen

Contents

PREFACE. 7
INTRODUCTION TO TWO TRAGEDIES IN ONE. 9
Two Lamentable Tragedies. 11
Two Tragedies in One. 12
INTRODUCTION TO THE CAPTIVES; OR, THE LOST RECOVERED. 124
THE CAPTIVES; OR, THE LOST RECOVERED. 127
INTRODUCTION TO THE COSTLIE WHORE. 262
THE COSTLIE WHORE. 265
INTRODUCTION TO EVERIE WOMAN 359
IN HER HUMOR. 359
EVERIE Woman in her Humor. 359
APPENDIX. 449

A COLLECTION OF OLD ENGLISH PLAYS, VOL. IV.

BY
Editor: A.H. Bullen

PREFACE.

The fourth and final volume of this Collection of Old Plays ought to have been issued many months ago. I dare not attempt to offer any excuses for the wholly unwarrantable delay.

In the preface to the third volume I stated that I hoped to be able to procure a transcript of an unpublished play (preserved in Eg. MS. 1,994) of Thomas Heywood. It affords me no slight pleasure to include this play in the present volume. Mr. JEAVES, of the Manuscript Department of the British Museum, undertook the labour of transcription and persevered to the end. As I have elsewhere stated, the play is written in a detestable hand; and few can appreciate the immense trouble that it cost Mr. JEAVES to make his transcript. Where Mr. JEAVES' labours ended mine began; I spent many days in minutely comparing the transcript with the original. There are still left passages that neither of us could decipher, but they are not numerous.

I may be pardoned for regarding the Collection with some pride. Six of the sixteen plays are absolutely new, printed for the first time; and I am speaking within bounds when I declare that no addition so substantial has been made to the Jacobean drama since the days of Humphrey Moseley and Francis Kirkman. ***Sir John Van Olden Barnavelt*** has been styled by Mr. Swinburne a "noble poem." Professor Delius urged that it should be translated into German; and I understand that an accomplished scholar, Dr. Gelbeke of St. Petersburg, has just completed an admirable translation. Meanwhile the English edition[1] has been reproduced in

Holland.

In the original announcement of this Collection I promised a reprint of ***Arden of Feversham*** from the quarto of 1592; I also proposed to include plays by Davenport, William Rowley, and Nabbes. After I had transcribed ***Arden of Feversham*** I determined not to include it in the present series. It occurred to me that I should enhance the value of these volumes by excluding such plays as were already accessible in modern editions. Accordingly I rejected Arden of Feversham, Sir John Oldcastle, Patient Grissel, ***and*** The Yorkshire Tragedy. The plays of Davenport, William Rowley, and Nabbes were excluded on other grounds. Several correspondents suggested to me that I should issue separately the complete works of each of these three dramatists; and, not without some misgivings, I adopted this suggestion.

I acknowledge with regret that the printing has not been as accurate as I should have desired. There have been too many misprints, especially in the first two volumes;[2] but in the eyes of generous and competent readers these blemishes (trivial for the most part) will not detract from the solid value of the Collection.

It remains that I should thank Mr. BERNARD QUARITCH, the most famous bibliopole of our age (or any age), for the kind interest that he has shewn in the progress of my undertaking. Of his own accord Mr. QUARITCH offered to subscribe for one third of the impression,--an offer which I gratefully accepted. I have to thank Mr. FLEAY for looking over the proof-sheets of a great part of the present volume and for aiding me with suggestions and corrections. To Dr. KOeHLER, librarian to the Grand Duke of Weimar, I am indebted for the true solution (see ***Appendix***) of the rebus at the end of ***The Distracted Emperor***. Mr. EBSWORTH, with his usual kindness, helped me to identify some of the songs mentioned in ***Everie Woman in Her Humor*** (see ***Appendix***).

17, SUMATRA ROAD, WEST HAMPSTEAD, N.W.

8th October, 1885.

INTRODUCTION TO *TWO TRAGEDIES IN ONE*.

Of Robert Yarington, the author of **Two Tragedies in One** absolutely nothing is known. There is no mention of him in Henslowe's Diary, and none of his contemporaries (so far as I can discover) make the slightest allusion to him. The **Two Tragedies** is of the highest rarity and has never been reprinted before.

There are two distinct plots in the present play. The one relates to the murder of Robert Beech, a chandler of Thames Street, and his boy, by a tavern-keeper named Thomas Merry; and the other is founded on a story which bears some resemblance to the well-known ballad of The Babes in the Wood. I have not been able to discover the source from which the playwright drew his account of the Thames Street murder. Holinshed and Stow are silent; and I have consulted without avail Antony Munday's "View of Sundry Examples," 1580, and "Sundry strange and inhumaine Murthers lately committed," 1591 (an excessively rare, if not unique, tract preserved at Lambeth). Yet the murder must have created some stir and was not lightly forgotten. From Henslowe's Diary[3] (ed. Collier, pp. 92-3) we learn that in 1599 Haughton and Day wrote a tragedy on the subject,--"the Tragedy of Thomas Merrye." The second plot was derived, I suppose, from some Italian story; and it is not improbable that the ballad of the ***Babes in the Wood*** (which was entered in the Stationers' Books in 1595, tho' the earliest printed copy extant is the black-letter broadside--circ. 1640?--in the Roxburghe Collection) was adapted from Yarington's play.

Although not published until 1601, the ***Two Tragedies*** would seem from internal evidence to have been written some years earlier. The language has a bald, antiquated look, and the stage-directions are amusingly simple. I once entertained a theory (which I cannot bring myself to wholly discard) that ***Arden of Feversham***, 1592, Warning for Fair Women***, 1599, and*** Two Tragedies in One, 1601, are all by the same hand; that the ***Warning*** and ***Two Tragedies***, though published later, were early essays by the author whose genius displayed its full power in ***Arden of Feversham***. A reader who will take the trouble to read the three plays together will discover many points of similarity between them. ***Arden*** is far more powerful than the two other plays; but I venture to think that the superiority lies rather in single scenes and detached passages than in general dramatic treatment. The noble scene of the quarrel and reconciliation between Alice Arden and Mosbie is incomparably finer than any scene in the ***Warning*** or ***Two Tragedies***; but I am not sure that Arden contains another scene which can be definitely pronounced to be beyond Yarington's ability, though there are many scattered passages displaying such poetry as we find nowhere in the ***Two Tragedies***. That Yarington could write vigorously is shown in the scene where Fallerio hires the two murderers (who remind us of Shagbag and Black Will in ***Arden***) to murder his nephew; and again in the quarrel between these two ruffians. Allenso's affection for his little cousin and solicitude at their parting are tenderly portrayed with homely touches of quiet pathos. The diction of the ***Two Tragedies*** is plain and unadorned. In reading ***Arden*** we sometimes feel that the simplicity of language has been deliberately adopted for artistic purposes; that the author held plenty of strength in reserve, and would not have been wanting if the argument had demanded a loftier style. In Yarington's case we have no such feeling. He seems to be giving us the best that he had to give; and it must be confessed that he is intolerably flat at times. It is difficult to resist a smile when the compassionate Neighbour (in his shirt), discovering poor Thomas Winchester with the hammer sticking in his head, delivers himself after this fashion:--

> "What cruell hand hath done so foule a deede,
> Thus to bemangle a distressed youth
> Without all pittie or a due remorse!
> See how the hammer sticketh in his head
> Wherewith this honest youth is done to death!
> Speak, honest *Thomas*, if any speach remaine:
> What cruell hand hath done this villanie?"

Merry's "last dying speech and confession" is as nasty as such things usually are.

In the introduction to **Arden of Feversham** I intend to return to the consideration of Yarington's *Two Tragedies*.

Two Lamentable Tragedies.

The one, of the Murther of **Maister** Beech A **Chaundler in** Thames-streete, and his boye, done by *Thomas Merry*.

The other of a Young childe murthered in a Wood by two Ruffins, with the consent of his Vnckle.

By ROB. YARINGTON.

LONDON.

Printed for **Mathew Lawe, and are to be solde at** his Shop in Paules Church-yarde neere vnto S. Austines Gate, at the signe of the Foxe. 1601.

Two Tragedies in One.

Enter Homicide, solus.

I have in vaine past through each stately streete,
And blinde-fold turning of this happie towne,
For wealth, for peace, and goodlie government,
Yet can I not finde out a minde, a heart
For blood and causelesse death to harbour in;
They all are bent with vertuous gainefull trade,
To get their needmentes for this mortall life,
And will not soile their well-addicted harts
With rape, extortion, murther, or the death
Of friend or foe, to gaine an Empery.
I cannot glut my blood-delighted eye
With mangled bodies which do gaspe and grone,
Readie to passe to faire Elizium,
Nor bath my greedie handes in reeking blood
Of fathers by their children murthered:

When all men else do weepe, lament and waile,
The sad exploites of fearefull tragedies,
It glads me so, that it delightes my heart,
To ad new tormentes to their bleeding smartes.

Enter Avarice.

But here comes *Avarice*, as if he sought,
Some busie worke for his pernicious thought:
Whether so fast, all-griping *Avarice*?

Ava. Why, what carst thou? I seeke for one I misse.

Ho. I may supplie the man you wish to have.

Ava. Thou seemes to be a bold audatious knave;
I doe not like intruding companie,
That seeke to undermine my secrecie.

Ho. Mistrust me not; I am thy faithfull friend.

Ava. Many say so, that prove false in the end.

Ho. But turne about and thou wilt know my face.

Ava. It may be so, and know thy want of grace.
What! *Homicide*? thou art the man I seeke:
I reconcile me thus upon thy cheeke.   [*Kisse, imbrace*.
Hadst thou nam'd blood and damn'd iniquitie,
I had forborne to bight so bitterlie.

Hom. Knowst thou a hart wide open to receive,

A plot of horred desolation?
Tell me of this, thou art my cheefest good,
And I will quaffe thy health in bowles of blood.

Ava. I know two men, that seem two innocents,
Whose lookes, surveied with iuditiall eyes,
Would seeme to beare the markes of honestie;
But snakes finde harbour mongst the fairest flowers,
Then never credit outward semblaunces.

   Enter[4] Trueth.

I know their harts relentlesse, mercilesse,
And will performe through hope of benefit:
More dreadfull things then can be thought upon.

Hom. If gaine will draw, I prethy then allure
Their hungrie harts with hope of recompence,
But tye dispaire unto those mooving hopes,
Unleast a deed of murther farther it,
Then blood on blood, shall overtake them all,
And we will make a bloodie feastivall.

Cove. The plots are laide, the keyes of golden coine,
Hath op'd the secret closets of their harts.
Inter [*sic*], insult, make captive at thy will,
Themselves, and friends, with deedes of damned ill:
Yonder is *Truth*, she commeth to bewaile,
The times and parties that we worke upon.

Hom. Why, let her weepe, lament and morne for me,
We are right bred of damn'd iniquitie,
And will go make a two-folde Tragedie.

[*Exeunt.*

Truth. Goe you disturbers of a quiet soule,
Sad, greedy, gaping, hungrie *Canibals*,
That ioy to practise others miseries.
Gentles, prepare your teare-bedecked eyes,
To see two shewes of lamentation,
Besprinckled every where with guiltlesse blood,
Of harmlesse youth, and pretie innocents.
Our Stage doth weare habilliments of woe,
Truth rues to tell the truth of these laments:
The one was done in famous London late,
Within that streete whose side the River Thames
Doth strive to wash from all impuritie:
But yet that silver stream can never wash,
The sad remembrance of that cursed deede,
Perform'd by cruell *Merry* on iust *Beech*,
And his true boye poore *Thomas Winchester*.
The most here present, know this to be true:
Would *Truth* were false, so this were but a tale!
The other further off, but yet too neere,
To those that felt and did the crueltie:
Neere *Padua* this wicked deed was done,
By a false Uncle, on his brothers sonne,
Left to his carefull education
By dying Parents, with as strict a charge
As ever yet death-breathing brother gave.
Looke for no mirth, unlesse you take delight,
In mangled bodies, and in gaping wounds,
Bloodily made by mercy-wanting hands.
Truth will not faine, but yet doth grieve to showe,
This deed of ruthe and miserable woe.

[*Exit*.

[ACT THE FIRST.]

[SCENE I.]

Enter Merry.

I live in meane and discontented state,
But wherefore should I think of discontent?
I am belov'd, I have a pretty house,
A loving sister, and a carefull man,
That doe not thinke their dayes worke well at end,
Except it bring me in some benefit:
And well frequented is my little house
With many guestes and honest passengers,

Enter Beech and a friend.

Which may in time advance my humble state
To greater wealth and reputation.
And here comes friends to drinke some beare or ale;   [*Sit in his Shop*.
They are my neighbours, they shall have the best.

Ne. Come neighbour *Beech*, lets have our mornings draught
And wele go drinke it at yong *Merries* house:
They say he hath the best in all this towne,
Besides they say he is an honest man,
And keepes good rule and orders in his house.

Beech. He's so indeede; his conversation
Is full of honest harmlesse curtesie:
I dare presume, if that he be within,
Hele serve us well, and keepe us company.
See where he is, go in, ile follow you;   [***Strive curtesies***.
Nay straine no curtesie, you shall goe before.

Mer. Your welcome, neighbour, you are welcome, sir;
I praie sit downe, your verie welcome both.

Beech. We thanke you for it, and we thinke no lesse.
Now fill two cans of your ould strongest beare;
That make so manie loose their little wits,
And make indentures as they go along.

Mer. Hoe, sister ***Rachell***!

Rach.   I come presently,

   Enter Rachell.

Mer. Goe draw these gentlemen two cans of beare.
Your negligence that cannot tend the shop,
Will make our customers forsake the house.
Wheres ***Harry Williams*** that he staies not here?

Rach. My selfe was busie dressing up the house:
As for your man he is not verie well,
But sitteth sleeping by the kitchen fier.

Mer. If you are busie, get you up againe;   [***Exit***.
Ile draw my neighbours then their drinke my selfe,

Ile warrant you as good as any mans,--
And yet no better; many have the like.
        [*Exit for Beare*.

Neigh. This showes him for a plain and honest man,
That will not flatter with too many wordes;
Some shriltong'd fellowes would have cogd and faind,
Saying, ile draw the best in Christendome.

Beech. Hees none of those, but beares an honest minde,
And shames to utter what he cannot prove.

  Enter Merry.

But here he comes: is that the best you have?

Mer. It is the best upon mine honest worde.

Beech. Then drinke to us.

Mer.   I drinke unto you both.

Nei. *Beech*. We pledge you both, and thanke you hartelie.

Beech. Heres to you sir.

Neigh.   I thank you.

  [*Maister Beech drinkes; drinke Neighbour*.

Neigh. Tis good indeed and I had rather drinke
Such beare as this as any *Gascoine* Wine:

But tis our *English* manner to affect
Strange things, and price them at a greater rate,
Then home-bred things of better consequence.

Mer. Tis true indeede; if all were of your mind,
My poore estate would sooner be advanc'd,
And our French Marchants seeke some other trade.

Beech. Your poore estate! nay, neighbour, say not so,
For God be thanked you are well to live.

Mer. Not so good neighbour, but a poore young man,
That would live better if I had the meanes:
But as I am I can content myselfe,
Till God amend my poore abilitie.

Neigh. In time no doubt; why, man, you are but young,
And God, assure your selfe, hath wealth in store,
If you awaight his will with patience.

Beech. Thankes be to God I live contentedlie,
And yet I cannot boast of mightie wealth:
But yet Gods blessings have beene infinit,
And farre beyond my expectations.
My shop is stor'd, I am not much in debt;
And here I speake it where I may be bold,
I have a score of poundes to helpe my neede,
If God should stretch his hand to visit me
With sicknesse or such like adversity.

Neigh. Enough for this; now, neighbour, whats to pay?

Mer. Two pence, good sir.

Beech. Nay, pray, sir, forbeare;
Ile pay this reckoning, for it is but small.

Neigh. I will not strive since yee will have it so.

Beech. Neighbour, farewell.

[*Exit Beech and Neigh*.

Mer. Farewell unto you both.
His shop is stor'd, he is not much in debt,
He hath a score of poundes to helpe his neede:
I and a score too if the trueth were known.
I would I had a shop so stor'd with wares,
And fortie poundes to buy a bargain with,
When as occasion should be offered me;
Ide live as merrie as the wealthiest man
That hath his being within London walles.
I cannot buy my beare, my bread, my meate,
My fagots, coales, and such like necessaries,
At the best hand, because I want the coine,
That manie misers cofer up in bagges,
Having enough to serve their turnes besides.
Ah for a tricke to make this ***Beeches*** trash
Forsake his cofer and to rest in mine!
I, marrie, sir, how may that tricke be done?
Marrie, with ease and great facilitie.
I will invent some new-found stratagem,
To bring his coyne to my possession.
What though his death relieve my povertie?
Gaine waites on courage, losse on cowardice.

[*Exit.*

[SCENE II.]

Enter Pandino and Armenia sicke on a bed, Pertillo their Sonne, Falleria his Brother, Sostrato his Wife, Alinso their Sonne, and a Scrivener with a Will, &c.

Pan. Brother and sister, pray you both drawe neere,
And heere my will which you have promised
Shall be performde with wished providence.
This little Orphant I must leave behinde,
By your direction to be governed.
As for my wife and I, we do awaite
The blessed houre when it shall please the Lord,
To take us to the iust *Ierusalem*.
Our chiefest care is for that tender boye,
Which we should leave discomfortlesse behinde,
But that we do assure us of your love
And care to guide his weake unhable youth
In pathes of knowledge, grace, and godlinesse.
As for the riches of this mortall life,
We leave enough; foure hundreth pounds a yeare,
Besides two thousand pounds to make a stocke,
In money, iewels, plate, and houshold stuffe,--
Which yearly rents and goods we leave to you,
To be surrendered into his hands,
When he attaines to yeeres of discreation.
My Will imports thus much, which you shall heare;
And you shall be my sole Executor.

Fall. Brother and sister, how my hart laments
To see your weake and sicke afflicted limmes
Neere overcome with dyrefull malladies,
The God of heaven can truly testifie,--
Which, to speake plaine, is nere a whit at all--
      [*To the people*.
Which knowes the secret corners of my heart;
But for the care you do impose on me,
For the tuition of your little sonne,
Thinke, my kinde brother, I will meditate,
Both day and night, how I may best fulfill,
The care and trust, reposed in your Will,--
And see him posted quickly after you.   [*To the people*.

Arm. Enough, kinde brother; we assure us so,
Else would we seeke another friend abroade,
To do our willes and dying Testament.
Nature and love will have a double care
To bring him up with carefull diligence,
As best beseemes one of such parentage.

Fall. Assure your selfe, the safest course I can,
Shall be provided for your little sonne,--
He shall be sent unto the King of Heaven.   [*To the people*.

Sostr. Feare not, good brother, and my loving sister,
But we will have as tender care of him
As if he were our owne ten thousand times:
God will be father of the fatherlesse,
And keepe him from all care and wretchednesse.

Allenso. Unckle and Aunt take comfort, I will see

My little coozen have no injurie.

Pan. *Ar*. We thanke you all, come let the Will be read,

Fall.--If it were seald, I would you both were dead.

Scrive. Then give attention, I will read the Will.
   Reade the Will.
In the name of God. Amen.--I, &c.

Pan. Thus, if my Sonne miscarry, my deare brother,
You and your sonne shall then enjoy the land
And all the goods which he should have possess'd.

Fall. If he miscarry, brother! God forbid!
God blesse mine Nephew, that thine eyes may see
Thy childrens children with prosperity!
I had rather see the little urchin hang'd   [*To the people*.
Then he should live and I forgoe the land.

Ar. Thankes, gentle brother; husband seale the will.

Pand. Give me a Pen and Inke first to subscribe;
I write so ill through very feeblenesse,
That I can scarcely know this hand for mine,
But that you all can witnesse that it is.

Scri. Give me the seale: I pray, sir, take it of.
This you deliver for your latest will,
And do confirme it for your Testament?

Pand. With all my hart; here, brother, keepe my Will,

And I referre me to the will of God,
Praying him deale as well with you and yours,
As you no doubt will deale with my poore child.
Come, my *Pertillo*, let me blesse thee, boy,
And lay my halfe-dead hand upon thy head.
God graunt those days that are cut off in me,
With ioy and peace may multiply in thee.
Be slowe to wrath, obey thy Unckle still,
Submit thy selfe unto Gods holy will,
In deede and word see thou be ever true;
So brother, childe, and kinsfolkes, all adue.   [*He dyeth*.

Per. Ah my deere Mother, is my father dead?

Ar. I, my sweete boye, his soule to heaven is fled,
But I shall after him immediatly.
Then take my latest blessing ere I dye:
Come, let me kisse thy little tender lips,
Cold death hath tane possession of thy mother;
Let me imbrace thee in my dying armes,
And pray the Lord protect thee from al harmes.
Brother, I feare, this Child when I am gone,
Wil have great cause of griefe and hideous feare:
You will protect him, but I prophecie,
His share will be of woe and misery:
But mothers feares do make these cares arise;
Come, boye, and close thy mothers dying eyes.
Brother and sister, here [*sic*] the latest words,
That your dead sister leaves for memory:
If you deale ill with this distressed boye,
God will revenge poore orphants iniuries,
If you deale well, as I do hope you will,
God will defend both you and yours from ill.

Farewell, farewell, now let me breath my last,
Into his dearest mouth, that wanteth breath,
And as we lov'd in life imbrace in death.
Brother and sister this is all I pray,
Tender my boye when we are laide in clay.   [*Dyeth*.

Allen. Gods holy Angell guide your loving soules
Unto a place of endlesse happinesse.

Sostr. Amen, Amen. Ah, what a care she had
Of her small Orphant! She did dying pray,
To love her Childe when she was laide in claye.

Scr. Ah blame her not although she held it deare;
She left him yonge, the greater cause of feare.

Fall. Knew she my mind, it would recall her life,   [*To the people*.
And like a staring Commet she would moove
Our harts to think of desolation.--
Scrivenor, have you certified the Will?

Scri. I have.

Fall. Then theres two Duckets for your paines.

Scri. Thankes, gentle sir, and for this time farewell.
                    [*Exit*.

Sost. Come pretty coozen, cozened by grim death
Of thy most carefull parents all too soone;
Weepe not, sweete boye, thou shalt have cause to say,
Thy Aunt was kinde, though parents lye in claye.

Pert. But give me leave first to lament the losse,
Of my deere parents, nature bindeth me,
To waile the death of those that gave me life,
And if I live untill I be a man,
I will erect a sumptuous monument,
And leave remembrance to ensuing times
Of kind *Pandino* and *Armenia*.

Allen. That shall not neede; my father will erect
That sad memoriall of their timeles[5] death,
And at that tombe we will lament and say
Soft lye the bones of faire *Armenia*.

Fall. Surcease, *Allenso*; thats a bootelesse cost,
The Will imports no such iniunction:
I will not spend my little Nephewes wealth,
In such vaine toyes; they shall have funerall,
But with no stately ceremoniall pompe,
Thats good for nought but fooles to gase uppon.
Live thou in hope to have thine unckles land.

Allen. His land! why, father, you have land enough,
And more by much then I do know to use:
I would his vertues would in me survive,
So should my Unckle seeme in me alive.
But to your will I doe submit my selfe;
Do what you please concerning funeralls.

Fall. Come then, away, that we may take in hand,
To have possession of my brothers land,
His goods and all untill he come of age
To rule and governe such possessions.--

That shalbe never, or ile misse my marke,
Till I surrender up my life to death:
And then my Sonne shalbe his fathers heire,
And mount aloft to honors happy chaire.

[*Exeunt omnes*.

[SCENE III.]

Enter Merry, solus.

Beech hath a score of pounds to helpe his neede,
And I may starve ere he will lend it me:
But in dispight ile have it ere I sleepe,
Although I send him to eternall rest.
But, shallow foole, thou talkst of mighty things,
And canst not compasse what thou dost conceive.
Stay, let me see, ile fetch him to my house,
And in my garret quickly murther him:
The night conceales all in her pitchie cloake,
And none can open what I meane to hide.
But then his boy will say I fetcht him foorth:
I am resolv'd he shall be murthered to [*sic*];
This toole shall write, subscribe, and seale their death
And send them safely to another world.
But then my sister, and my man at home,
Will not conceale it when the deede is done.
Tush, one for love, the other for reward,
Will never tell the world my close intent.
My conscience saith it is a damned deede

To traine one foorth, and slay him privily.
Peace, conscience, peace, thou art too scripulous [*sic*];
Gaine doth attend[6] this resolution.
Hence, dastard feare! I must, I can, I will,
Kill my best friend to get a bag of gold.
They shall dye both, had they a thousand lives;
And therefore I will place this hammer here,
And take it as I follow *Beech* up staires,
That suddenlie, before he is aware,
I may with blowes dash out his hatefull braines.--
Hoe, *Rachell*, bring my cloake; look to the house,
I will returne againe immediately.

Rach. Here it is brother, I pray you stay not long;
Guesse[7] will come in, 'tis almost supper time.
            [*Ex. Ra*.

Mer. Let others suppe, ile make a bloudier feast
Then ever yet was drest in *Merryes* house.
Be like thy selfe then, have a merrie hart,
Thou shalt have gold to mend thy povertie,
And after this live ever wealthilie.

   Then Merry must passe to Beeches shoppe,
   who must sit in his shop, and Winchester
   his boy stand by: Beech reading.

What, neighbour *Beech*, so godly occupied?

Beech. I, maister *Merry*; it were better reade,
Then meditate on idle fantasies.

Mer. You speake the trueth; there is a friend or two
Of yours making merry in my house,
And would desire to have your company.

Beech. Know you their names?

Mer. No truely, nor the men.
I never stoode to question them of that,
But they desire your presence earnestlie.

Beech. I pray you tell them that I cannot come,
Tis supper time, and many will resort
For ware at this time, above all other times;
Tis Friday night besides, and Bartholomew eve,
Therefore good neighbour make my just excuse.

Mer. In trueth they told me that you should not stay,
Goe but to drinke, you may come quick againe,--
But not and if my hand and hammer hold.   [(To the) people.

Beech. I am unwilling, but I do not care,
And if I go to see the Company.

Mer. Come quickly then, they think we stay too long.

Beech. Ile cut a peece of cheese to drink withall.

Mer. I, take the farewell of your cutting knife,
Here is a hand shall helpe to cut your throate,
And give my selfe a fairing[8] from your chest.--
What are you ready, will you goe along?

Beech. I, now I am; boy, looke you tend the shoppe;
If any aske, come for me to the ***Bull***.
I wonder who they are that aske for me.

Mer. I know not that, you shall see presentlie.
Goe up those staires, your friends do stay above.--
Here is that friend shall shake you by the head,
And make you stagger ere he speake to you.

>Then being in the upper Rome Merry strickes
>him in the head fifteene times.

Now you are safe, I would the boy were so;
But wherefore wish I, for he shall not live?
For if he doe, I shall not live myselfe.

>[Merry wiped [sic] his face from blood.

Lets see what mony he hath in his purse.
Masse heres ten groates, heres something for my pains.
But I must be rewarded better yet.

Enter Rachell and Harry Williams.

Wil. Who was it, ***Rachell***, that went up the staires?

Rach. It was my brother, and a little man
Of black complexion, but I know him not.

Wil. Why do you not then carry up a light,
But suffer them to tarry in the darke?

Rach. I had forgot, but I will beare one up.   [*Exit up*.

Wil. Do so, I prethee; he will chide anon.   [*Exit*.

[**Rachell speaketh to her Brother**.

Rach. Oh brother, brother, what have you done?

Mer. Why, murtherd one that would have murtherd me.

Rach. We are undone, brother, we are undone.
What shall I say, for we are quite undone?

Mer. Quiet thy selfe, sister; all shalbe well.
But see in any case you do not tell,
This deede to *Williams* nor to any one.

Rach. No, no, I will not; was't not maister *Beech*?

Mer. It was, it is, and I will kill his man,   [*Exit Rach*.
Or in attempting doe the best I can.

Enter Williams and Rachell.

Wil. What was the matter that you cride so lowde?

Rach. I must not tell you, but we are undone.

Wil. You must not tell me, but we are undone!
Ile know the cause wherefore we are undone.   [*Exit up*.

Rach. Oh would the thing were but to doe againe!

The thought thereof doth rent my hart in twaine.   [*She goes up*.

Williams to Merry above.

Wil. Oh maister, maister, what have you done?

Mer. Why slaine a knave that would have murtherd me;
Better to kill, then to be kild my selfe.

Wil. With what? wherewith? how have you slaine the man?

Mer. Why, with this hammer I knockt out his braines.

Wil. Oh it was beastly so to butcher him.
If any quarrell were twixt him and you,
You should have bad him meete you in the field,
Not like a coward under your owne roofe
To knock him downe as he had bin an oxe,
Or silly sheepe prepard for slaughter house.
The Lord is just, and will revenge his blood,
On you and yours for this extremitie.
I will not stay an hower within your house,
It is the wickedst deed that ere was done.

Mer. Oh, sir, content your selfe, all shall be well;
Whats done already cannot be undone.

Rach. Oh would to God, the deed were now to do,
And I were privie to your ill intent,
You should not do it then for all the world.
But prethie, *Harry*, do not leave the house,
For then suspition will arise thereof,
And if the thing be knowne we are undone.

Wil. Forsake the house! I will not stay all night,
Though you will give the wealth of Christendome.

Mer. But yet conceale it, for the love of God;
If otherwise, I know not what to do.

Wil. Here is my hand, ile never utter it;
Assure your selfe of that, and so farewell.

Mer. But sweare to me, as God shall help thy soule,
Thou wilt not tell it unto any one.

Wil. I will not sweare, but take my honest worde,
And so farewell. My soule assureth me   [*Exit Merry and Rach*.
God will revenge this damn'd iniquitie.
What shall become of me unhappie wretch?
I dare not lodge within my Maisters house,
For feare his murthrous hand should kill me too.
I will go walke and wander up and downe,
And seeke some rest, untill the day appeare.
At the *Three Cranes*,[9] in some Haye loft ile lye,
And waile my maisters comming miserie.

[*Exit*.

[SCENE IV.]

Enter Fallerio solus.

Fall. I have possession of my brothers goods;
His tennants pay me rent, acknowledge me
To be their Landlord; they frequent my house,
With Turkeys, Capons, Pigeons, Pigges and Geese,
And all to game my favour and goodwill.
His plate, his iewels, hangings, household stuffe,
May well beseeme to fit a demie King;
His stately buildings, his delightfull walkes,
His fertile meadowes, and rich ploughed lands,
His well-growne woods and stor'd fishing ponds,
Brings endlesse wealth, besides continuall helpe,
To keepe a good and hospitable house:
And shall I ioy these pleasures but a time?
Nay brother, sister, all shall pardon me,
Before ile sell my selfe to penurie.
The world doth know thy brother but resigned
The lands and goods untill his sonne attain'de
To riper years to weld [*sic*] and governe them.
Then openly thou canst not do him wrong,
He living: theres the burthen of the song.
Call it a burthen, for it seemes so great
And heavie burthen, that the boy should live
And thrust me from this height of happinesse,
That I will not indure so heavie waight,
But shake it off, and live at libertie,
Free from the yoake of such subjection.
The boy shall dye, were he my fathers sonne,
Before ile part with my possession.
Ile call my sonne, and aske his good advice,
How I may best dispatch this serious cause.--
Hoe, sir, *Allenso*!

Alle. Father.

Fall.   Hearken, sonne.
I must intreate your furtherance and advise
About a thing that doth concerne us neere.
First tell me how thou doost affect in heart
Little *Pertillo*, thy dead Unckles sonne.

Allen. So well, good father, that I cannot tell,
Whether I love him dearer then my selfe;
And yet if that my heart were calde to count,
I thinke it would surrender me to death,
Ere young *Pertillo* should sustain a wrong.

Fall. How got his safetie such a deepe regarde
Within your heart, that you affect it so?

Allen. Nature gave roote; love, and the dying charge,
Of his dead father, gives such store of sap
Unto this tree of my affection
That it will never wither till I dye.

Fall. But nature, love, and reason, tells thee thus,
Thy selfe must yet be neerest to thyselfe.

Allen. His love dooth not estrange me from my selfe,
But doth confirme my strength with multitudes
Of benefits his love will yeelde to me.

Fall. Beware to foster such pernicious snakes
Within thy bosome, which will poyson thee.

Allen. He is a Dove, a childe, an innocent,

And cannot poyson, father, though he would.

Fall. I will be plainer: know, ***Pertillos*** life,
Which thou doost call a dove, an innocent,
A harmlesse childe, and, and I know not what,
Will harm thee more, than any Serpent can,
I, then the very sight of Basiliskes.

Allen. Father you tell me of a strange discourse.
How can his life produce such detriment,
As Basiliskes, whose only sight is death?

Fall. Hearken to me, and I will tell thee how;
Thou knowst his fathers goods, his houses, lands,
Have much advaunc'd our reputation,
In having but their usage for a time.
If the boy live, then like to sencelesse beasts,
Like longd-eard Asses and riche-laden Mules,
We must resign these treasures to a boye,
And we like Asses feede on simple haye:
Make him away, they shall continue ours
By vertue of his fathers Testament,--
The iewels, castles, medowes, houses, lands,
Which thy small cozen should defeate thee of,
Be still thine owne, and thou advance thy selfe,
Above the height of all thine Auncestours.

Allen. But if I mount by murther and deceite,
Iustice will thrust aspiring thoughts belowe,
And make me caper for to breake my neck,
After some wofull lamentation
Of my obedience to unlawfulnesse.
I tell you plaine, I would not have him dye,

Might I enjoy the *Soldans* Emperie.

Fall. What, wilt thou barre thy selfe of happinesse?
Stop the large streame of pleasures which would flowe,
And still attend on thee like Servingmen?
Preferre the life of him that loves thee not
Before thine owne and my felicitie?

Allen. Ide rather choose to feede on carefulnesse,
To ditche, to delve, and labour for my bread,
Nay rather choose to begge from doore to doore,
Then condiscend to offer violence
To young *Pertillo* in his innocence.
I know you speake, to sound what mightie share
Pertillo hath in my affection.

Fall. In faith I do not; therefore, prethie, say,
Wilt thou consent to have him made away?

Allen. Why, then in faithe I am ashamde to think,
I had my being from so foule a lumpe
Of adulation and unthankfulnesse.
Ah, had their dying praiers no availe
Within your hart? no, damnd extorcion
Hath left no roome for grace to harbor in!
Audacious sinne, how canst thou make him say
Consent to make my brothers sonne away?

Fall. Nay if you ginne to brawle, withdrawe your selfe,
But utter not the motion[10] that I made,
As you love me, or do regarde your life.

Allen. And as you love my safetie and your soule,

Let grace and feare of God, such thoughts controule.

Fall. Still pratling! let your grace and feare alone,
And leave me quickly to my private thoughts,
Or with my sword ile open wide a gate,
For wrath and bloudie death to enter in.

Allen. Better you gave me death and buriall,
Then such foule deeds should overthrow us all.

Fall. Still are you wagging that rebellious tounge!
Ile dig it out for Crowes to feede upon,
If thou continue longer in my sight.   [*Exit Allenso*.
He loves him better then he loves his life!
Heres repetition of my brothers care,
Of sisters chardge, of grace, and feare of God.
Feare dastards, cowards, faint hart runawayes!
Ile feare no coulours[11] to obteine my will,
Though all the fiends in hell were opposite.
Ide rather loose mine eye, my hand, my foote,
Be blinde, wante senses, and be ever lame,
Then be tormented with such discontent
This resignation would afflict me with.
Be blithe, my boy, thy life shall sure be done,
Before the setting of the morrowe sunne.
          [*Exit*.

Enter Avarice and Homicide bloody.

Hom. Make hast, runne headlong to destruction!
I like thy temper that canst change a heart
From yeelding flesh to Flinte and Adamant.
Thou hitst it home, where thou doost fasten holde;

Nothing can separate the love of golde.

Ava. Feare no relenting, I dare pawne my soule,
(And thats no gadge, it is the divels due)
He shall imbrew his greedie griping hands
In the dead bosome of the bloodie boy,
And winde himselfe, his sonne, and harmlesse wife,
In endlesse foldes of sure destruction.
Now, *Homicide*, thy lookes are like thyselfe,
For blood and death are thy companions.
Let my confounding plots but goe before,
And thou shalt wade up to the chin in gore.

Homi. I finde it true, for where thou art let in,
There is no scruple made of any sinne;
The world may see thou art the roote of ill,
For but for thee poore *Beech* had lived still.

[*Exeunt*.

[ACT THE SECOND.]

[SCENE I.]

Enter Rachell and Merry.

Rach. Oh my deare brother, what a heap of woe,
Your rashnesse hath powrd downe upon your head!
Where shall we hide this trumpet of your shame,

This timelesse ougly map of crueltie?
Brother, if *Williams* do reveale the truth,
Then brother, then, begins our sceane of ruthe.

Mer. I feare not *Williams*, but I feare the boy,
Who knew I fetcht his maister to my house.

Rach. What, doth the boy know whereabouts you dwell?

Mer. I, that tormentes me worse than panges of hell:--
He must be slaine to, else hele utter all.

Rach. Harke, brother, harke, me thinkes I here on[12] call.

Mer. Go downe and see; pray God my man keep close;
If he prove long-tongd then my daies are done.
The boy must die, there is no helpe at all;
For on his life my verie life dependes.
Besides I cannot compasse what I would,
Unlesse the boy be quicklie made away.
This that abridgde his haplesse maisters daies,
Shall leave such sound memorials one [*sic*] his head,
That he shall quite forget who did him harme,
Or train'd his master to this bloodie feast.--
Why, how now, *Rachell*? who did call below?

Enter Rachell.

Rach. A maide that came to have a pennie loafe.

Mer. I would a pennie loafe cost me a pound,
Provided *Beeches* boy had eate his last.

Rach. Perchance the boy doth not remember you.

Mer. It may be so,--but ile remember him.   [*To people*.
And send him quicklie with a bloodie scrowle,
To greete his maister in another world.

Rach. Ile go to **Beeches** on a faind excuse,
To see if he will ask me for his maister.

Mer. No, get you up, you shall not stir abroade,
And when I call, come quicklie to the dore.

Rach. Brother, or that, or any thing beside,
To please your mind, or ease your miserie.   [*Exit*.

Mer. I am knee-deepe, ile wade up to the wast,
To end my hart of feare, and to atteine
The hoped end of my intention.
But I maie see, if I have eyes to see,
And if my understanding be not blind,
How manie dangers do alreadie waight,
Upon my steppes of bold securitie.
Williams is fled, perchaunce to utter all;
Thats but perchance, naie rather flatlie no.
But should he tell, I can but die a death;
Should he conceale, the boy would utter it;
The boy must die, there is no remedie.

   [*The boy sitting at his maisters dore*.

Win. I wonder that my maister staies so long;

He had not wont to be abroade so late.
Yonder comes one; I thinke that same is he.

Mer. I see the boye sits at his maisters doore.
Or now, or never; *Merry*, stir thy selfe,
And rid thy hart from feare and jealousie.--
Thomas Winchester, go quicklie to your shoppe:
What, sit you still? your maister is at hand.

> [When the boy goeth into the shoppe Merrie striketh six blowes on his head & with the seaventh leaves the hammer sticking in his head; the boy groaning must be heard by a maide who must crye to her Maister.
>
> > [Merrie flieth.

Mai. Oh God I thinke theres theeves in **Beeches** shop.

> Enter one in his shirt and a maide, and comming to Beeches shop findes the boy murthered.

Nei. What cruell hand hath done so foule a deede,
Thus to bemangle a distressed youth
Without all pittie or a due remorse!
See how the hammer sticketh in his head,
Wherewith this honest youth is done to death!
Speak, honest *Thomas*, if any speach remaine:
What cruell hand hath done this villanie?
He cannot speake, his senses are bereft.
Hoe, neighbour **Loney**! pray come downe with speede,
Your tennant **Beeches** man is murthered.

Loney sleeping. What, would you have some mustard?

Nei. Your tennant *Beeches* man, is murthered.

Lo. Whose smothered, I thinke you lack your wit
What, neighbor? what make[13] you here so late?   [*Out at a window*.

Nei. I was affrighted by a sodaine crie,
And comming downe saw maister *Beeches* man,
Thus with a hammer sticking in his head.   [*Comes to win*.

Loney. Ah wo is me for *Thomas Winchester*,
The truest soule that ever maister had!
Wheres maister *Beech*?

Neigh. Nay, no body can tell:
Did you see any running from the dore,
When you lookt out and heard the youngman crie?

Maid. Yes I saw two trulie to my thinking, but they ranne away as fast as their hands could beare them.--By my troth twas so darke I could see no bodie.--[*To people*. Praie God Maister *Beech* hath not hurt his boy in his patience and if he have he must be hangd in his choller.

Lo. I dare be sworne he would not strike him thus,
Praie God his Maister be not slaine himselfe.
The night growes late, and we will have this course
Be watch'd all night; to morrow we shall see
Whence sprang this strange uncivill crueltie.

Nei. Neighbour good night.

Lon. Neighbors all good night.

Ma. Praie God I never see so sad a sight.

[*Exeunt omnes*.

Enter Merry knocking at the doore, and Rachell comes downe.

Mer. Oh sister, sister, now I am pursu'd!
The mightie clamour that the boy did make,
Hath raisde the neighbours round about the street:
So that I know not where to hide my selfe.

Ra. What, brother! have you kild *Beeches* boy?

Mer. No, no, not I, but yet another hath.
Come, come to bed, for feare we be descri'd:
The fearfullest night that ever *Merry* knew!

[*Exeunt*.

[SCENE II.]

Enter Falleria and two Ruffaines.

Fall. Seeme it not strange, resolved gentlemen,[14]
That I thus privatelie have severed you,
To open secret furrowes of my hart.
Think not I do intend to undermine,
Your passed lives, although you know I am

A man to whom the true unpartiall sworde,
Of equall justice is delivered.
Therefore sweare both, as you respect your soules,
At the last dreadfull sessions held in heaven,
First to conceale, and next to execute,
What I reveale, and shall enioyne you to.

Both. So you rewarde us, whatsoever it be,
We vowe performance, and true secrecie.

Fall. There go aside, yee seeming semblances,
Of equall justice, and true pietie,
And lay my hearts corrupted Cytadell
Wide open to your thoughts to look into.
Know I am named *Fallerio* to deceive
The world with shew of truth and honestie,
But yet nor truth, nor honestie abides
Within my thoughts, but falshood, crueltie,
Blood-sucking *Avarice*, and all the sinnes,
That hale men on to bloodie stratagems,
Like to your selves, which care not how you gaine,
By blood, extorcion, falshood, periurie,
So you may have a pleasing recompence: [*They start*.
Start not aside, depart not from your selves,
I know your composition is as mine,
Of bloud, extortion, falshood, periurie,
True-branded with the marke of wickednesse.

1 *Ruffin*. Be not so bitter; we are they indeede,
That would deprive our fathers of their lives,
So we were sure to have a benefit:
I way no more the murthring of a child,
Drag'd from the sucking bosome of his mother,

Then I respect to quaffe a boule of wine,
Unto his health, that dearely loveth me.

2 *Ruff*. Where golde rewardeth, were apparent death,
Before mine eyes, bolde, hartie, visible,
Ide wrastle with him for a deadly fall,
Or I would loose my guerdon promised.
Ide hang my brother for to wear his coate,
That all that saw me might have cause to say,
There is a hart more firme then Adamant,
To practise execrable butcheries.

Fall. I know that well, for were I not assur'd
Of your performance in this enterprice,
I would not ope the closet of my brest,
To let you know my close intention.
There is a little boy, an urchin lad,
That stands betweene me and the glorious rayes,
Of my soule-wishing sunne of happinesse.
There is a thicket ten miles from this place,
Whose secret ambush and unused wayes
Doth seeme to ioyne with our conspiracie:
There murther him, and when the deed is done,
Cast his dead body in some durtie ditch,
And leave him for the fowles to feed upon.
Do this, here is two hundreth markes in golde,
To harten on your resolution:
Two hundreth more, after the deed is done,
Ile pay you more for satisfaction.

1 *Ruff*. Swones her's rewards would make one kill himselfe,
To leave his progenie so rich a prize!
Were twentie lives engadged for this coine,

Ide end them all, to have the money mine.

2 *Ruff*. Who would not hazard life nay soule and all,
For such a franke and bounteous pay-maister?
Sblood! what labor is't to kill a boy?
It is but thus, and then the taske is done.
It grieves me most, that when this taske is past,
I have no more to occupie my selfe.
Two hundred markes to give a paltrie stab!
I am impatient till I see the brat.

Fall. That must be done with cunning secrecie,
I have devisde to send the boye abroade,
With this excuse, to have him fostered,
In better manners than this place affoords.
My wife, though loath indeed to part with him,
Yet for his good, she will forgoe her joy,
With hope in time to have more firme delights,
Which she expects from young *Pertillos* life.

2 *Ruff*. Call you him *Pertillo*, faith leave out the *T*.

Fall. Why so?

Ruff. Because *Perillo* will remaine,
For he shall surely perish if I live.
What do you call the father of the child?

Fall. Why man, he hath no father left alive.

1 *Ruff*.--Yes, such a father, that doth see and know,
How we do plot this little infants woe.   [*To the people*.

2 *Ruff*. Why, then his little sonne is much to blame,
That doth not keepe his father company.
When shall we have deliverie of the boy?

***Fall*.** To morrow morning by the breake of day:
And you must sweare youle see him safely brought,
Unto the place that I do send him to.

2 *Ruff*. That may we safely, for you meane to send
Him to the wood and there his journey end.[15]
Both soule and limbes shall have a place to rest,
In earth the last, the first in ***Abrams*** brest.

***Fall*.** Come gentlemen, this night go rest with me,
To morrow end ***Pertillos*** tragedie.

[*Exeunt omnes*.

[SCENE III.]

Enter Merry and Rachell.

***Mer*.** Sister, now all my golde-expected hopes
Of future good is plainely vanished,
And in her stead grim-visadged dispaire,
Hath tane possession of my guiltie heart.
Desire to gaine began this desperate acte;
Now plaine apparance of destruction,
Of soule and body, waights upon my sinne.
Although we hide our sinnes from mortall men,

Whose glasse of knowledge is the face of man,
The eye of heaven beholdes our wickednesse,
And will no doubt revenge the innocent,

Rach. Ah, do not so disconsolate your selfe,
Nor adde new streames of sorrow to your griefe,
Which like a spring tide over-swels the bankes,
Least you do make an inundation
And so be borne away with swiftest tides
Of ugly feare and strong dispairing thoughts.
I am your sister; though a silly Maide,
Ile be your true and faithfull comforter.

Mer. *Rachell*, I see thy love is infinite,
And sorrow hath so borne my thoughts away,
That I had almost quite forgot my selfe.
Helpe me, deare sister, to convey from hence
The spectacle of inhumanitie.

Rach. Whether would you convey this lumpe of dust
Untimely murthered by your lucklesse hand?

Mer. To the lowe roome, where we will cover it,
With Fagots, till the evening doe approche:
In the meane time I will bethinke my selfe,
How I may best convey it foorth of doores;
For if we keepe it longer in the house,
The savour will be felt throughout the streete,
Which will betray us to destruction.
Oh what a horror brings this beastlinesse,
This chiefe of sinnes, this self-accusing crime
Of murther! now I shame to know my selfe,
That am estrang'd so much from that I was,

True, harmlesse, honest, full of curtesie,
Now false, deceitfull, full of injurie.
Hould thou his heeles, ile bear his wounded head:
Would he did live, so I myself were dead!

[*Bring down the body, and cover it over with Faggots himselfe*.

Rach. Those little stickes, do hide the murthred course,
But stickes, nor ought besides, can hide the sinne.
He sits on high, whose quick all-seeing eye,
Cannot be blinded by mans subtilties.

Mer. Look every where, can you discerne him now?

Rach. Not with mine eye, but with my heart I can.

Mer. That is because thou knowest I laide him there:
To guiltinesse each thought begetteth feare.
But go, my true, though wofull comforter,
Wipe up the blood in every place above,
So that no drop be found about the house:
I know all houses will be searcht anon.
Then burne the clothes, with which you wipe the ground
That no apparant signe of blood be found.

Rach. I will, I will; oh, would to God I could
As cleerely wash your conscience from the deed
As I can cleanse the house from least suspect
Of murthrous deed, and beastly crueltie!

Mer. Cease to wish vainely, let us seeke to save
Our names, our fames, our lives and all we have.

[*Exeunt.*

[SCENE IV.]

Enter three or foure neighbours together.

1 *Neigh*. Neighbours, tis bruted all about the towne
That **Robert Beech**, a honest Chaundelor,
Had his man deadly wounded yester night,
At twelve a clock, when all men were a sleepe.

2. Where was his maister, when the deed was done?

3. No man can tell, for he is missing to,
Some men suspect that he hath done the fact,
And that for feare the man is fled away;
Others, that knew his honest harmlesse life,
Feare that himselfe is likewise made away.

4. Then let commaundement every where be given,
That sinkes and gutters, privies, crevises,
And every place where blood may be conceald,
Be throughly searcht, swept, washt, and neerely sought,
To see if we can finde the murther out.
And least that **Beech** be throwne into the *Thames*,
Let charge be given unto the watermen
That, if they see the body of a man,
Floting in any place about the *Thames*,
That straight they bring it unto **Lambert Hill**,
Where **Beech** did dwell when he did live in health.

1 *Neigh*. Ile see this charge performd immediatly.

4. Now let us go to Maister *Beeches* shop,   [*Exit*.
To see if that the boy can give us light,
Of those suspitions which this cause doth yeeld.

2. This is the house; call Maister *Loney* forth.

3. Hoe, Maister *Loney*! doth the boy yet live?

   Enter Loney.

Or can he utter who hath done him wrong.

Lo. He is not dead but hath a dying life,
For neither speech, nor any sense at all,
Abideth in the poore unhappie youth.

4. Here [*sic*] you of anie where his Maister is?

Lo. No, would we could; we all, that knew his life,
Suspect him not for any such offence.

4. Bring forth the boy, that we may see his wounds.

   [Bringes him forth in a chaire with a hammer sticking
   in his head.

What say the Surgeons to the youngmans woundes?

Lo. They give him over, saying everie wound,

Of sixe, whereof theres seav'n in his head,
Are mortall woundes and all incurable.

[*They survey his woundes*.

Enter Merrie and Williams.

Mer. How now, good **Harry**, hast thou hid my fault?
The boy that knew I train'd his Maister forth,
Lies speechlesse, and even at the point of death.
If you prove true, I hope to scape the brunt.

Will. Whie, feare not me, I have conceal'd it yet,
And will conceale it, have no doubt of me.

Mer. Thanks, gentle **Harry**, thou shalt never lacke;
But thou and I will live as faithfull friendes,
And what I have, shalbe thine owne to use.
There is some monie for to spend to-day,
I know you meane to goe and see the faire.

Will. I faine would go, but that I want a cloake.

Mer. Thou shalt not want a cloake, or ought beside,
So thou wilt promise to be secret.   [**Gives him his cloake**.
Here, take my Cloake, ile weare my best my selfe.
But where did you lie this last night?

Wil. At the **three Cranes**, in a Carmans hay loft,
But ile have better lodging soone at night.

Mer. Thou wilt be secret. I will go and see,   [**Exit Willi**.

What stir they keepe about **Beeches** shop,
Because I would avoyde suspition.   [**Go to them**.
God save you, Gentlemen! is this the boy
That is reported to be murthered?

4. He is not dead outright, but pleas'd it God,
Twere better he had left this wicked world,
Then to live thus in this extremitie.

Mer. A cruell hand no doubt that did the deede.
Whie pull you not the hammer from his head?

4. That must not be before the youth be dead,
Because the crowner and his quest may see,
The manner how he did receive his death.
Beare hence the bodie, and endevor all,
To finde them out that did the villanie.

[**Exeunt omnes: manet Merrie**.

Mer. Do what you can, cast all your wits about,
Rake kennells, gutters, seeke in everie place,
Yet I will overgoe your cunning heads,
If **Williams** and my sister hold their tongues.
My neighbours holdes not me in least suspect,
Weighing of my former conversation.
Were **Beeches** boy well conveid awaie,
Ide hope to overblow this stormie day.

[*Exit*.

[SCENE V.]

    Enter Falleria, Sostrata, Allenso, Pertillo,
    and two Murtherers booted.

Fall. Now little cooze, you are content to goe,
From me your Unckle and your loving Aunt,
Your faithfull cozen, and your dearest friendes:
And all to come to be a skilfull man,
In learned artes and happy sciences?

Per, I am content, because it pleaseth you.
My father bid I should obey your will,
And yeelde my selfe to your discretion:
Besides my cozen gave me yesternight,
A prettie nag to ride to *Padua*.
Of all my friends *Allenso* loves me best.

Fall. I thinke thou art inspir'd with prophesie: [*To the people*.
He loves thee better then I would he did.--
Why, wherefore think you so, my prettie Nephew?

Per. Because he taught me how to say my prayers,
To ride a horse, to start the fearfull hare.
He gave this dagger to me yester night,
This little Ring, and many pretie things;
For which, kind cooze, I rest your true debtor,
And one day I will make you recompence.

Fall. I, with thy lands and goods thou leav'st behinde.

Allen. Pray, father, let me go along with him.--
Now, by the Saviour of my sinfull soule,   [*To the people*.
I do not like those fellowes countenance.

Fall. Sonne be content, weele go a seavenight hence,
And see him in his universitie weedes.
These will conduct him safely to the place;
Be well assured they'l have a care of him--
That you shall never see *Pertillo* more.   [*To the people*.

Allen. Father, I pray you to withdraw your selfe,
Ide have a word or two in secresie.

[*They speake together*.

Sost. Come living image of thy dead mother,
And take my loving farewell, ere we part.
I love thee dearly for thy fathers sake,
But for thy mothers dote with jealousie.
Oh I do feare, before I see thy face,
Or thou or I shall taste of bitternesse.
Kisse me, sweete boy, and, kissing, folde thine Aunte
Within the circle of thy little armes.
I neede not feare, death cannot offer wrong;
The majestie of thy presaging face,
Would vanquish him, though nere so terrible.
The angry Lionesse that is bereav'd
Of her imperious crew of forrest kings,
Would leave her furie, and defend thee safe
From Wolves, from Panthers, Leopards, and Shee Beares,
That live by rapine, stealth and crueltie.
Therefore to God I do commend thy state,
Who will be sure to guard thee tenderly.

And now to you, that carry hence this wealth,
This precious Jewell, this unprized good,
Have a regarde to use him carefully,
When he is parted from that serious care,
Which was imployde for his securitie.
I urge it not, that I misdoubt your truth;
I hope his Unckle doth perswade himselfe
You will be courteous, kinde, and affable.
Ther's some rewarde for hoped carefulnesse.

Allen. Now by my soule I do suspect the men,
Especially the lower of the two:
See, what a hollow discontented looke
He casts, which brings apparant cause of feare:
The other, though he seeme more courteous,
Yet dooth his lookes presadge this thought in me.
As if he scorn'd to thinke on courtesie.

Fall. Upon my life, my sonne you are to blame,
The gentlemen are honest, vertuous,
And will protect *Pertillo* happily.
These thoughts proceed out of aboundant love,
Because you grieve to leave his company.
If ought betide him otherwise then well,
Let God require due vengaunce on my head,
And cut my hopes from all prosperitie.

Allen. A heavie sentence, full of wondrous feare:
I cannot choose but credit such a vowe.
Come hether then, my joy, my chiefest hopes,
My second selfe, my earthly happinesse,
Lend me thy little prety cherry lip,
To kisse me, cozen; lay thy little hand

Upon my cheeke, and hug me tenderly.
Would the cleere rayes of thy two glorious sunnes
Could penetrate the corners of my heart,
That thou might see how much I tender thee.
My friends, beholde, within this little bulke
Two perfect bodyes are incorporate;
His life holdes mine, his heart conteines my hart,
His every lim containes my every part;
Without his being I can never be,
He being dead, prepare to bury me.
Oh thou immortall mover of the spheares
Within their circled revolusions,
Whose glorious image this small orphant beares,
Wrought by thy all-sufficient majestie,
Oh never suffer any wicked hand
To harme this heavenly workmanship of thine,
But let him live, great God, to honor thee
With vertuous life and spotlesse pietie!

Per. Cease, my kind cooze; I cannot choose but weepe,
To see your care of my securitie.

Allen.--Knewst thou my reason, that perswades my hart,
Thou wouldst not wonder, why I grieve to part:
But yet I would suspect my fathers vowe,
Did any other make it by your leave.

Fall. What have you done? this lothnesse to depart,
Seemes you were trained up in tediousnesse,
Thou knowst not when and where to make an end.
Take him my friends, I know you will discharge
The hope and trust that I repose in you.

Both. Assure your selfe, in every circumstance.

Fall. Then to your horses quicklie, speedily,
Else we shall put our fingers in the eye,
And weepe for kindnesse till tomorrow morne.

Per. Farewell good Unckle, Aunt, and loving cooze.

[*Sostratus* [sic] *kisseth the boy weeping.*

Allen. Farewell.--I fear me everlastinglie.

[***Exeunt Sostratus and Allenso.***

[**One of the Murtherers takes Falleria by the sleeve.**

1 *mu*. You meane not now to have him murthered?

Fall. Not murthered, what else? kill him, I say:
But wherefore makes thou question of my will?

Mur. Because you wisht that God should be revenged,
If any ill betide the innocent.

Fall. Oh that was nothing but to blind the eyes
Of my fond sonne, which loves him too too well.

Mer. It is enough, it shall be surely done.

[***Exeunt om.***

[SCENE VI.]

Enter Merry and Rachel with a bag.

Mer. What, hast thou sped? have you bought the bag?

Rach. I, brother, here it is; what is't to do?

Mer. To beare hence **Beeches** body in the night.

Rach. You cannot beare so great a waight your selfe,
And tis no trusting of another man.

Mer. Yes well enough, as I will order it.
Ile cut him peece-meale; first his head and legs
Will be one burthen; then the mangled rest,
Will be another, which I will transport,
Beyond the water in a Ferryboate,
And throw it into **Paris-garden** ditch,[16]
Fetch me the chopping knife, and in the meane
Ile move the fagots that do cover him.
              [*Remove the Fagots*.

Rach. Oh can you finde in hart to cut and carve,
His stone-colde flesh, and rob the greedy grave,
Of his dissevered blood-besprinkled lims?

Mer. I, mary can I:--fetch the chopping knife.

Rach. This deed is worse, then when you took his life.   [*Exit*.

Mer. But worse, or better, now it must be so,
Better do thus than feele a greater woe.

Enter Rach.

Here is the knife, I cannot stay to see
This barbarous deed of inhumanitie.   [*Exit Rachel*.

> [Merry begins to cut the body, and bindes the armes
> behinde his back with Beeches garters; leaves out the
> body, covers the head and legs againe.

Enter Truth.

Yee glorious beames of that bright-shining lampe
That lights the starre-bespangled firmament,
And dimnes the glimmering shadowes of the night,
Why doost thou lend assistance to this wretch,
To shamble forth with bold audacitie
His lims, that beares thy makers semblance!
All you the sad spectators of this Acte,
Whose harts do taste a feeling pensivenesse
Of this unheard of, savadge massacre,
Oh be farre of to harbour such a thought
As this audacious murtherer put in ure![17]
I see your sorrowes flowe up to the brim,
And overflowe your cheekes with brinish teares,
But though this sight bring surfet to the eye,
Delight your eares with pleasing harmonie,[18]
That eares may counterchecke your eyes, and say,
Why shed you teares, this deede is but a playe?
His worke is done, he seekes to hide his sinne;

Ile waile his woe before his woe begin.   [*Exit Trueth*.

Mer. Now will I high me to the water side,
And fling this heavie burthen in a ditche,
Whereof my soule doth feele so great a waight
That it doth almost presse me downe with feare.

[ACT THE THIRD.]

[SCENE I.]

Enter Rachell.

Harke, *Rachell*, I will crosse the water straight
And fling this middle mention of a man
Into some ditch; then high me home againe,
To rid my house of that is left behinde.

Rach. Where have you laid the legs & battered head?

Mer. Under the fagots where it lay before.
Helpe me to put this trunk into the bag.

Rach. My heart will not endure to handle it,
The sight hereof doth make me quake for feare,

Mer. Ile do't my selfe; onely drie up the blood,
And burne the clothes as you have done before.   [*Exit*.

Rach. I feare thy soule will burne in flames of hell,
Unless repentance wash wash away thy sinne
With clensing teares of true contrition.
Ah, did not nature oversway my will,
The world should know this plot of damned ill.

[*Exit*.

[SCENE II.]

Enter two Murtherers with Pertillo.

Per. I am so wearie in this combrous wood,
That I must needes go sit me downe and rest.

1 ***Mur***. What were we best? to kill him unawares,
Or give him notice what we doe intend?

2 ***Mur***. Whie then belike you meane to do your charge,
And feel no tast of pittie in your hart.

1 ***Mur***. Of pittie, man! that never enters heere,
And if it should, Ide threat my craven heart
To stab it home for harbouring such a thought.
I see no reason whie I should relent;
It is a charitable vertuous deede,
To end this princkocke[19] from this sinfull world.

2 ***Mur***. Such charitie will never have reward,
Unlesse it be with sting of conscience;

And thats a torment worse than Sisipus,
That rowles a restlesse stone against the hill.

1 *Mur*. My conscience is not prickt with such conceit.

2 *Mur*. That shews thee further off from hoped grace.

1 *Mur*. Grace me no graces, I respect no grace,
But with a grace, to give a gracelesse stab;
To chop folkes legges and armes off by the stumpes,
To see what shift theile make to scramble home;
Pick out mens eyes, and tell them thats the sport
Of hood-man-blinde, without all sportivenesse.
If with a grace I can perform such pranckes,
My hart will give mine agents many thankes.

2 *Mur*. Then God forbid I should consort my selfe
With one so far from grace and pietie,
Least being found within thy companie,
I should be partner of thy punishment.

1 *Mur*. When wee have done what we have vowed to do,
My hart desires to have no fellowship
With those that talk of grace or godlinesse.
I nam'd not God, unleast twere with an othe,
Sence the first hour that I could walk alone;
And you that make so much of conscience,
By heaven thou art a damned hipocrite,
For thou hast vow'd to kill that sleeping boy,
And all to gaine two hundreth markes in gold.
I know this purenesse comes of pure deceit,
To draw me from from the murthering of the child,
That you alone might have the benefit.

You are too shallow; if you gull me so,
Chop of my head to make a Sowsing-tub,
And fill it full of tripes and chitterlinges.

2 *Mur*. That thou shalt see my hart is far from fraud,
Or vaine illusion in this enterprize,
Which doth import the safetie of our soules,
There take my earnest of impietie.   [*Give him his mony*.
Onely forbeare to lay thy ruder handes
Upon the poore mistrustlesse tender child.
As for our vowes, feare not their violence;
God will forgive on hartie penitence.

1 *Mur*. Thou Eunuch, Capon, Dastard, fast and loose,
Thou weathercocke of mutabilitie,
White-livered Paisant, wilt thou vowe and sweare,
Face and make semblance with thy bagpipe othes
Of that thou never meanst to execute?
Pure cowardice, for feare to cracke thy necke
With the huge Caos of thy bodies waight,
Hath sure begot this true contrition.
Then fast and pray, and see if thou canst winne,
A goodlie pardon for thy hainous sinne.
As for the boy, this fatall instrument
Was mark'd by heaven to cut his line[20] of life,
And must supplie the knife of *Atropos*,
And if it doe not, let this maister-piece
(Which nature lent the world to wonder at)
Be slit in Carbonadoes[21] for the jawes
Of some men-eating hungrie Canniball.
By heaven ile kill him onely for this cause,
For that he came of vertuous Auncestors.

2 m. But by that God which made that wondrous globe,
Wherein is seene his powerfull dietie,[22]
Thou shalt not kill him maugre all thy spight.
Sweare, and forsweare thyselfe ten thousand times.
Awake *Pertillo*, for thou art betrai'd;
This bloody slave intends to murther thee.   [*Draw both*.

1 mur. Both him, and all, that dare to rescue him.

Per. Wherefore? because I slept without your leave?
Forgive my fault, ile never sleepe againe.

2 Mur. No Child, thy wicked Unckle hath suborn'd
Both him and me to take thy life away,
Which I would save, but that this hellish impe
Will not content to spare thy guiltlesse blood.

Per. Why should *Falleria* seeke to have my life?

2 mur. The lands and goods, thy father left his sonne,
Do hale thee on to thy destruction.

Per. Oh needy treasure, harme-begetting good!
That safety[23] should procure the losse of blood!

2 mur. Those lands and goods, thy father got with paine,
Are swords wherewith his little sonne is slaine.

1 mu. Then let our swords let out his guiltlesse life.

Per. Sweete, sowre, kinde, cruell, hold thy murthering knife,
And here [*sic*] me speake, before you murther me.

2 *mu*. Feare not, sweet child, he shall not murther thee.

1 *mu*. No, but my sword shall let his puddings forth.

Per. First here me speake, thou map of Butcherie:
Tis but my goods and lands my Unckle seekes;
Having that safely, he desires no more.
I do protest by my dead parents soules,
By the deare love of false **Fallerios** sonne,
Whose heart, my heart assures me, will be griev'd
To heare his fathers inhumanitie,
I will forsake my countrie, goods, and lands,
I, and my selfe will even change my selfe,
In name, in life, in habit, and in all,
And live in some farre-moved continent,
So you will spare my weake and tender youth,
Which cannot entertaine the stroake of death
In budding yeares and verie spring of life.

1 *Mur*. Leave of these bootlesse protestations,
And use no ruth-enticing argumentes,
For if you do, ile lop you lim by lim,
And torture you for childish eloquence.

2 *Mur*. Thou shalt not make his little finger ake.

1 *Mur*. Yes, every part, and this shall proove it true.
　　　　[**Runnes Perillo in with his sworde**.

Per. Oh I am slaine, the Lord forgive thy fact!
And give thee grace to dye with penitence.　　[**Dyeth**.

2 Mur. A treacherous villaine, full of cowardise!
Ile make thee know that thou hast done amisse.

1 m. Teach me that knowledge when you will or dare.

[They fight and kill one another; the relenter
having some more life, and the other dyeth.

1 mur. Swoones, I am peppered, I had need have salt,
Or else to morrow I shall yeeld a stincke,
Worse then a heape of dirty excrements.
Now by this Hilt, this golde was earn'd too deare:
Ah, how now death, wilt thou be conquerour?
Then vengeance light on them that made me so,
And ther's another farewell ere I goe.
             [**Stab the other murtherer againe**.

2 mur. Enough, enough, I had my death before.

[**A hunt within**.

Enter the Duke of Padua, Turqualo, Vesuvio, Alberto, &c.

Duke. How now my Lords, was't not a gallant course,
Beleeve me sirs, I never saw a wretch,
Make better shift to save her little life.
The thickets full of buskes,[24] and scratching bryers,
A mightie dewe,[25] a many deepe mouth'd hounds,
Let loose in every place to crosse their course,--
And yet the Hare got cleanly from them all.
I would not for a hundred pound in faith,

But that she had escaped with her life;
For we will winde a merry hunters home,
And starte her once again tomorrow morne.

Turq. In troth my Lord, the little flocked[26] hound,
That had but three good legs to further him,
Twas formost still, and surer of his sent,
Then any one in all the crie besides.

Vesu. But yet **Pendragon** gave the Hare more turnes.

Alber. That was because he was more polliticke,
And eyed her closely in her coverts still:
They all did well, and once more we will trie,
The subtile creature with a greater crie.

Enter Allenso, booted.

Duke. But say, what well accomplished Gentleman
Is that that comes into our company?

Vesu. I know him well, it is **Fallerios** sonne,
Pandynos brother (a kinde Gentleman)
That dyed and left his little pretty sonne,
Unto his brother's[27] good direction.

Duke. Stand close awhile, and overheare his wordes;
He seemes much over-gone with passion.

Allen. Yee timorous thoughts that guide my giddy steps
In unknowne pathes of dreadfull wildernesse,
Why traitor-like do you conspire to holde
My pained heart twixt feare and jealousie?

My too much care hath brought me carelesly,
Into this woody savadge labyrinth,
And I can finde no way to issue out;
Feare hath so dazeled all my better part,
That reason hath forgot discreations art.
But in good time, see where is company.--
Kinde Gentlemen, if you, unlike my selfe,
Are not incumbred with the circling wayes
Of this erronious winding wildernesse,
I pray you to direct me foorth this wood
And showe the pathe that leades to *Padua*.

Duke. We all are *Paduans*, and we all intend
To passe forthwith with speed to *Padua*.

Allen. I will attend upon you presently.   [*See the bodyes*.

Duke. Come then away:--but, gentlemen beholde,
A bloody sight, and murtherous spectacle!

2 *Mur*. Oh, God, forgive me all my wickednesse
And take me to eternall happinesse!

Duke. Harke one of them hath some small sparke of life,
To kindle knowledge of their sad mishaps.

Allen. Ah gratious Lord, I know this wretched child,
And these two men that here lye murthered.

Vesu. Do you, *Allenso*?

Allen. I, my gracious Lord:

It was *Pertillo* my dead Unckles sonne.
Now have my feares brought forth this fearefull childe
Of endlesse care, and everlasting griefe!

Duke. Lay hands upon *Allenso*, Gentlemen.
Your presence doth confirme you had a share
In the performance of this crueltie.

Allen. I do confesse I have so great a share
In this mishap, that I will give him thankes,
That will let foorth my sorrow-wounded soule
From out this goale of lamentation.

Duke. Tis now too late to wish for hadiwist.[28]
Had you withheld your hand from this attempt,
Sorrow had never so imprisoned you.

Allen. Oh my good Lord, do not mistake my case,
And yet my griefe is sure infallible.
The Lord of heaven can witnesse with my soule,
That I am guiltelesse of your wrong suspect,
But yet not griefelesse that the deed is done.

Duke. Nay if you stand to justifie your selfe,
This gentleman whose life dooth seeme to stay,
Within his body till[29] he tell your shame,
Shall testifie of your integritie:
Speake then, thou sad Anatomy of death,
Who were the Agents of your wofulnesse?

2 *Mur*. O be not blinded with a false surmise,
For least my tongue should faile to end the tale
Of our untimely fate-appointed death,

Know young ***Allenso*** is as innocent
As is ***Fallerio*** guiltie of the crime.
He, he it was, that with foure hundredth markes,
Whereof two hundred he paide presently,
Did hire[30] this damn'd villaine and my selfe
To massacre this harmelesse innocent:
But yet my conscience, toucht with some remorse,
Would faine have sav'd the young ***Pertillos*** life,
But he remorselesse would not let him live,
But unawares thrust in his harmelesse brest
That life-bereaving fatall instrument:
Which cruell deede I seeking to revenge,
Have lost my life and paid the slave his due
Rewarde for spilling blood of innocents.
Surprise ***Fallerio***, author of this ill;
Save young ***Allenso***, he is guiltlesse still.   [***Dyeth***.

Allen. Oh sweetest honie mixt with bitter gall,
Oh Nightingale combinde with Ravens notes,
Thy speech is like a woodward that should say,--
Let the tree live, but take the root away.
As though my life were ought but miserie,
Having my father slaine for infamie!

Duke. What should incite ***Fallerio*** to devise,
The overthrowe of this unhappie boy?

Vesu. That may be easily guest, my gracious Lord,
To be the lands ***Pandino*** left his sonne,
Which, after that the boy were murthered,
Discend to him by due inheritance.

Duke. You deeme aright. See, gentlemen, the fruites,

Of coveting to have anothers right.
Oh wicked thought of greedie covetice!
Could neither nature, feare of punishment,
Scandall to wife and children, nor the feare,
Of Gods confounding strict severitie,
Allay the head-strong furie of thy will?
Beware, my friends, to wish unlawfull gaine;
It will beget strange actions full of feare,
And overthrowe the actor unawares.
For first *Fallerios* life must satisfie
The large effusion of their guiltlesse bloods,
Traind on by him to these extremities;
Next, wife and children must be disposest,
Of lands and goods, and turnde to beggerie;
But most of all, his great and hainous sinne,
Will be an eye-sore to his guiltlesse kinne.
Beare hence away these models of his shame,
And let us prosecute the murtherer
With all the care and diligence we can.

[*Two must be carrying away Pertillo*

Allen. Forbeare awhile to beare away my joy,
Which now is vanisht since his life is fled;
And give me leave to wash his deadly wound
With hartie teares, outflowing from those eyes
Which lov'd his sight, more then the sight of heaven.
Forgive me God for this idolatrie!
Thou ugly monster, grim imperious death,
Thou raw-bonde lumpe of foule deformitie,
Reguardlesse instrument of cruell fate,
Unparciall Sergeant, full of treacherie,
Why didst thou flatter my ill-boding thoughts,

And flesh my hopes with vaine illusions?
Why didst thou say, *Pertillo* should not dye,
And yet, oh yet, hast done it cruelly?
Oh but beholde, with what a smiling cheere,
He intertain'd thy bloody harbinger!
See, thou transformer of a heavenly face
To Ashie palenesse and unpleasing lookes,
That his fair countenance still retaineth grace
Of perfect beauty in the very grave.
The world would say such beauty should not dye;
Yet like a theefe thou didst it cruelly.
Ah, had thy eyes, deepe-sunke into thy head,
Beene able to perceive his vertuous minde,
Where vertue sat inthroned in a chaire,
With awfull grace and pleasing maiestie,
Thou wouldest not then have let *Pertillo* die,
Nor like a theefe have slaine him cruellie.
Inevitable fates, could you devise,
No means to bring me to this pilgrimage,
Full of great woes and sad calamities,
But that the father should be principall,
To plot the present downfall of the sonne?
Come then kind death and give me leave to die,
Since thou hast slaine *Pertillo* cruellie.

Du. Forbeare, *Allenso*; hearken to my doome,
Which doth concerne thy fathers apprehension.
First we enjoyne thee, upon paine of death,
To give no succour to thy wicked sire,
But let him perrish in his damned sinne,
And pay the price of such a treacherie.
See that with speede the monster be attach'd,
And bring him safe to suffer punishment.

Prevent it not, nor seeke not to delude
The Officers to whom this charge is given;
For if thou doe, as sure as God doth live,
Thy selfe shall satisfie the lawes contempt.
Therefore forward about this punishment.

[*Exeunt omnes: manet Allenso*.

Al. Thankes, gratious God, that thou hast left the meanes
To end my soule from this perplexitie.
Not succour him on paine of present death!
That is no paine; death is a welcome guest
To those whose hearts are overwhelm'd with griefe.
My woes are done, I having leave to die
And after death live ever joyfullie.   [*Exit*.

Enter Murther and Covetousnesse.

Mur. Now, *Avarice*, I have well satisfied
My hungrie thoughtes with blood and crueltie;
Now all my melanchollie discontent
Is shaken off, and I am throughlie pleas'd,
With what thy pollicie hath brought to passe.
Yet am I not so throughlie satisfied
Untill I bring the purple actors forth.
And cause them quaffe a bowle of bitternesse,
That father sonne, and sister brother may
Bring to their deathes with most assur'd decay.

Ava. That wilbe done without all question,
For thou hast slaine **Allenso** with the boy,
And **Rachell** doth not wish to overlive
The sad remembrance of her brothers sinne.

Leave faithfull love to teach them how to dye,
That they may share their kinsfolkes miserie.

[*Exeunt.*

[ACT THE FOURTH.]

[SCENE I.]

Enter Merrie and Rachell uncovering the head and legges.

Mer. I have bestow'd a watrie funerall
On the halfe bodie of my butchered friend.
The head and legges Ile leave in some darke place;
I care not if they finde them yea or no.

Ra. Where do you meane to leave the head and legs?

Mer. In some darke place nere to **Bainardes Castle**.[31]

Ra. But doe it closelie that you be not seene;
For all this while you are without suspect.

Mer. Take you no thought, Ile have a care of that;
Onelie take heede you have a speciall care
To make no shew of any discontent
Nor use too many words to any one.
    [**Puts on his Cloake; taketh up the bag**.
I will returne when I have left my loade.

Be merrie, **Rachell**; halfe the feare is past.   [*Exit.*

Ra. But I shall never thinke my selfe secure.
This deede would trouble any quiet soule,
To thinke thereof, much more to see it done;
Such cruell deedes can never long be hid,
Although we practice nere so cunningly.
Let others open what I doe conceale;
Lo he is my brother, I will cover it,
And rather dye than have it spoken rife,--
Lo where she goes, betrai'd her brothers life.

[*Exit.*

[SCENE II.]

Enter Williams and Cowley.

Co. Why, how now, **Harry**, what should be the cause,
That you are growne so discontent of late?
Your sighes do shew some inward heavinesse;
Your heavy lookes, your eyes brimfull of teares,
Beares testimonie of some secret griefe.
Reveale it, **Harry**; I will be thy friend,
And helpe thee to my poore habillity.

Wil. If I am heavie, if I often sigh,
And if my eyes beare recordes of my woe,
Condemne me not, for I have mightie cause,
More then I will impart to any one.

Co. Do you misdoubt me, that you dare not tell
That woe to me that moves your discontent?

Wil. Good Maister **Cowley**, you were ever kinde,
But pardon me; I will not utter it
To any one, for I have past my worde;
And therefore urge me not to tell my griefe.

Cow. But those that smother griefe too secretly,
May wast themselves in silent anguishment,
And bring their bodies to so low an ebb,
That all the world can never make it flowe,
Unto the happy hight of former health.
Then be not [so] iniurious to thy selfe,
To wast thy strength in lamentation,
But tell thy case; wele seeke some remedie.

Wil. My cause of griefe is now remedilesse,
And all the world can never lessen it;
Then since no meanes can make my sorrowes lesse,
Suffer me waile a woe which wants redresse.

Cow. Yet let me beare a part in thy lamentes,
I love thee not so ill but I will mone
Thy heavie haps; thou shalt not sigh alone.

Wil. Nay, if you are so curious to intrude
Your selfe to sorrow, where you have no share,
I will frequent some unfrequented place
Where none shall here nor see my lamentations.   [*Exit*.

Cow. And I will follow wheresoever thou goe;

I will be a partner of thy helplesse woe.

[*Exit*.

[SCENE III.]

Enter two Watermen.

1. **Will**, ist not time we should go to our boates,
And give attendance for this **Bartlemew** tide?
Folkes will be stirring early in the morning.

2. By my troth I am indifferent whether I go or no. If a fare come, why so; if not, why so; if I have not their money, they shall have none of my labour.

1. But we that live by our labours, must give attendance.
But where lyes thy Boate?

2. At **Baynards Castle** staires.

1. So do's mine, then lets go together.

2. Come, I am indifferent, I care not so much for going; but if I go with you, why so; if not, why so.   [**He falls over the bag**.
Sblood, what rascall hath laide this in my way!

1. A[32] was not very indifferent that did so, but you are so permentorie, to say, why so, and why so, that every one is glad to do you iniurie. But lets see: what is it?

[*Taking the Sack by the end, one of the legs and head drops out*.

Good Lord deliver us! a mans legges, and a head with manie wounds!

2. Whats that so much? I am indifferent, yet for mine owne part, I understand the miserie of it; if you doe, why so, if not, why so.

1. By my troth I understand no other mistery but this:
It is a strange and very rufull sight.
But, prethee, what doost thou conceit of it?

2. In troth I am indifferent, for if I tell you, why so, if not why so.

1. If thou tell me, Ile thanke thee; therefore I prethee tell me.

2. I tell you I am indifferent; but to be plaine with you, I am greeved to stumble at the hangmans budget.

1. At the hangmans budget? why, this is a sack.

2. And to speake indifferently, it is the hangman's Budget; and because he thought too much of his labour to set this head upon the bridge, and the legs upon the gates, he flings them into the streete for men to stumble at, but If I get him in my boate, Ile so belabour him in a stretcher, that he had better be stretcht in one of his owne halfepeny halters. If this be a good conceit, why so; if not, why so.

1. Thou art deceiv'd, this head hath many wounds,
And hoase and shoes remaining on the legs.
Bull always strips all quartered traitors quite.

2. I am indifferent whether you beleeve me or no; these were not worth

taking of, and therefore he left them on. If this be likely why so;
if not, why so.

1. Nay, then I see you growe from worse to worse.
I heard last night, that one neere **Lambert Hill**
Was missing, and his boy was murthered.
It may be this is a part of that same man;
What ere it be, ile beare it to that place.

2. Masse I am indifferent; ile go along with you, if it be so, why so;
if not why so.

    [*Exeunt.*

[SCENE IV.]

    Enter three neighbors knocking at Loneys doore: Loney comes.

1. Hoe, Maister Loney! here you any newes
What is become of your Tennant **Beech**?

Lon. No truely, sir, not any newes at all.

2. What, hath the boy recovered any speach,
To give us light of these suggestions
That do arise upon this accident?

Lon. There is no hope he should recover speech;
The wives do say he's ready now to leave
This greevous world, full-fraught with treacherie.

3. Methinkes if **Beech** himselfe be innocent,
That then the murtherer should not dwell farre off;
The hammer that is sticking in his head,
Was borrowed of a Cutler dwelling by,
But he remembers not who borrowed it:
He is committed that did owe[33] the hammer,
But yet he standes uppon his innocence;
And **Beeches** absence causeth great suspition.

Lo. If **Beech** be faulty, as I do not thinke,
I never was so much deceiv'd before.
Oh had you knowne his conversation,
You would not have him in suspition.

3. Divels seeme Saints, and in these[34] hatefull times,
Deceite can beare apparraunt signes of trueth,
And vice beare shew of vertues excellence.

   Enter the two Watermen.

1. Pray is this Maister **Beeches** house?

Lo. My friend this same was maister **Beeches** shop:
We cannot tell whether he live or no.

1. Know you his head and if I shew it you?
Or can you tell me what hose or shooes he ware,
At that same time when he forsooke the shoppe?

3. What, have you head, and hose, and shooes to show,
And want the body that should use the same?

1. Behold this head, these legges, these hose and shooes,
And see if they were **Beeches**, yea or no.

Lo. They are the same; alas, what is become,
Of the remainder of this wretched man!

1 *Wat*. Nay that I know not; onelie these we found,
As we were comming up a narrow lane,
Neere **Baynardes Castle**, where we two did dwell;
And heering that a man was missing hence,
We thought it good to bring these to this place,

3. Thankes, my good friendes; ther's some thing for your paines.

2 *Wat*. We are indifferent, whether you give us anything or nothing;
and if you had not, why so; but since you have, why so.

1 *Wat*. Leave your repining: Sir, we thanke you hartely.

3. Farewell good fellowes.--Neighbour, now be bold: [*Exeunt Watermen*.
They dwell not farre that did this bloodie deed,
As God no doubt will at the last reveale,
Though they conceale it nere so cunninglie.
All houses, gutters, sincks and crevices
Have carefully been sought for, for the blood;
Yet theres no instaunce found in any place.

   Enter a Porter and a Gentleman.

But who is that that brings a heavy loade,
Behinde him on a painefull porters backe?

Gen. Praie, Gentlemen, which call you **Beeches** shoppe?

2 *Neig*. This is the place; what wold you with the man?

Gen. Nothing with him; I heare the man is dead,
And if he be not, I have lost my paines.

Lo. Hees dead indeede, but yet we cannot finde
What is become of halfe his hopelesse bodie.
His head and legges are found, but for the rest,
No man can tell what is become of it.

Gen. Then I doe thinke I can resolve your doubt
And bring you certain tydings of the rest,
And if you know his doublet and his shirt.
As for the bodie it is so abus'd
That no man can take notice whoes it was.
Set downe this burden of anothers shame.
What, do you know the doublet and the shirt?

[*Ex. Porter*.

Lo. This is the doublet, these the seuered limmes,
Which late were ioyned to that mangled trunke:
Lay them together, see if they can make
Among them all a sound and solid man.

3 *neigh*. They all agree, but yet they cannot make
That sound and whole which a remorsles hand
Hath severed with a knife of crueltie.
But say, good sir, where did you finde this out?

Gent. Walking betime by *Paris Garden* ditch,
Having my Water Spaniell by my side,

When we approach'd unto that haplesse place
Where this same trunke lay drowned in a ditch,
My Spaniell gan to sent, to bark, to plunge
Into the water, and came foorth againe,
And fawnd one me, as if a man should say,
Helpe out a man that heere lyes murthered.
At first I tooke delight to see the dog,
Thinking in vaine some game did there lye hid
Amongst the Nettles growing neere the banke;
But when no game, nor anything appear'd,
That might produce the Spaniell to this sport,
I gan to rate and beate the harmlesse Cur,
Thinking to make him leave to follow me;
But words, nor blowes, could moove the dog away,
But still he plung'd, he div'd, he barkt, he ran
Still to my side, as if it were for helpe.
I seeing this, did make the ditch be dragd,
Where then was found this body as you see,
With great amazement to the lookers on.

3. Beholde the mightie miracles of God,
That sencelesse things should propagate their sinne
That are more bestiall farre then beastlinesse
Of any creature most insensible!

2. **Neigh**. Cease we to wonder at Gods wondrous works,
And let us labour for to bring to light
Those masked fiends that thus dishonor him.
This sack is new, and, loe! beholde his marke
Remaines upon it, which did sell the bag.
Amongst the Salters we shall finde it out
When, and to whom, this bloody bag was sold.

3. Tis very likely, let no paines be spar'd,
To bring it out, if it be possible;
Twere pitty such a murther should remaine
Unpunished mongst Turkes and Infidels.

1. *neigh*. Sirs, I do know the man that solde this bag,
And if you please, Ile fetch him presently?

Gent. With all our hearts. How say you gentlemen?
Perchance the murther thus may come to light.

3. I pray you do it, we will tarry heere: [*Exit 1. neigh*.
And let the eyes of every passenger
Be satisfied, which may example be
How they commit such dreadfull wickednesse.

Ent. wom. And please your maisterships, the boy is dead.

3. *neigh*. Tis very strange that having many wounds
So terrible, so ghastlie; which is more,
Having the hammer sticking in his head;
That he should live and stirre from *Friday* night,
To *Sunday* morning, and even then depart,
When that his Maisters mangled course were found.
Bring him foorth too; perchance the murtherers
May have their hearts touched with due remorse,
Viewing their deeds of damned wickednesse.
  [*Bring forth the boye and laye him by Beech*.

1 *neigh*. Here is the Salters man that solde the bag.

Gent. My friend, how long since did you sell that bag?

And unto whom, if you remember it?

Sal. I sould the bag, good sir, but yesterday,
Unto a maide; I do not know her name.

3 *neigh*. Nor where she dwels.

Sal. No certeinly.

2 *neigh*. But what apparell had she on her back?

Sal. I do not well remember what she wore,
But if I saw her I should know her sure.

3 *neigh*. Go round about to every neighbours house,
And will them shew their maides immediately:
God grant we may finde out the murtherers.
    [*Go to one house, and knock at doore, asking*.
Bring forth such maides as are within your house!

1 *housekeeper*. I have but one, ile send her down to you.

3 *neigh*. Is this the maide?   [*Come out maide*.

Salt. No, sir, this is not she.   [*Go to another, &c*.
How many maides do dwell within this house?

2 *house*. Her's nere a woman here, except my wife.   [*Go to Merryes*.

3 *neigh*. Whose house is this?

Lo. An honest civill mans, cald Maister *Merry*,

Who I dare be sworne, would never do so great a murther;
But you may aske heere to for fashion sake.

[*Rachell sits in the shop*.

3. How now, faire maide, dwels any here but you?
Thou hast too true a face for such a deed.

Rach. No, gentle sir; my brother keepes no more.

3 *neigh*. This is not she?

Salt.   No truly, gentleman.

[*Ex. R*.

3. This will not serve; we cannot finde her out.
Bring in those bodyes, it growes towards night;
God bring these damn'd murtherers at length to light!

[*Exeunt omnes*.

[SCENE V.]

Enter Merry and Rachell.

Mer. Why go the neighbours round about the streete
To every house? what hast thou heard the cause?

Rach. They go about with that same Salters man,

Of whom I bought the bag but yesterday,
To see if he can know the maide againe
Which bought it: this I think the very cause.

Mer. How were my senses overcome with feare,
That I could not foresee this jeopardy!
For had I brought the bag away with me,
They had not had this meanes to finde it out.
Hide thee above least that the Salters man
Take notice of thee that thou art the maide,
And by that knowledge we be all undone.

Rach. That feare is past, I sawe, I spake with him,
Yet he denies that I did buy the bag;
Besides the neighbours have no doubt of you,
Saying you are an honest harmelesse man,
And made enquirie heere for fashion sake.

Mer. My former life deserves their good conceits,
Which is not blemisht with this treacherie.
My heart is merier then it was before,
For now I hope the greatest feare is past.
The hammer is denyed, the bag unknowne;
Now there is left no meanes to bring it out,
Unless our selves proove Traitors to our selves.

Rach. When saw you **Hary Williams**?

Me. Why, to day;
I met him comming home from **Powles Crosse**,
Where he had beene to heare a Sermon.

Rach. Why brought you not the man along with you

To come to dinner, that we might perswade
Him to continue in his secrecie?

Mer. I did intreate him, but he would not come,
But vow'd to be as secret as my selfe.

Rach. What, did he sweare?

Mer. What neede you aske me that?
You know we never heard him sweare an othe.
But since he hath conceal'd the thing thus long,
I hope in God he will conceale it still.

Rach. Pray God he do, and then I have no doubt
But God will overpasse this greevous sinne,
If you lament with true unfained teares
And seeke to live the remnant of your yeares
In Gods true feare with upright conscience.

Mer. If it would please him pardon this amisse
And rid my body from the open shame
That doth attend this deed, being brought to light,
I would endevour all my comming dayes
To please my maker and exalt his praise.
But it growes late, come bring me to my bed,
That I may rest my sorrow-charged head.

Rach. Rest still in calme secure tranquillitie,
And over-blowe this storme of mightie feare
With pleasant gales of hoped quietnesse.
Go when you will; I will attend, and pray
To send this wofull night a cheerfull day.

[*Exeunt*.

[SCENE VI.]

Enter Falleria and Sostrata weeping.

Fall. Passe ore these rugged furrowes of laments
And come to plainer pathes of cheerefulnesse;
Cease thy continuall showers of thy woe.
And let my pleasing wordes of comfort chase
These[35] duskie cloudes of thy uniust dispaire
Farre from thy hart, and let a pleasing hope
Of young *Pertillos* happy safe returne
Establish all your ill-devining thoughts;
So shall you make me cheerfull that am sad,--
And feede your hopes with fond illusions.

Sos. I could be so; but my divided soule,
Twixt feare and hope of young *Pertillos* life,
Cannot arrive at the desired port
Of firme beleefe, until mine eyes do see
Him that I sent to know the certainetie.

Fal. To know the certaintie! of whom, of what?
Whome, whether, when, or whereabout, I praie,
Have you dispatcht a frustrate messenger?--
By heaven, and earth, my heart misgiveth[36] me,
They will prevent my cunning pollicie.   [*To the people*.
Why speake you not? what winged Pegasus
Is posted for your satisfaction?

Sos. Me thinkes my speach reveales a hidden feare,
And that feare telles me that the childe is dead.

Fall. By sweete **S. Andrew** and my fathers soule,
I thinke the peevish boy be too too well
But speake, who was your passions harbinger?

Sos. One that did kindle my misdoubting thoughts,
With the large flame of his timiddity.

Fall. Oh then I know the tinder of your feare.
Was young **Allenso** your white[37] honnie sonne.
Confusion light upon his timerous head,
For broching this large streame of fearefulnesse!
And all the plagues that damned furies feele
For their forepassed bold iniquities,
Afflict you both for thus preventing me!

Sos. Preventing you! of what? **Fallerio**, speake,
For if you doe not my poore hart will breake.

Fall. Why of the good that I had purposed,
To young **Pertillo**, which I would conceale
From you and him until the deed were done.

Sost. If it were good, then we affect him deare,
And would add furtherance to your enterprise.

Fall. I say your close eaves-dropping[38] pollicies
Have hindred him of greater benefits
Then I can ever do him after this.--

If he live long, and growe to riper sinne,   [*To the people*.
Heele cursse you both, that thus have hindered
His freedom from this goale of sinfull flesh.--
But let that passe, when went your harebrainde sonne,
That Cuckow, vertue-singing, hatefull byrde,
To guarde the safetie of his better part,
Which he hath pend within the childish coope
Of young *Pertillos* sweete securitie?

Sost. That lovely sonne, that comfort of my life,
The root of vertuous magnamitie,
That doth affect with an unfained love,
That tender boy, which under heavens bright eye,
Deserveth most to be affected deare,
Went some two houres after the little boy
Was sent away to keepe[39] at *Padua*.

Fall. What, is a lovelie? he's a loathsome toade,
A one eyde *Cyclops*, a stigmaticke[40] brat,
That durst attempt to contradict my will,
And prie into my close intendements.

   Enter Alenso sad.

Mas, here a comes: his downcast sullen looke,
Is over-waigh'd with mightie discontent.--
I hope the brat is posted to his sire,
That he is growne so lazie of his pace;
Forgetfull of his dutie, and his tongue
Is even fast tyde with strings of heavinesse.--
Come hether, boye! sawst thou my obstacle,
That little *Dromus* that crept into my sonne,
With friendly hand remoov'd and thrust away?

Say, I, and please me with the sweetest note
That ever relisht in a mortals mouth.

Allen. I am a Swan that singe, before I dye,
Your note of shame and comming miserie.

Fall. Speake softly, sonne, let not thy mother heare;
She was almost dead before for very feare.

Allen. Would I could roare as instruments of warre,
Wall-battring Cannons, when the Gun powder
Is toucht with part of *Etnas* Element!
Would I could bellow like enraged Buls,
Whose harts are full of indignation,
To be captiv'd by humaine pollicie!
Would I could thunder like Almightie *Ioue*,
That sends his farre-heard voice to terrifie
The wicked hearts of earthly citizens!
Then roaring, bellowing, thundring, I would say,
Mother, lament, *Pertillos* made away!

Sost. What, is he dead? God give me leave to die,
And him repentance for his treacherie!
         [*Falleth down and dyeth*.

Fall. Never the like impietie was done:
A mother slaine, with terror of the sonne!
Helpe to repaire the damadge thou hast made,
And seeke to call back life with dilligence.

Allen. Call back a happy creature to more woe!
That were a sinne: good Father, let her go.

O happy I, if my tormenting smart,
Could rend like her's, my griefe-afflicted heart!
Would your hard hart extend unto your wife,
To make her live an everdying life?
What, is she dead? oh, then thrice happy she,
Whose eyes are bard from our callamitie!

Fall. I, all too soone, thou viper, paracide!
But for thy tongue thy mother had not dyde:
That belching voice, that harsh night-raven sound,
Untimely sent thy mother to the ground:
Upbraid my fault, I did deceive my brother;
Cut out thy tongue, that slue thy carefull mother.

Allen. God love my soule, as I in heart rejoyce
To have such power in my death-bringing voice,
See how in steade of teares and hartie sighes;
Of foulded armes and sorrow-speaking lookes,
I doe behold with cheerefull countenance
The livelesse roote of my nativitie,
And thanke her hasty soule that thence did goe
To keep her from her sonne and husbandes woe.--
Now, father, give attention to my tale;
I will not dip my griefe-deciphering tongue
In bitter wordes of reprehension.
Your deeds have throwne more mischiefes on your head
Then wit or reason can remove againe;
For to be briefe, *Pertillo*, (oh that name
Cannot be nam'de without a hearty sigh!)
Is murthered, and--

Fal. What and? this newes is good.

Allen. The men which you suborn'd to murther him--

Fal. Better and better, then it cannot out,
Unlesse your love will be so scripulous [*sic*]
That it will overthrowe your selfe and me.

Allen. The best is last, and yet you hinder me.
The Duke of *Padua* hunting in the wood,
Accompanied with Lordes and Gentlemen--

Fal. Swones what of that? what good can come of that?

Allen. Was made acquainted by the one of them,
(That had some little remnant of his life)
With all your practice and conspiracie.

Fall. I would that remnant had fled quicke to hell,
To fetch fierce fi[e]ndes to rend their carcases,
Rather then bring my life in ieopardie!
Is this the best? swones, doe you mocke me, sonne,
And make a iest at my calamitie?

Allen. Not I, good father; I will ease your woe,
If you but yeeld unto my pollicie.

Fal. Declare it then, my wits are now to seeke;
That peece of life hath so confounded mee
That I am wholly overcome with feare.

Allen. The Duke hath vow'd to prosecute your life,
With all the strict severitie he can;
But I will crosse his resolution

And keepe you from his furie well enough.
Ile weare your habit, I will seeme the man
That did suborne the bloodie murtherers;
I will not stir from out this house of woe,
But waight the comming of the officers,
And answere for you fore the angrie Duke,
And, if neede be, suffer your punishment.

Fall. Ile none of that; I do not like the last;
I love thee dearer then I doe my life,
And all I did, was to advance thy state
To sunne-bright beames of shining happinesse.

Allen. Doubte not my life, for when I doe appeare
Before the Duke, I being not the man,
He can inflict no punishment on mee.

Fall. Mas, thou saiest true, a cannot punish thee;
Thou wert no actor of their Tragaedie.
But for my beard thou canst not counterfet
And bring gray haires uppon thy downy chinne;
White frostes are never seene in summers spring.

Allen. I bought a beard this day at *Padua*,
Such as our common actors use to weare
When youth would put on ages countenance;
So like in shape, in colour, and in all,
To that which growes upon your aged face,
That were I dressed in your abilimentes,
Your selfe would scarcely know me from your selfe.

Fall. That's excellent. What shape hast thou devis'd,
To be my vizard to delude the worlde?

Allen. Why thus: ile presentlie shave off your haire,
And dresse you in a lowlie shepheardes weede;
Then you will seeme to have the carefull charge
Of some wealth-bringing, rich, and fleecy flocke,
And so passe currant from suspition.

Fall. This care of thine, my sonne, doth testifie,
Nature in thee hath firme predominance,
That neither losse of friend, nor vile reproch,
Can shake thee with their strongest violence:
In this disguise, ile see the end of thee,
That thou, acquited, then maist succour me.

Allen. I am assur'd to be exempt from woe:--
This plot will worke my certaine overthrowe.   [(To the) People.

Fall. I will beare hence thy mother, and my wife,
Untimely murthered with true sorrowes knife.   [***Exit***.

Allen. Untimely murthered! happy was that griefe,
Which hath abridg'd whole numbers numberlesse
Of hart-surcharging deplorations.
She shall have due and Christian funerall,
And rest in peace amongst her auncestors.
As for our bodies, they shall be inter'd,
In ravening mawes, of Ravens, Puttockes, Crowes,
Of tatlin[g] Magpies, and deathes harbingers,
That wilbe glutted with winde-shaken limmes
Of blood-delighting hatefull murtherers.
And yet these many winged sepulchers,
Shall turne to earth, so I and father shall,
At last attaine to earth by funerall.

Well I will prosecute my pollicy,
That wished death may end my miseries.

[*Exit*.

[SCENE VII.]

Enter Cowley and Williams.

Cow. Still in your dumpes, good **Harry**? yet at last,
Utter your motive of this heavinesse.
Why go you not unto your maisters house?
What, are you parted? if that be the cause,
I will provide you of a better place.

Wil. Who roves all day, at length may hit the marke;
That is the cause,--because I cannot stay
With him whose love is dearer then my life.

Cow. Why fell you out? why did you part so soone?

Wil. We fell not out, but feare hath parted us.

Cow. What, did he feare your truth or honest life?

Wil. No, no, your understanding is but dimme,
That farre-remooved cannot iudge the feare.
We both were fearefull, and we both did part,
Because indeed we both were timerous.

Cow. What accident begot your mutuall feare?

Wil. That which my hart hath promis'd to conceale.

Cow. Why, now you fall into your auncient vaine.

Wil. Tis vaine to urge me from this silent vaine;
I will conceale it, though it breed my paine.

Cow. It seemes to be a thing of consequence,
And therefore prithie, **Harry**, for my love,
Open this close fast-clasped mysterie.

Wil. Were I assur'd my hart should have release
Of secret torment and distemperature,
I would reveale it to you specially
Whom I have found my faithfull favorite.

Cow. Good **Harrie Williams**, make no doubt of that;
Besides your griefe reveald may have reliefe,
Beyond your present expectation.
Then tell it, **Harry**, what soere it be,
And ease your hart of horror, me of doubt.

Wil. Then have you heard of **Beech** of **Lambert Hill**,
And of his boy which late were murthered?

Cow. I heard, and sawe their mangled carcases.

Will. But have you heard of them that murthered them?

Cow. No, would I had, for then Ide blaze their shame,

And make them pay due penance for their sinne.

Wil. This I misdoubted, therefore will forbeare
To utter what I thought to have reveald.

Cow. Knowst thou the actors of this murthrous deed,
And wilt conceale it now the deed is done?
Alas, poore man, thou knowest not what thou doost!
Thou hast incur'd the danger of the lawe
And thou mongst them must suffer punishment,
Unlesse thou do confesse it presentlie.

Wil. What? shall I then betray my maisters life?

Cow. Better then hazard both thy life and soule
To boulster out such barbarous villanie.
Why, then belike your maister did the deed?

Wil. My maister unawares escapt my mouth;
But what the Lord doth please shall come to light,
Cannot be hid by humaine pollicie:
His haplesse hand hath wrought the fatall end
Of *Robert Beech* and *Thomas Winchester*.

Cow. Could he alone do both those men to death?
Hadst thou no share in execution?

Wil. Nor knew not of it, till the deed was done.

Cow. If this be true, thou maist escape with life:
Confesse the truth unto the officers,
And thou shalt finde the favour of the lawe.

Wil. If I offended, 'twas my Maister's love
That made me hide his great transgressions:
But I will be directed as you please.
So save me God, as I am innocent!

[*Exeunt.*

[SCENE VIII.]

Enter Alenso in Falleriaes apparell and berd;
Falleria shaven in shepheards habilliments.

Fal. Part of my selfe, now seemst thou wholy me,
And I seeme neither like my selfe nor thee,
Thankes to thy care and this unknown disguise.
I like a shepheard now must learn to know,
When to lead foorth my little bleating flock,
To pleasing pastures, and well-fatting walkes;
In stormie time to drive them to the lee;
To cheere the pretie Lambes, whose bleating voice
Doth crave the wished comfort of their dams;
To sound my merry Bag-pipe on the downes,
In shearing times, poore Shepheards festivals;
And lastlie, how to drive the Wolfe away,
That seeke to make the little Lambes their pray.

Allen. Ah, have you care to drive the Wolfe away
From sillie creatures wanting intellecte,
And yet would suffer your devouring thoughts,
To suck the blood of your dead brothers sonne!

As pure and innocent as any Lambe
Pertillo was, which you have fed upon.
But things past helpe may better be bewaild
With carefull teares, then finde a remedie;
Therefore, for feare our practise be espide,
Let us to question of our husbandrie.
How many Lambes fell from the middle flock,
Since I myselfe did take the latter view?

   Enter Vesuvio, Turqual, Alberto.

Fall. Some vive and twenty, whereof two are dead.
But three and twenty scud about the fields,
That glads my hart to ze their iollitie.

Vesu. This is the man, conferring of his Lambes,
That slew a Lambe worth all his flock besides.

Allen. What is the time to let the Weathers blood?
The forward spring, that hath such store of grasse,
Hath fild them full of ranke unwholsome blood,
Which must be purg'd; else, when the winter comes,
The rot will leave me nothing but their skinnes.

Fall. Chil let om blood, but yet it is no time,
Untill the zygne be gone below the hart.[41]

Vesu. Forbeare a while this idle businesse,
And talke of matters of more consequence.

Fall. Che tell you plaine, you are no honest man,
To call a sheapheards care an idle toye.
What though we have a little merry sport

With flowrie gyrlonds, and an Oaten pipe,
And jolly friskins on a holly-day,
Yet is a shepheards cure a greater carke
Then sweating Plough-men with their busie warke.

Vesu. Hence! leave your sheepish ceremoniall!--
And now, *Fallerio*, in the Princes name,
I do arrest you, for the cruell murther
Of young *Pertillo*, left unto your charge,
Which you discharged with a bloody writ,
Sign'd by the hands of those you did suborne.
Nay, looke not strange, we have such evidence,
To ratifie your *Stigian* cruelty,
That cannot be deluded any way.

Allen. Alas, my Lords, I know not what you say!
As for my Nephew, he, I hope, is well:
I sent him yesterday to *Padua*.

Alber. I, he is well, in such a vengers handes,
As will not winck at your iniquitie.

Allen. By heaven and earth my soule is innocent!
Say what you will, I know my conscience.

Fal.--To be afflicted with a scourge of care,
Which my oreweaning rashnesse did infflict.

Turq. Come, beare him hence! expostulate no more;
That heart that could invent such treachery,
Can teach his face to brave it cunninglie.

Alen. I do defie your accusations;
Let me have justice, I will answere it.

Vesuv. So, beare him hence! I meane to stay behinde,
To take possession of his goods and landes
For the Dukes use: it is too manifest.

Allen. I hope youle answere anything you doe.
My Lord *Vesuvio*, you shall answere it,
And all the rest that use extremities.

Alber. I, to the Dukes Exchecker, not to you.

[*Exeunt omnes; manet Falleria*.

Fal. Thus shades are caught when substances are fled.
Indeede they have my garments, but my selfe
Am close enough from their discoverie;
But not so close but that my verie soule,
Is ract with tormentes for *Pertillos* death.
I am *Acteon*; I doe beare about,
My hornes of shame and inhumanitie.
My thoughts, like hounds which late did flatter me
With hope of great succeeding benefits,
Now gin to teare my care-tormented heart
With feare of death and tortring punishment.
These are the stings whenas our consciences
Are stuf'd and clogd with close-concealed crimes.
Well, I must smoather all these discontentes,
And strive to beare a smoother countenaunce
Then rugged care would willingly permit.
Ile to the Court to see *Allenso* free,
That he may then relieve my povertie.

[*Exit*.

[SCENE IX.]

 Enter Constable, three watchmen with halberdes.

Con. Who would have thought of all the men alive
That *Thomas Merry* would have done this deede
So full of ruth and monstrous wickednesse!

1 *wat*. Of all the men that live in *London* walles,
I would have thought that *Merry* had bin free.

2 *wat*. Is this the fruites of Saint-like Puritans?
I never like such damn'd hipocrisie.

3 *wat*. He would not loase a sermon for a pound,
An oath he thought would rend his iawes in twaine,
An idle word did whet Gods vengeance on;
And yet two murthers were not scripulous.
Such close illusions God will bring to light,
And overthrowe the workers with his might.

Con. This is the house; come let us knocke at dore;
I see a light, they are not all in bed:
   [*Knockes; Rachell comes downe*.
How now, faire maide? is your brother up?

Rach. He's not within, sir; would you speake with him?

Con. You doe but iest; I know he is within,
And I must needes go uppe and speake with him.

Rach. In deede, good sir, he is in bed a sleepe,
And I was loath to trouble him to-night.

Con. Well, sister, I am sorry for your sake;
But for your brother, he is knowne to be
A damned villaine and an hipocrite.
Rachell, I charge thee in her highnesse name,
To go with us to prison presently.

Rach. To prison, sir? alas, what have I done?

Con. You know that best, but every one doe know
You and your brother murthered Maister *Beech*,
And his poore boy that dwelt at *Lambert hill*.

Rach. I murthered? my brother knowes that I,
Did not consent to either of their deathes.

Con. That must be tride; where doth your brother lye?

Rach. Here in his bed; me thinks he's not a sleepe.

Con. Now, Maister *Merry*, are you in a sweate?
      [**Throwes his night cap away**.

Merry sigh. No verily, I am not in a sweate.

Con. Some sodaine feare affrights you; whats the cause?

Mer. Nothing but that you wak'd me unawares.

Con. In the Queenes name I doe commaund you rise,
And presently to goe along with us.
                [*Riseth up*.

Mer. With all my hart; what, doe you know the cause?

Con. We partly doe; when saw you maister *Beech*?

Mer. I doe not well remember who you meane.

Con. Not *Beech*, the Chaundler upon *Lambert hill*?

Mer. I know the man, but saw him not this fortnight.

Con. I would you had not, for your sisters sake,
For yours, for his, and for his harmlesse boy.
Be not obdurate in your wickednesse;
Confession drawes repentance after it.

Mer. Well, maister Constable, I doe confesse,
I was the man that did them both to death:
As for my sister and my harmlesse man,
I doe protest they both are innocent.

Con. Your man is fast in hold, and hath confest
The manner how, and where, the deede was done;
Therefore twere vaine to colour anything.
Bring them away.

Rach. Ah brother, woe is me!

Mer. I comfortlesse will helpe to comfort thee.

[*Exeunt*.

Enter Trueth.

Weepe, weepe poor soules, & enterchange your woes;
Now, *Merry*, change thy name and countenance;
Smile not, thou wretched creature, least in scorne
Thou smile to thinke on thy extremities.
Thy woes were countlesse for thy wicked deedes,
Thy sisters death neede not increase the coumpt,
For thou couldst never number them before.--
Gentles, helpe out with this suppose, I pray,
And thinke it truth, for Truth dooth tell the tale.
Merry, by lawe convict as principall,
Receives his doome, to hang till he be dead,
And afterwards for to be hangd in chaines.
Williams and ***Rachell*** likewise are convict
For their concealment; ***Williams*** craves his booke[42]
And so receaves a brond[43] of infamie;
But wretched ***Rachels*** sexe denies that grace,
And therefore dooth receive a doome of death
To dye with him whose sinnes she did conceale.
Your eyes shall witnesse of their shaded tipes,
Which many heere did see perform'd indeed.
As for *Fallerio*, not his homelie weedes,
His beardlesse face, nor counterfetted speech,
Can shield him from deserved punishment;

But what he thinkes shall rid him from suspect,
Shall drench him in more waves of wretchednesse,
Pulling his sonne into relentlesse iawes,
Of hungrie death, on tree of infamie.
Heere comes the Duke that doomes them both to die;
Next *Merries* death shall end this Tragedie.

[*Exit.*

[ACT THE FIFTH.]

[SCENE I.]

Enter Duke, Vesuvio, Turq., Alberto: and Fallerio disguised.

Duke. Where is that *Syren*, that incarnate fiend,
Monster of Nature, spectacle of shame,
Blot and confusion of his familie,
False-seeming semblance of true-dealing trust,
I meane *Fallerio*, bloody murtherer:
Hath he confest his cursed treacherie,
Or will he stand to proove his innocence?

Vesu. We have attach'de *Fallerio*, gracious lord,
And did accuse him with *Pertillos* death;
But he remote will not confesse himselfe
Neither the meanes nor author of the same.
His mightie vowes and protestations
Do almost seeme to pleade integritie,

But that we all do know the contrarie.

Fall.--I know your error stricks your knowledge blinde;
His seeming me, doth so delude your minde.   [(To the) People.

Duke. Then bring him forth, to answer for himselfe,
Since he stands stoutly to denie the deed:

[*Alberto and other fetch Alenso*.

His sonne can witnesse that the dying man
Accusde *Fallerio* for his treacherie.--
Stand forth thou close disguised hipocrite,
And speake directlie to these articles:
First, didst thou hire two bloodie murtherers
To massacre *Pertillo* in a wood?

Alen. I never did suborne such murtherers,
But ever lov'd *Pertillo* as my life.

Duke. Thy sonne can witnesse to the contrarie.

Alen. I have no sonne to testifie so much.

Fal.--No, for his gravitie is counterfeit,
Pluck off his beard, and you will sweare it so.

Vesu. Have you no sonne? doth not *Alenso* live?

Alen. *Alenso* lives, but is no sonne of mine.

Alber. Indeed his better part had not his source

From thy corrupted vice-affecting hart,
For vertue is the marke he aimeth at.

Duke. I dare be sworne that *Sostrata* would blush,
Shouldst thou deny *Alenso* for thy sonne.

Alen. Nay, did she live, she would not challenge me
To be the father of that haplesse sonne.

Turq. Nay, then anon you will denie your selfe
To be your selfe, unjust *Fallerio*.

Alen. I do confesse my selfe to be my selfe,
But will not answere to *Fallerio*.

Duke. Not to *Fallerio*? this is excellent!
You are the man was cal'd *Fallerio*.

Alen. He never breathed yet that cal'd me so,
Except he were deceiv'd as you are now.

Duke. This impudence shall not excuse your fault;
You are well knowne to be *Fallerio*,
The wicked husband of dead *Sostrata*
And father to the vertuous *Alenso*;
And even as sure as all these certeinties,
Thou didst contrive thy little Nephewes death.

Alen. True, for I am nor false *Fallerio*,
Husband, nor father, as you do suggest,
And therefore did not hire the murtherers;
Which to be true acknowledge with your eyes.

[*Puls off his disguise.*

Duke. How now, my Lords! this is a myracle,
To shake off thirtie yeares so sodeinlie
And turne from feeble age to flourishing youth!

Alb. But he my Lord that wrought this miracle,
Is not of power to free himselfe from death,
Through the performance of this suddaine change.

Duke. No, were he the chiefest hope of Christendome,
He should not live for this presumption:
Use no excuse, ***Alenso***, for thy life;
My doome of death shall be irrevocable.

Alen. Ill fare his soule that would extenuate
The rigor of your life-confounding doome!
I am prepar'd with all my hart to die,
For thats th' end of humaine miserie.

Duke. Then thus: you shall be hang'd immediately,
For your illusion of the Magistrates
With borrowed shapes of false antiquitie.

Alen. Thrice-happy sentence, which I do imbrace
With a more fervent and unfained zeale
Then an ambicious rule-desiring man
Would do a Iem-bedecked Diadem,
Which brings more watchfull cares and discontent
Then pompe or honor can remunerate.
When I am dead, let it be said of me,
Alenso died to set his father free.

Fal. That were a freedome worse than servitude
To cruell Turke or damned Infidell.
Most righteous Judge, I do appeale for Iustice,
Justice on him that hath deserved death,
Not on *Alenso*; he is innocent.

Alen. But I am guiltie of abetting him,
Contrarie to his Maiestie's Edict,
And therefore death is meritorious.

Fall. I am the wretch that did subborne the slaves,
To murther poore *Pertillo* in the wood.
Spare, spare *Alenso*! he is innocent.

Duke. What strange appeale is this! we know thee not:
None but *Fallerio* is accusde hereof.

Alen. Then, father, get you hence, depart in time,
Least being knowne you suffer for the crime.

Fal. Depart, and leave thee clad in horrors cloake,
And suffer death for true affection!
Although my soule be guiltie of more sinne,
Then ever sinfull soule were guiltie of,
Yet fiends of hell would never suffer this.
I am thy father, though unworthy so:
Oh, still I see these weeds do feare your eyes.
I am *Fallerio*, make no doubt of me,   [*Put off*.
Though thus disguisde, in habite, countenance,
Only to scape the terror of the lawe.

Alen. And I *Alenso* that did succour him

Gainst your commaundement, mightie Soveraigne.
Ponder your oath, your vowe, as God did live,
I should not live, if I did rescue him.
I did, God lives, and will revenge it home,
If you defer my condigne punishment.

Duke. Assure your selves, you both shall suffer death:
But for *Fallerio*, he shall hang in chaines
After he's dead, for he was principall.

Fall. Unsaverie Woormewood, Hemlock, bitter gall,
Brings no such bad, unrelisht, sower taste,
Unto the tongue as this death-boding voice,
Brings to the eares of poore *Fallerio*,
Not for myselfe but for *Allensoes* sake,
Whome I have murthered by my trechery.
Ah my dread Lord, if any little sparke
Of melting pittie doth remaine alive,
And not extinguisht by my impious deedes,
Oh kindle it unto a happie flame,
To light *Allenso* from this miserie
Which through dim death he's like to fall into.

Allen. That were to overthrow my soule and all.
Should you reverse this sentence of my death,
My selfe would play the death-man on my selfe
And overtake your swift and winged soule,
Ere churlish *Caron* had transported you
Unto the fields of sad *Proserpina*.

Duke. Cease, cease, *Fallerio*, in thy bootlesse prayers.
I am resolv'd, I am inexorable.

Vesuvio, see their judgement be performde,
And use *Alenso* with all clemencie,
Provided that the lawe be satisfied.

[*Exit Duke and Alberto*.

Vesu. It shall be done with all respectivenesse;
Have you no doubt of that, my gratious Lord.

Fall. Here is a mercie mixt with equitie,
To show him favour but cut off his head.

Alen. My reverend father pacifie yourselfe;
I can, and will, indure the stroake of death,
Were his appearance nere so horrible,
To meete *Pertillo* in another world.

Fal. Thou shouldst have tarried untill natures course
Had been extinct, that thou oregrowne with age,
Mightst die the death of thy progenitors;
Twas not thy meanes he died so soddenly,
But mine, that causing his, have murthered thee.

Alen. But yet I slew my mother, did I not?

Fal. I, with reporting of my villanie.
The very audit of my wickednesse,
Had force enough to give a sodaine death.
Ah sister, sister, now I call to minde,
Thy dying wordes now prov'd a prophesie,
If you deale ill with this distressed childe,
God will no doubt revenge the innocent.
I have delt ill, and God hath tane revenge.

Allen. Now let us leave remembrance of past deedes,
And thinke on that which more concerneth us.

Fal. With all my hart; thou ever wert the spur
Which prict me on to any godlinesse;
And now thou doest indevor to incite
Me make my parting peace with God and men.
I doe confesse, even from my verie soule,
My hainous sinne and grievous wickednesse
Against my maker manie thousand waies:
Ab imo cordis I repent my selfe
Of all my sinnes against his maiestie;
And, heavenly father, lay not to my charge
The death of poore ***Pertillo*** and those men
Which I suborn'd to be his murtherers,
When I appeare before thy heavenlie throne
To have my sentence or of life or death.

Vesu. Amen, amen, and God continue still
These mercie-moving meditations.

Allen. And thou, great God, which art omnipotent,
Powerful! enough for to redeeme our soules
Even from the verie gates of gaping hell,
Forgive our sinnes and wash away our faults
In the sweete river of that precious blood
Which thy deare sonne did shed in ***Galgotha***,
For the remission of all contrite soules.

Fal. Forgive thy death, my thrice-beloved sonne.

Allen. I doe, and, father, pardon my misdeedes

Of disobedience and unthankfullnesse.

Fal. Thou never yet wert disobedient,
Unlesse I did commaund unlawfulnesse.
Ungratefulnesse did never trouble thee;
Thou art too bounteous thus to guerdon me.

Allen. Come, let us kisse and thus imbrace in death.
Even when you will, come, bring us to the place,
Where we may consumate our wretchednesse,
And change it for eternall hapinesse.

[*Exeunt omnes*.

[SCENE II.]

Enter Merry and Rachel to execution with Officers
with Halberdes, the Hangman with a lather [sic] &c.

Mer. Now, sister *Rachell*, is the houre come
Wherein we both must satisfie the law
For *Beeches* death and harmelesse *Winchester*.
Weepe not sweete sister, for that cannot helpe:
I doe confesse fore all this company
That thou wert never privie to their deaths,
But onelie helpest me, when the deede was done,
To wipe the blood and hide away my sinne;
And since this fault hath brought thee to this shame,
I doe intreate thee on my bended knee
To pardon me for thus offending thee.

Rach. I doe forgive you from my verie soule,
And thinke not that I shed these store of teares,
For that I price my life, or feare to dye,
Though I confesse the manner of my death
Is much more grievous then my death it selfe;
But I lament for that it hath beene said
I was the author of this crueltie
And did produce you to this wicked deede,
Whereof God knowes that I am innocent.

Mer. Indeede thou art; thy conscience is at peace,
[*Goe up the lather*.
And feeles no terror for such wickednesse;
Mine hath beene vexed but is now at rest,
For that I am assur'd my hainous sinne
Shall never rise in judgement gainst my soule,
But that the blood of *Jesus Christ* hath power
To make my purple sinne as white as Snowe.
One thing, good people, witnesse here with me,
That I doe dye in perfect charitie,
And do forgive, as I would be forgiven
First of my God and then of all the world.
Cease publishing that I have beene a man
Train'd up in murther or in crueltie,
For fore this time, this time is all too soone,
I never slue or did consent to kill;
So helpe me God as this I speake is true!
I could say something of my innocence,
In fornication and adulterie,
But I confesse the iustest man alive,
That beares about the frailtie of a man,
Cannot excuse himselfe from daily sinne
In thought, in word, and deed. Such was my life.

I never hated *Beech* in all my life,
Onely desire of money which he had,
And the inciting of that foe of man,
That greedie gulfe, that great *Leviathan*,
Did halle [*sic*] me on to these callamities;
For which, even now my very soule dooth bleede.
God strengthen me with patience to endure
This chastisement, which I confesse too small
A punishment for this my hainous sinne.
Oh be couragious, sister! fight it well!
We shall be crown'd with immortallitie.

Rach. I will not faint, but combat manfully;
Christ is of power to helpe and strengthen me.

Officer. I pray make hast; the hower is almost past.

Mer. I am prepar'd; oh God, receive my soule;
Forgive my sinnes, for they are numberlesse.
Receive me, God, for now I come to thee!
  [*Turne of the Lather. Rachel shrinketh*.

Offi. Nay shrinke not, woman; have a cheerefull hart.

Rach. I, so I do, and yet this sinfull flesh
Will be rebellious gainst my willing spirit.
Come, let me clime these steps that lead to heaven,
Although they seeme the staires of infamie:
Let me be merror to ensuing times,
And teach all sisters how they do conceale,
The wicked deeds of brethren, or of friends.
I not repent me of my love to him,
But that thereby I have provoked God

To heavie wrath and indignation;
Which turne away, great God, for Christes sake.
Ah, **Harry Williams**, thou wert chiefest cause,
That I doe drinke of this most bitter cup,
For hadst thou opened **Beeches** death at first,
The boy had liv'd and thou hadst sav'd my life.
But thou art branded with a marke of shame,
And I forgive thee from my very soule.
Let him and me learn all that heare of this
To utter brothers or their maisters misse;
Conceale no murthers, lest it do beget
More bloody deeds of like deformitie.
Thus God forgive my sinnes, receive my soule!
And though my dinner be of bitter death,
I hope my soule shall sup with Jesus Christ,
And see his presence everlastingly.   [*Dyeth*.

Offi. The Lord of heaven have mercy on her soule,
And teach all others by this spectacle,
To shunne such dangers as she ran into,
By her misguided taciturnitie:
Cut downe their bodies, give hers funerall,
But let his body be conveyed hence,
To **Mile-end** greene, and there be hang'd in chaines.

[*Exeunt omnes*.

Enter Truthe.

Tru. See here the end of lucre and desire
Of riches, gotten by unlawfull meanes.
What monstrous evils this hath brought to passe,
Your scarce-drie eyes give testimoniall;

The father sonne, the sister brother brings,
To open scandall and contemptuous death.

Enter Homicide and Covetousnesse.

But heere come they that wrought these deeds of ruthe,
As if they meant to plot new wickednesse.
Whether so fast, you damned miscreants,
Yee vaine deluders of the credulous,
That seeke to traine men to destruction?

Mur. Why, we will on, to set more harmes a flote,
That I may swim in rivers of warme blood,
Out-flowing from the sides of Innocents.

Cove. I will entice the greedie-minded soule,
To pull the fruite from the forbidden tree;
Yet *Tantall*-like, he shall but glut his eye,
Nor feede his body with salubrious fruite.

Tru. Hence Stigmaticks, you shall not harbor heare,
To practice execrable butcheries!
My selfe will bring your close designes to light,
And overthrow your vilde conspiracies.
No hart shall intertaine a murthrous thought
Within the sea-imbracing continent,
Where faire *Eliza*, Prince of pietie,
Doth weare the peace-adorned Diadem.

Cove. Mauger the worst, I will have many harts
That shall affect my secret whisperings;
And chinck of golde is such a pleasing crie,
That all men wish to heare such harmony,

And I will place stern *Murther* by my side,
That we may do more harmes then haughty pride.

Homi. Truth, now farewell; hereafter thou shalt see
Ile vexe thee more with many tragedies.

Truth. The more the pitty; would the hart of man
Were not so open wide to entertaine
The harmfull baites of selfe-devouring sinne!
But from the first unto the latter times,
It hath and will be so eternally.----
Now it remaines to have your good advice
Unto a motion of some consequence.
There is a Barke thats newly rigd for sea,
Unmand, unfurnishd with munition:
She must incounter with a greater foe
Then great *Alcydes* slue in *Lerna* Lake
Would you be pleasd to man this willing barke
With good conceits of her intencion;
To store her with the thundring furniture
Of smoothest smiles, and pleasing plaudiats;
She shall be able to endure the shock
Of snarling *Zoylus*, and his cursed crue,
That seekes to sincke her in reproches waves;
And may perchance obteine a victorie
Gainst curious carpes, and fawning parasites:
But if you suffer her, for want of ayde,
To be orewhelmed by her insulting foes,
Oh then she sinckes, that meant to passe the flood
With stronger force to do her countrie good.
It resteth thus; whether she live or dye,
She is your Beades-man everlastinglie.

Finis--Rob. Yarington.

Laus Deo

INTRODUCTION TO THE CAPTIVES; OR, THE LOST RECOVERED.

In Sir Henry Herbert's MS. Office-Book, under date Sept. 3rd, 1624, is the entry:--"for the Cock-pit Company[44] a new play called the Captive [*sic*] or the Lost Recovered, written by Hayward," i.e., Heywood. The lost recovered! Lost for two centuries and a half was this comedy of dear Tom Heywood, until I recovered it from Egerton MS. 1994. I am proud to have rendered this service to a gentle poet who has given me many hours of delight.

The play is without title or author's name in the MS. After reading the first page I judged that the author was Heywood, and this impression was soon confirmed beyond all doubt. In the MS. the present play is immediately followed by a piece called *Calisto*, which consists of scenes from Heywood's *Golden Age* and *Silver Age*. I have elsewhere mentioned (Vol. ii. p. 419) that *Calisto* and *The Captives* are written in the same desperately difficult handwriting,--peculiar to these two plays, and not found in any other part of the volume. There can be no doubt that whoever transcribed *Calisto* transcribed also The Captives. But from internal evidence alone--putting aside the testimony afforded by the handwriting, and ignoring the entry in Sir Henry Herbert's Office-Book--any competent reader could plainly perceive that the play is Heywood's. In the very first scene--in the conversation between Treadway and Raphael--we feel at once the charm of that hearty "Christianism" which is never absent from Heywood's work. There is no affectation in Heywood; he is always natural and simple, though occasionally the writing sprawls.

Everybody knows the droll description in Heywood's ***English Traveller*** of the "Shipwreck by Drink,"[45]--how some unthrift youths, carousing deeply, chanced to turn their talk on ships and storms at sea; whereupon one giddy member of the company suddenly conceived that the room was a pinnace, that the sounds of revelry were the bawlings of sailors, and that his unsteady footing was due to the wildness of the tempest; the illusion spread among his companions, and a scene of whimsical confusion followed. In ***The Captives***, ii. 2, we have a similar conceit suggested:--

Scrib. Such was the grace heaven sent us, who from perill,
Danger of lyfe, the extreamest of all extreames
Hathe brought us to the happy patronage
Of this most reverent abbott.

Clowne. What dangers? what extreames?

Scrib. From the sea's fury, drowneing; for last night
Our shipp was splitt, wee cast upon these rocks.

Clowne. Sayd in a jest, in deede! Shipwreck by land! I perceive you tooke the wooden waggen for a ship and the violent rayne for the sea, and by cause some one of the wheels broake and you cast into some water plashe, you thought the shipp had splitt and you had bene in danger of drowneinge.

The main story of ***The Captives*** is borrowed from Plautus's ***Rudens***, many passages being translated almost word for word. It will be remembered that in the ***English Traveller*** Heywood was indebted to another of Plautus's plays--the ***Mostellaria***. I have not been able to discover the source of the very curious underplot of ***The Captives***.

The MS. from which the play is printed bears every appearance of being a play-house copy. Numerous passages have been cancelled, seemingly (for the most part) by the hand of some reviser. In most instances I have restored the cancelled passages to the text--though the task of deciphering them has been cruelly difficult.

THE CAPTIVES; OR, THE LOST RECOVERED.

A Comedy by THOMAS HEYWOOD.

Licensed by Sir Henry Herbert in 1624,
and now first printed from Egerton MS. 1994.

Actus primus.

SCENA PR.

    Enter Mr. Raphael a younge marchaunt, Mr. Treadway
    his companione and frend.

Raphael. You talke to one thats deaf; I am resolv'd.

Treadway. I knwe [*sic*] you are not of that stupid sence
But you will lyst to reason.

Raphael. Alls but vayne.

Treadway. You saye shees fayre.

Raphael. And there-fore to bee lov'd.

Treadway.[46] No consequent
To trust to collour. Are not the bewtyous lyllyes,
The gardens pryde and glorye of the feilds,
Thoughe to the eye fayre and delectable,
Yet ranke in smell? the stayneles swanne
With all the Oceans water cannot wash
The blacknes from her feete, tis borne with her.
Oft painted vessayles bringe in poysond cates,
And the blackest serpents weare the goldenst scales;
And woman, made mans helper at the fyrst,
Dothe oft proove his destroyer.

Raphael. Saye perhapps
Some frend of yours miscarried in his choyse,
Will you condeme all women for that one?
Bycause we reade one **Lais** was unchast,
Are all Corinthian Ladyes cortesans?
Shall I, bycause my neighbours house was burnt,
Condeme the necessary use of fyre?
One surfeitts, and shall I refuse to eate?
That marchant man by shipwreck lost his goodds;
Shall I, bycause hee perisht in the sea,
Abiure the gainfull trade of merchandyse,
Despoyle my shipps, and unbecom [?] the deepes
Of theire fayre Sayles and tackles?

Treadway. Not so, frend.[47]
Althoughe her person may perhapps content,
Consider but the place.

Raphael. I knwe it badd,
Nay woorst of Ills.

Treadway. A howse of prostitution
And common brothellrie.

Raphael. Which coold not stand
But that her vertue guards it and protects it
From blastinges and heavens thunders. There shee lyves
Lyke to a ritche and pretious Jewell lost,
Fownd shyninge on a doonge-hill, yet the gemme
No wyse disparadged of his former worthe
Nor bated of his glory; out of this fyre
Of lust and black temptation sheis [*sic*] returned
Lyke gold repur'd and tryde.

Treadway. Of what byrthe is shee?

Raphael. Unknwne to mee or any: shee protests,
Neye to her self; what neede I question that?
Sure sutche sweete features, goodnes, modesty
Such gentlenes, such vertue cannot bee
Deryvd from base and obscure parentadge.

Treadway. Whats then your end and purpose?

Raphael. To redeeme her
Out of this gayle of sinne and leprosye,
This mart of all diseases, where shee lyves
Still under the comande and Tyrany
Of a most base hee-bawde: about which busines
Wee have allready traffict.

Treadway. Well, if so,
And to dispose her elsewhere to her goodd,
Provided still that vertue be your ayme,

I cannot but commende your charity
And to my power I'l seeke to further it.

Raphael. You so intyre mee to you. Within theire!

Enter the Clowne.

Clowne. Within theire is nowe without heare: your worshipps pleasure?

Raphael. Hye to the next key and inquire for one cald Seignior *Mildewe* and resolve him from mee that I have kept apointment: the somms redy and present to bee tendred.

Clowne. Who? the *Frenshe* monster,[48] *Neapolitan* Seignor, the man-makarel[49] and marchant of madens-fleshe that deales altogether in flawed ware and crackt comodityes? the bawdy broker, I meanes, where a man for his dollers may have choyse of diseases, and som tymes the pox too, if hee will leeve beehind him a good pawne for it.

Raphael. How thou drummst.

Clowne. Marry qothe hee. So I may happen to bringe it awaye in my nose. Well I smell some bawdy business or other in hand. They call this place *Marcellis* Roade, the cheiff haven towne in *France*, but hee keepes a road[50] in his oune howse wherein have ridd and bin ridd more leakinge vessayles, more panderly pinks,[51] pimps and punkes, more rotten bottoms ballanst, more fly-boates[52] laden and unladen every morninge and evenning tyde then weare able to fill the huge greate baye of *Portingall*. Is this all, syr?

Raphael. Yes all, and heares the somme.

Clowne. A small somme of that is worthe all the busines that I am sent about, for the all in all on't is I am afrayde that all will proove woorthe nothinge.

Treadway. And yet mee thinkes ere folly you conclude
You should a little stagger.

Raphael. Should? wherein?

Treadway. For many reasons: Il alleadge som fewe.
Who knwes but this your fayre and seeminge saynt,
Thoughe disposd well and in her owne condition
Of promisinge goodnes, yet livinge in the seminary
Of all libidinous actions, spectars, sights,
Even in the open market where sinne's sould
Where lust and all uncleanes are commerst
As freely as comodityes are vended
Amongst the noblest marchants,--who I saye
So confident that dare presume a virgin
Of such a soft and maiden temperature,
Deyly and howerly still sollicited
By gallants of all nations, all degrees,
Allmost all ages, even from upright youth
To the stoopinge and decrepitt--

Raphael. Heare mee nowe.

Treadway. Two woords and I have doone: the place considered,
The basenes of the person under whome
Shee lyves opprest, a slave of sordid lyfe,
Conditiond with the devill, tempting still
Sometymes by fayre means, then againe by foul,
To prostitute her for his servyle gaynes;

And next the dissolute crewe with which shees hows'd
Ech night, ech deye perswedinge boathe with toonge
And lewde example; all these circonstances
Duly considered, I shoold dowbt at least,
If not presume, the woorst.

Raphael. Oh you have pleasd mee,
And in proposinge all these difficultyes
Given of her graces ample testimony.
Shee is that miracle, that only one
That cann doo these; wear't comon in the sexe
Twold not appeare to mee so admirable;
It is for these I love her.

Treadway. You are resolvd
And I'l not staye your purpose.

    Enter the Clowne with Mildewe and Sarleboys his
    guest and frende.

Clowne. I have brought this flesh-fly whome as soone as the butchers wyves sawe comminge throwghe the shambles, they all of them stood with theire flapps in theire hands like fanns. I, demandinge the reason itt was answerd me againe itt was to keepe away his infectious breath least it should fill theire meate with fly-blowes.

Raphael. Well, mett, good Mr. **Mildewe**.

Mildewe. My returne
Of your salutes I cast belowe your feete.

Raphael. Syr, I am yours to treade on. You will then
Stand to your former bargen?

Mildewe. I weare else
Not woorthy to bee stil'd what I am tearmd,
A trewe venereall broaker.

Clowne. That's in *Italian*
A damnable hee bawde.

Mildewe Y'have such a bargen
Marcellis, nor all France, shall yeild the like.
Tis such a deynty peece of purity
Such a coy thinge that[53] hee unto whose lott
She shall hereafter fall may boast himself
To bee a happy husband. For our trade
Shees out at that: neather promises, rewards,
Example or Intreaty, fayre, fowle meanes,
Gaine present or the hope of future goodd,
Can force from her a presens; then much lesse
A frendly prostitution.

Raphael. Hearst thou this?

Treadway. Yes[54] and comende it in her, if that toonge,
Even from his fyrst of speakinge traind to lye,
Can now at lengthe speake truth.

Clowne. Ay theres the dowbt.

Sarly. This too yeares I have quested to his howse,
And knwe all this most certeine.

Raphael. Witnes too.

Mildewe. I doo protest she spoyles my family
And rather growne a hyndrance to my trade
Then benefitt; so that, if not to losse,
I wishe that I were clerly ridd of her,
For shee hathe gott a trick to[55] my whores;
And such as of themselves are impudent,
When shee but coms in presens she makes blushe,
As if ashamd of what they late had doon
Or are about to doo.

Clowne. Well sayde, ould sinner.

Raphael. See, heeres the sum, 3 hundred crownes.

Mildewe. O'th somme.

Raphael. All currant and full weight.

Mildewe. I'l fetch my doughter
That hath no lightnes in her, currant too
As any lasse i'th cittye.

Raphael. *Mildewe*, staye.

Clowne. Staye, oh thou father of fornication and marchant of nothinge but mesteryes and mischeife; whele about, thou dung[c]art of diseases; sayle this way thoue galley foyst[56] of galls and garbadge! Dost not heare my master? staye!

Mildewe. Why, did his worshippe call?

Clowne. Didst thou not heare him call, and mee cry out upon thee?

Mildewe. His pleasure then?

Raphael. I have bethought mee better nowe to keepe
This business secrett, least it chance to arryve
To th'eares of some of my most noble frends;
And not to make it publicke and this honest
Purpose of myne by that meanes misreated,[57]
Heare lett her stay till night bycause I am loath
In th'eye of day to move her through the streetes.

Mildewe. Good, syr.

Raphael. Nwe [Now] in the villaige by, that fronts the sea,
Som halff league off where stands the monastery,
I have bespoake a place to sojorn her.
There I this evening do intend[58] a feast
Where only wee and som fewe private frends
Have purpost to bee jhoviall. To that place
I prithee, with what pryvacy thou canst,
Conduct her and so add unto our guests.

Mildewe. The place I knwe, the tyme is perfect with mee,
And for the feast you saye you have prepared
I shall provyde a stomacke.

Raphael. Her caskett, and such other necessaryes
Included in our bargen, bring alonge
Or lett her mayde do'ot for thee.

Mildewe. I'l not bate her
A ruff or ragge; no pinne that's usefull too her
Will I keepe backe.

Raphael. To this you are witnes, frend.

Treadway. I am, Syr.

Mildewe. So's my guest.

Clowne. And lookes as if with me
Hee only could write witlesse.

Raphael. Supper tyme
You will remember, *Mildewe*.

Mildewe. Possible
I should forgett to eate of others' cost?
It never was my custom.

Clowne. Choake you for't.

Raphael. Come, frend, mee thinks I have doone a deede this day
Crownes all my better actions, for I have raised
An Innocent from the hands of an Infidell agent.

Clowne. Farewell, rott, farewell murreine, adiewe.

Mildewe. Farewell till soone.

    [*Exeunt Raphael, Treadway, and Clowne*.

Sarleb. And do you meane to keepe your promisse then,
And doo as you have sayde?

Mildewe. Why not, I prithee?

What else canst thou advyse mee?

Sarleb. Are not wee
Boathe of a rotten conscience, men debosht,
Secluded from the company of such
As either are or else would stryve to bee
Reputed honest? wherefore then should wee
Keepe tutche with any that professe themselves
Not to bee of our ranke?

Mildewe. Proceede, good frend:
Thou hast putt project in my brayne allredy,
Small tyme woold better fashion.

Sarleb. What if I
Laye such a plotte that you shall gayne these crownes
These full three hundred to your proper use,
And of these peevishe harletryes at home
Make a much greater market?

Mildewe. Marry, syr,
That were a tale worth listeninge.

Sarleb. These crowns
Are all your owne in your possession,
So are the maydes. I knowe you ritche besydes
In coyne and jewells; heere you lyve despysed,
And whats this clime to us of more esteme
Then any forreine region? whores and bawdes
May lyve in every corner of the woorld,
We knowe tis full of sinners. This, this day
Letts hyre a bark; wee dwell upon the haven,
And instantly 'tis done. Shipp all your goods

With these shee-chatteyles; putt this night to sea--
England they saye is full of whormasters;
There will bee vent for such comoditye,
There strompett them where they (you saye) weare born,
Else you in *Spayne* may sell them to the stewes,
Venyce or any place of *Italy*;
They are everywhere good chaffer. If not these,
What saye you to *Morocho, Fesse, Algiers*?
Faith these are wares in all parts vendible,
No matter thoughe to *Turke* and infidell,
So itt bringe gayne and profitt.

Mildewe. Lett me hugg thee
For this, deare frend; heareafter I will style thee
My better genius; thou hast monied mee in this,
Nay landed me, made me thy braynes executor,
And putt mee in a lardge possession.
Go hyre a barke.

Sarlab. I shall.

Mildewe. And instantly.

Sarlab. I shall.

Mildewe. Ere night wee'l putt into a sea
No larger then our full stretcht consciences.
Lett mee once more Imbrace thee.
      [*Exeunt*.

SCENA 2.

Enter an Abbot with his covent[59] of Fryars, amongst them Fryar Jhon, and Fryar Ritchard.

Abbot. As I have heare priority of place,
Boathe by our patrons favour and your voyce,
So give me leave to arbitrate amongst you.

Fr. Jhon. Without respect of person wee acknowledge you.
Our prince and cheiff.

Fr. Rich. And to your fatherly
And grave advyse humbly submitt our selves.

Abbot. Knwe then in this small covent, which consysts
Only of 12 in nomber, fryars I meane
And us the Abbat, I have fownde amongst you
Many and grosse abuses; yet for the present
I will insist on fewe. Quarrells, debates,
Whisperinge, supplantinges, private calumnyes,
These ought not bee in such a brotherhood.
Of these Fryar ***Jhon*** and thou Fryar ***Richard*** are
Accused to bee most guilty, ever jarring
And opposite to peace.

Fr. Jhon. The faults in him.

Fr. Rich. As in all other thinges, so even in this
Hee still is apt to wronge mee.

Fr. Jhon. Hee that fyrst gives th'occasion, fyrst complaines:
It ever was his fashion.

Fr. Rich. Never myne:
I appeale to the whole covent.

Abbot. Mallyce rooted,
I finde, is woondrous hard to bee supprest.
But knwe where consell and advise preveyle not,
The fayrest meanes that I can wourk your peace,
I'l take upon mee my authority,
And where I finde in you the least contempt
I shall severely punishe.

Fr. Jhon. I submitt.

Fr. Rich. I yeeld myself to your grave fatherhood.

Abbot. Consider, sonnes, this cloystered place of ours
Is but newe reared; the founder, hee still lyves,
A souldier once and eminent in the feild,
And after many battayles nowe retyrd
In peace to lyve a lyff contemplative.
Mongst many other charitable deedes,
Unto religion hee hathe vowed this howse,
Next to his owne fayre mantion that adjoynes
And parted only by a slender wall.
Who knwes but that hee neighboring us so neare
And havinge doone this unto pious ends,
May carry over us and our behavioures
An austere eye of censure?

Fr. Jhon. Fitt therefore
Wee should bee in our actions cautelous.[60]

Fr. Rich. And carefull least wee may incurr displeasure
Of such a noble patron.

Abbot. Well observ'd.
His bewtious Lady--

Fr. Jhon. A sweete soule indeede.

Fr. Rich. On whom Fryar *Jhon* casts many a leering eye:
I have observd that too.

Abbot. Boath for her outward feature
And for her inward graces excellent
Beyond compare, shee lykewyse is to us
A worthy benefactor.

Fr. Rich. Tis confest.

Fr. Jhon. Would I might com to bee her confessor:
It is a fayre sweete lady.

Fr. Rich.[61] Howe the lecher
Hugges at the very name.

Abbot. Morninge and eveninge
They deyly com to mattens and to evensonge;
Such and so greate is theire devotion.
That, if not crasd or feylinge in theire healthe,
They do not misse us any hower of prayer;
And therefore it behooves us all in generall
To sett a carefull watche upon our deedes,
Least we that are proffest religious
Bee in the least deffective.

Fr. Richard. Noate, Fryar *Jhon*,
Howe hee makes anticke faces and in scorne
Of this your reverent counsell.

Fr. Jhon. I, alas?
A weaknes from my childhood, I confesse,
I ever had and cannott helpe it nowe,
To have a trobled countenance. I make mouthes?
This (most observed father) but approoves
My innosens and his envye. Markt you that?
Fryar *Richard* bent his fyst and threatned mee.
I call all these to witnesse.

Fr. Rich. No such thinge.
I have a crampe oft takes me in this hand
And makes mee weare clutcht ringers, and that passion
Now came upon mee; but for meanacinge him
It ever was farr from mee. This but showes
His owld inveterate mallice, which in charity
I wishe might heare lye buried.--Syrrah, anon
I'l have you by the eares.

Fr. Jhon. Doo if thou darst;
We'll tugge it out by the teeth.

Fr. Rich. Meete me i'th orchard
Just after even song.

Fr. Jhon. I will make short prayers
Bycause I'l keepe appointment.

Abbot. I am playne

And breife with all: eather betwixt you too [*sic*]
Make frendly reconsilement, and in presence
Of this your brotherhood (for what is fryar
But *frater*, and that's brother?), or my selfe
Out of my power will putt you to a penance
Shall make you in one weeke fyve fasting-dayes.

Fr. Jhon. Oh terrible!

Abbot. Or, if that will not tame you,
I will complayne to'th fownder of your loosenes,
Your riotts, and disorders, and petition
That you, as sowers off seditious hatred[62]
And sole disturbers of our common peace,
Maye bee excluded this society,
Banisht by common barre-law, and shutt out
To publick shame and beggerye.

Fr. Rich. Horrible!

Fr. Jhon. Fyrst then to showe my submisse willingnes
And forwardnes withall: with as much charity
As any new reformed man maye doo,
I with a zeale and hart new reconsiled
Thus humbly begge his love.
(Y'are a rogue, *Ritchard*.)

Fr. Rich. To meete his trewe
And most unfeigned affection, heare in face
And viewe of this our holly brotherhoode,
As if in open coort with this mi[63] breath
I heare confine all hatred.
(*Jhon*, y'are a Jack sauce, I meane a sawcye Jacke.)

Fr. Jhon. The orchard.

Fr. Rich. Theare.

Abbot. Why, this is as it should bee, and becomes
A trew religious order. Such as are sequestred
And vowed unto a strict monasticke lyfe,
Ought to putt off these grosse and prophane sinnes
Most frequent amongst laye-men. Unity,
Due conformation and fraternall love.
Devotion, hott zeale, and obediens; these
Are vertues that become a cloyster best.
Nowe lett's retyre unto our oresons
And p[r]eye for our good fownders; may they still
Grow to our wishe and thryve to theire owne will.

[*Exeunt all but Friar Jhon.*

Fr. Jhon. More then I woold to have my wishe on thee,
Richard, though I have a good stomacke too't,
Ey, and to baste thee sowndly, I woold nowe
To have my will one her. Tis a sweete creature;
Our patron owld, shee younge; som hope in that.
Besydes, shee's woondrous kind and affable;
And when we duck or congee, smiles as if
Shee tooke som pleasure in our shaven crownes.
I am the fyrst that every morninge, when
Shee passes through the cloyster to her prayers,
Attend her with good morrowe, pray for her health.
For her content and pleasure, such as canott bee
Hop't or expected from her husband's age;
And these my frendly wishes she returnes

Not only in kind language but sweete smiles,
The least of which breede som Incoradgement.
I will, if shee persist to proove thus kind,
If not to speeke my thoughts, to wryte my mynd.

[*Exit.*

SCENA TERTIA.

Thunder.

Enter after a greate Tempestuous storme Mr. Ashburne
an Englishe marchant and his man Godfrey.

Ashburne. Was ever knowne such a tempestuous night
Of thunder, hayle, wynd, lightninge! Twas as if
The fower seditious brothers threatned warr
And weare but nowe at battayle.

Godfrey. The fower winds you meane; blusteringe fellowes they are.
Preye God all be well at sea, for I am sure the roofes tyles and
ridges have payde for it a shewer.[64]

Ashb. The very rafters of the howses bend;
Some breake and are demolisht; barnes blowne downe;
The very chimneyes rattle ore our heads;
The strongest buildinges tremble just as if
Theire is above a tempest, so belowe
There weare a fearefull earth-quake.

Godfrey. All our howses
Are nothinge nowe but windowes, broad bay windowes
So spatious that carts laded may drive throughe
And neather loush oth' topp or eathere syde.
Lights every where, we shall have lightnes inoughe:
Heares stupid woork for daubers!

Ashburne. We are forct
All to forsake the villaige and to fly
Unto the feilds for succor.

Godfrey. Syr, it putt me
In minde of the greate King *Agathocles*,
Who was, as I have heard you oft relate,
Brain'd with a Tyle. Why may not meaner men
Then feare the fall of brick batts?

Enter Raphael, Treadway, and the Clowne.

Treadway. A strange night
And full of terror; yet, thanks heaven, well past.

Raphael. Oh, but I feare the greater storms to come,
A gust that will more shake mee.

Clowne. More, quothe hee; I can scarce see howe that well can bee, for I can assure you the garrett that I laye in putt mee in mind of myne infancye, for I lye all the night longe as if I had bin rockt in a cradle.

Raphael. Oh, frend, I feare this false and perjur'd slave,
That hathe not kept apointment, hath deceiv'd mee
Boathe of my coyne and pretious marchandyse.

Clowne. Did you ever looke for better from a Judas [?] of his he[yre]?[65]

Raphael. Which if hee have--

Clowne. Why then hee hathe, and the mends is in y'r owne hands: that's all that I can say too't.

Raphael. Hee hathe undone mee dubly.

Treadway. Hope the best.
Perhapps the threatninge weather kept him backe:
Itt was a trobled skye, the soon set blusheing,
The rack cam swiftly rushing from the west;
And these presadges of a future storme,
Unwillinge for to trust her tendernes
Unto such feares, might make him fayle his hower;
And yet with purpose what hee slack't last night
Howe to make goodd this morninge.

Raphael. Oh you tent[66]
My woonds too gently, dally with my dowbts
And flutter my trewe feares: the even was calme,
The skye untrobled, and the soon went downe
Without disturbance in a temperate ayr.
No, not the least conjecture coold be made
Of such a suddeine storme, of which the woorld
Till after midnight was not sensible.
His hower was supper, and in faylinge that--

Clowne. Ey, nowe begin I to feare too for thee. Breake his woord if it bee to com to dinner or supper! I'l never trust his bond for the valewe of a threepenny ordenarye after.

Raphael. Post you back to the citty; make inquiries
And most strickt search to find that *Mildewe* out;
Whom if you meete, fyrst rate his last neclect,
Then hasten his repayer. Heare you shall finde mee
Or in the waye home; for in all this villaige
I woll not leave a howse, a place unsearcht.
If where hee dwells you misse him, then demande
Att every bey what shippinge late went out.
If any vowed love still remane betwixt us,
Make it appear nowe in your present care
And expedition.

Treadw. I'l be your *Mercury*,
Not fayle you in the least.

Raphael. And so betwixt us
Increase a frendshipp that was never flawed.

[Exit[67] Treadway.

Ashburne. This gentleman, itt seemes, hathe in this tempest
Sustein'd som losse, he appears so much disturb'd.

Clowne. See, syr, heare are some it may bee beelonge to this
villadge; you had best aske of them.

Raphael. And well advysed. Hayle, father!

Godfrey. No more hayle if you love mee; we had too much of that
last night.

Ashburne. Of what sexe are you that you call me so?
I have bene father of a doughter once,
Though not these many yeares blest with her sight,
But of a soone yet never.

Raphael. What you have lost
May you in som most fayer and fortunate hower
Againe find to your comfort.

Ashburne. You wishe well.

Raphael. Sawe you not bowte this villadge late last night,
Or early now i'th morninge, a short fellowe
Thin heyred, flat nosed, sand-bearded and squint eyde?

Clowne. The mapp of misfortune and very picture of ill luck.

Raphael. Grosse-wasted, gowty-legg'd.

Clowne. Whose face is puft up like a bladder and whose belly
lyke a toonne.

Raphael. Owld, graye and hoary.

Clowne. And withall cheatinge, cousininge, and crafty; a remarkable
raskall, a damnable deceiver, and a most substantiall cinner.

Ashburne. By such I have much suffred in my state,
Opprest almost to utmost penury
In my once better fortune; but so late
I sawe not any such.

Raphael. Hee was expected
To bee attended by too [*sic*] handsome gurles,
Boathe younge, boathe fayre, but th'one unparreld [*sic*];
Neather of which by computation
Hathe told so hye as twenty.

Ashb. If such I chance to meete by accident
I'l send you notyce. Please you leave your name
And place of your abode.

Raphael. *Raphael* I am cald,
A marchant in *Marcellis*, and my lodginge
Is at the *Parratt* in the markett-place;
There you shall finde mee knowne.

Ashb. And by that name
Presume I'l not forgett you.

Raph. For which curtesy,
Fare you well, syr;
You shall oblighe mee to you. If not heare
Weele seeke her further; *France* shall not conteine them
But I will finde theire start-holes.

Ashb. Good speede with you.

Clowne. If I weare a dogge nowe and coold hunt dry foote[68]
I could smell them out presently.

[Exeunt[69] Raphael and Clown.

Ashb. Come lett us mount ourselfes upon these rockes

And, havinge feelinge of our hurts at land,
Letts see what shyppes have ben distrest at sea,
If any shaken in this storme or wreckt;
And though wee cannot help the miserable
Yet lett them taste our pittye.

Godfrey. Sir, content; but I hope your fishermen have not putt to sea this night. If they have I sweare they have showed themselves much madder then the tempest.

Ashb. I hope they have bin more discreate and wyse
Then with the hazard of my boates and netts
To indanger theire owne lyves.

Godfr. See: do you see, Syr?

Ashb. What?

Godfr. Why, yonder.

Ashb. Where?

Godfr. There towards yon shore.

Ashb. A shipp laboringe for liffe
Nowe cast upon the rocks, nowe splitt, nowe sinkinge,
Nowe dasht to peeces.

Godfr. I see all mischeifes do not com by land,
Som's doone upon the water.

Ashb. Though theire goodes perishe,

Yet in thy mercy, heaven, protect theire lyves.
Som sitt upon the planks, som on the masts,
Som hange upon the cables, and som few
Have only gott the cock-boat; others swimme.
Oh that wee shoold beehold theire misery
And want power to assiste them!

Godfr. Sure, syr, it was som shipp of passengers,
For see you not too women? daynty ducks!
Would they coold swime as ducks can, see how they spread
And cast theire legges abroad lyke naked frogges!
See howe they spread theire armes and stryve for lyfe!
I[70] would I weare som Dolphin or some whayle
That they might sitt astryde upon my backe
To beare them safe ashore; but I as yet
Could neare indure still water. See yet still,
Still theire coates beare them upp, keepe them aloft;
The modest ayer not willinge to discover
That which the bawdy waves shame not belowe
Rudely to lifte and handle.

Ashb. Blesse them heaven!
The wind and tyde still beate them towards the shore,
But oh that cursed billowe hath devyded
And parted them asunder. Yet all's well;
They still beare upp. If they but scape the next
There may bee hope of safetye.

Godfr. One's driven this way,
The tother that; the men shift for themselves,
Howe shall we save thes women?

Ashb. No meanes unlesse we leape downe from the rockes,

And that's meare desperation. Yet to showe
Our charityes to wretches thus extreame,
Lett's see if wee can find the least descent
And hasten to theire suckor.

Godfr. By your favour,
I had rather they with brine shoold break their bellys
Then I my neck with clamberinge.

Explicit Actus primus.

Actus 2.

SCENA PRIMA.

    Storme continewed. Enter Palestra all well, as newly shipwreckd and escapt the fury of the seas.

Palestra.[71] Is this then the reward of Innocense,
Of goodness to our selfes, namely chast lyfe,
Pietye to our parents, love to all,
And above all our Christian zeale towardes heaven?
But why shoold wee poore wretches thus contest
Against the powers above us, when even they
That are the best amongst us are servd badd?
Alas, I never yet wrongd man or child,
Woman or babe; never supplanted frend
Or sought revendge upon an enemy.
You see yet howe we suffer; howe shall they then

That false their faythes, that are of uncleane lyfe
And then not only sinne unto them selves
But tempt and persuade others? what shall I thinke
Becoms of my base guardian? though the waves
Have spared the guiltles, sure his putrid s[oule][72]
Cannot escape heavens justyce! wee poor wretches
Are punishe [*sic*] for his grosse impietyes,
They mov'd heavens wrathe, who stir'd the winds and waves
Stryvinge whose fury should destroy us fyrst.
These boathe conspyringe in our ruinne, th'one
Beate us belowe the billowes whilst the other
Swallowed boathe shippe and goodes; [amongst] the rest
A[73] budget or portmantau which includes
All the bawdes wealth. But that weare nothinge to mee
Though he had vowed and sworne to make mee his heyer;
The losse I so lament is a small caskett
Kept by him from my childhood, and packt up
Amongst his treasure; and that perishinge,
I forfett the longe expectation
Ever to knowe my parents, therefore wishe
With it I had i'th sea been buried.

   Enter Scribonia.

Scrib. With perill of oft fallinge and the danger
Of second deathe, having new scapt the fyrst,
I have with feare and terror clim'd these rocks,
And these too past I feare to meete a thyrd.
I spy no howse, no harbor, meete no creature
To point mee to some shelter; therefore heare
Must starve by famine or expire by could.
O'th sea the whystlinge winds still threaten wreckes,
And flyinge nowe for refuge to the lande

Find nought save desolation. Thoughe these three,
Three dreadfull deaths all spare mee, yeat a fowerth,
I cannot shoone [shun] in my *Palestras* losse,
More[74] deare to mee then all the world besides,
For the best blood of myne runns in her veynes,
This lyfe breath in her bosom. Oh my *Palestra*!

Palestr. Numnes and feare, hungar and sollitude,
Besydes my casket, my *Scribonia's* losse,
All these at once afflict mee.

Scrib. Notheinge mee
More than *Palestra's* deathe. Ha, who's that spake?
Suer twas som womans voyce! if my *Palestra*
Only for her sake I coulde wishe to live.

Pal. Then lyve, my deere *Scribonia*, synce I am only
Spar'd to partake with thee newe miseryes.

Scrib. Scarce can I bee perswaded you are shee:
But, bee yt but her shadowe, give mee leave
For her remembrance to imbrace it thus.

Palest. These armes at once locke all my lyvinge hopes
In my restored *Scribonia*.

Scrib. Nowe I perceave
My comfort is not meare imaginary
But reall and effectuall. Lyve you then?

Pal. To triumphe in your safety.

Scrib. Possible
That mongst these desert unfrequented rocks
Thou can imadgine such a thing can be
As that which you call safety?

Pal. Yes, *Scribonia*,
And comfort too; for, see, I spy a villadge,
A maner and a fayre built monastery,
Just at the foott of this descendeinge hill.
And where, if not amongst religious men,
Shoold we find that's calld charity?

Scrib. Thether, then:
Lett[75] us make hast with all the speede we can:
Fyre at the least I hope it [is?] well assured,
Besydes releiffe and harbor.

Pal. Can you begge?

Scrib. What will not rude necessity compell
Distressed folke to doo? We'll not doo't basely,
For beinge brought upp to musick and to sing,
Demandinge in that kind there charity,
And they perceivinge us much better bred
Then these our present fortunes might deserve,
May move in them compassions.

Pal. Lett's retyre
To the backe gate then, there complane our wants
And that which others doo with impudence
Lett us in shame and blushes.

Scrib. Som sweete echo

Speake from these walls and answer to our wants,
And eather lend som comfort to our grieffs
Or send us hence dispayringe and asham'd.

[*They go in*.

Pal. Oh charity where art thou fled,
And nowe how longe hast thou been dead?

Answer within. Oh many many many hundred yeares

Scrib. In villadge, borrough, towne or citty
Remaines there yet no grace, no pitty?

Answ. Not in sighes, not in want, not in teares.

Pal. Cold comfort in this answer; but proceede.

Above. we see a threatninge skye.

Answ. Beelowe the winds and gusts blowe hye,
And all all to fright hence this same juell.

Scrib. The lightninges blast, the thunders cracke,
The billows menace nought save wracke.

Answ. And yet man is then these much more crewell.

Pal. Unless my judgment quite miscarry,
Shee may lyve in som monastery.

Answ. Tis a place too that was fyrst assigned her.

Scrib. If not amongst religious men,
Yett where, where shall wee seeks her then?

Answ. Yet even there, there, you scarce scarce can find her.

Pal. If chastity and Innocens tryde
Have boathe escaped wind and tyde--

Answ. Yet oh why should the land, land these cherish?

Scrib. Of whome even billowes have a care,
Whom seas preserve, whom tempests spare--

Answ. Yet these these amongst men may perishe.

Pal. Uncharitable echo! from a place
Of pure devotion canst thou answer that?
If not in these religious monasteries,
In what place can we find could charity?

Scrib. Where ere wee meete her shee is lyke our selfes,
Bare, without harbor, weake and comfortles.

   Enter Fryer John.

Fr. Jhon. What singeinge beggers were those at the gate
That would so early rowse our charity,
Before it was half styrringe or awake?

   Enter Fryer Richard.

I thinke I answerd them in such a way
As I beleeve scarce pleas'd them.

Fr. Rich. What sweete musick
Was that at the back gate hath cald mee upp
Somwhat before my hower?

Fr. Jhon. Morrow, fryar ***Richard***:
Howe did you lyke our last night's buffetinge?
Whilst all the rest of our fraternity
In feare of that greate tempest weare att prayers,
Wee too pickt out that tyme of least suspition
And in the orchard hand to hand weare att it.

Fr. Rich. Tis trew for blooddy noses; and, Fryar ***Jhon***,
As you lyke that which is allredy past
So chalendge mee hereafter. But whence cam
Those sweete and delicate voyces?

Fr. Jhon. I bare part
In theire sadd quire though none of these yet knw't.
But peace: our Father Abbat.

Enter the Abbot with other fryars.

Abbott. Morrow, soonns,
An early blessinge on you, if as the larke
Rysen beetymes still to salute the soon,
So your devotion pluckes you from your bedds
Beefore your hower unto your orisons.
Did you not heare a musicall complaynt
Of women that in sadd and mournefull tones
Bewayld theire late disasters, harshly answerd
By a churlish echo?

Fr. Jhon. Som such thinge wee heard.

Fr. Rich. The noates still persist with mee.

Pal. There appeares
In his grave lookes bothe zeele and charity;
Letts to his sight boldly expose ourselfes.
Hayle, reverent father!

Abbot. What are you poore soules
Thus wett and wether-bitt?

Scrib. Ere you demand
Further from us, letts tast your Christian charity,
Som fyare, som harbor, least ere our sadd tale
Bee fully tould wee perishe.

Abbot. Why, whence came you?

Pal. From sea; our shipp last night in the great storme
Cast on these rocks and split; this the fyrst place
Exposed unto our eyes to begge releiff.
But oh I faynt.

Abbot. Some[76] faggotts instantly:
Hott brothes, hott water for them, and warme cloathes.
Whome the high powers miraculously preserve,
Whome even the merciles waves have borne ashore,
Shall we soe sinke a land? Even wee our selfes
That lyve and eate by others charity,
To others shall not wee bee charitable?
All succor, all supply that can be given,
They from our hands shall tast.

Fr. Jhon. Shall we remove them
Into the cloyster?

Fr. Rich. Tis agaynst our oath
On any, though the great'st, extremity
To addmitt women thether.

Abbot. That I knowe:
Yet in som out-office see them chear'd,
Want nothinge that the cloyster can affourd.
Theire bewtyes, though my eye be bleynd at them,
Deserve no lesse; I looke on theire distresse
And that I pitty. Ech one lend a hand
To take off from theire present misery
And ease theire tender shoulders; when they are cheer'd
And better comforted, I'l finde occatione
To enquire further from them.

Pal. Heaven be as kind
To you as you to us!

Abb. Feare not fayre damselles:
This place, though not within the monastery,
Yet stands within the cloysters previledge
And shallbee unto you a sanctuary.

Scrib. No other wee expect it.

Abb. Guide them in: [***Bell ring***.
Bewty and youthe to pitty 'tis no sinne.

   The bell ringes to mattens. Enter the Lord de Averne

and his Lady. Dennis and others.

Fr. Jhon. Harke, the bell ringes to mattens.

Fr. Rich. See withall
Our noble patron with his lovely lady
Prepare for theire devotion. Nowe, Friar *Jhon*,
Your letcherous eye is conninge.

Fr. Jhon. I knowe my place.

Abbott. Way for our noble founder!

L. Aberne. Morrowe, father;
So to the rest of all the brotherhood.

[The quire and musick; the fryars make a lane with ducks and obeysance.

Voyces. Te tuosque semper, oh semper beamus,
Et salvos vos venisse, o venisse gaudeamus.

Fr. Jhon. Good daye to our fayre foundresse!

Lady. Mercy, Fryar *Jhon*;
Above the rest you are still dutifull,
For which wee kindly thanke you.

[*Exeunt: manet Jhon*.

Fr. Jhon. Kindly thanke you!
Nay, smyld withall! allthough that I have more

Then a monthes mind[77] to these younge harletryes
Yet heares the grownd on which I fyrst must build
And ryse my fortunes many steepes[78] hye.
Nay, I perhapps, ere they can drye there smocks,
Will putt th'affayre in motion, whyle these are
Att solleme mattens. I'l take pen and wryte,
And sett my mind downe in so quaint a strayne
Shall make her laughe and tickle, whylst I laughe
And tickle with the thought on't, still presuminge
These lookes, these smyles, these favours, this sweete language
Could never breathe, butt have theire byrthe from love.
But how to ha'tt delivered? there's the dowbt.
Tush I have plott for that too; hee, no questione,
That sett mee on to compasse this my will,
May when the up-shoote comes assist mee still.

[*Exit.*

SCENA 2.

[*Tempest. Thunder.*

Enter 2 Fishermen.

1st Fish. The trobled sea is yet scarce navigable
Synce the last tempest: yet wee that only lyv
By our owne sweatt and labour, nor cann eate
Beffore[79] wee fetch our foode out of the sea,
Must ventur thoughe with daunger or bee suer
With empty stomakes go unsupt to bed.

2nd Fish. And so it often happens.

1 Fish. See the cordaige
Be stronge and tight, the netts with all theire stringes,
Plometts, and corks, well plac't for hookes and bates,
This daye wee shall have little use of them:
The wind's still hye, beare but a gentle sayle
And hazard not the channele. Keepe alonge
Close by the shoare, the rocks will shelter us
And may perhapps affoord us lobsters, praunes,
Shrimps, crabbes, and such lyke shell fishe; hence[80] we may
Hunt the sea urchen, and with safety too;
There's many holde hime for a dayntye fishe,
Hee sells well in the markett. That poore men
Are forct too, for a slender competens,
A little to prolonge a wretched lyfe!

2 Fish. Com then lett us weighe anchor and aboord:
The soone is upp allredy.

Enter the Clowne.

Clowne. If ever menn weare madd then suer my master is not well in his witts, and all about this wenshe; here's such sendeinge and seekeinge, hurriinge and posteinge, and all to no purpose. I have nowe some thyrty errands to deliver and knowe not to whome nor where, what nor to which place fyrst; hee's gone on to the citty and sent mee back to the villaige, whither his frend travelled[81] one waye, hee another, and I a thyrd contrary from them boathe; he cannott beleeve his inquiry to be well doone but hee must send me to doo't over againe. I have asked all I mett and demanded of all I have seene.[82] But what are theese? these should bee fishermen. Good morrowe, you sea theeves.[83]

1 Fish. You call us theeves that may proove honester
Than many goe for trewe[84] men on the shore.

Clowne. Sawe[85] you not passe this [way] an ould bald fellowe hutch-shoolderd, crooked nos'd, beetle browd, with a visadge lowreing and a looke skowlinge; one that heaven hates and every good man abhors; a cheatinge raskall and an ugly slave,--did note such passe you?

1 Fish. If such a one as you describe you inquire for,
Mee thinks, my frend, thou hast mistooke thy way;
Thou shouldst have sought him at the gallowes rather,
There such are soonest fownd.

Clowne. Byrlady, worst answered of a playne fellowe; but that you may knowe him the better, hee had too handsome streete-singing-fact lasses in his companye.

2 Fish. And for such creatures y'had best search the stewes
O'th citty; this our villadge yields none such.
This fellowe doth but flowte us; letts aboord.

1 Fish. Inquire for us of wenshes? tush, wee fishe
For no such perewinkles; farewell flesh mongere.

[*Ex. Fish*.

Clowne. No wonder these fellowes pretend to be witty; for understandinge, so manye have lost there witts as ... they have fisht for it and in som drawenett or other have caught it. But where might these lost shrewes bee? I suspect this pestiferous *Je vous prie* hathe putt some slovenly tricke or other to cheate my mayster boathe of his ware and mony.

Enter Scribonia with an empty pale to y̅e Clow.

Scribon. Thus beinge chered with warmth, and change of clothes,
With all such comforts as the cloyster yeelds,
I am dyrected to a neighbours by
For water to refreshe and wash our selves.
And this shoold bee the howse.

Clowne. What! not ***Scribonia***,
One of the flock that's missing?

Scrib. Oh sweete ***Jayms***,
Where is your noble maister?

Clowne. Nay, sweete rogue,
Where is his bewteous mystresse?

Scrib. Heare within.

Clowne. In this place joyninge to the monastery?
And ***Mildewe*** too?

Scrib. Rott on that villeyne! no.

Clowne. Hee promist to bringe you too alonge and meete with my master and som others of his frends att supper.

Scrib. Can such men, ever false unto theire God,
Keepe faythe with men at any tyme?

Clowne. But staye, staye, there's one riddle I cannot expound: howe

com thou so suddenly to lepp out of a howse of roguery into a howse of
religion, from a stewes to a cloyster, from beastleness to blessednes
and from a sacrilegious place to a sanctuary?

Scrib. Such was the grace heaven sent us, who from perill,
Danger of lyfe, the extreamest of all extreames
Hathe brought us to the happy patronage
Of this most reverent abbott.

Clowne. What dangers? what extreames?

Scrib. From the sea's fury, drowneing; for last night
Our shipp was splitt, wee cast upon these rocks.

Clowne. Sayd in a jest, in deede! Shipwreck by land![86] I perceive
you tooke the woodden waggen for a ship and the violent rayne for the
sea, and by cause some one of the wheeles broake and you cast into some
water plashe, you thought the shipp had splitt and you had bene in
danger of drowneinge.

Scrib. Are you then ignorant how, late in the even,
With purpose to make better sale of us
And to defraude thy maister, hee shipt us
With all the gold and jewels that hee had,
All which save wee are perisht?

Clowne. But that caterpiller, that ould catamiting cankerworme,
what's become of him?

Scrib. Dead I hope, with drinkinge of salte water.

Clowne. I would all of his profession had pledged him the same
healthe. But how doth *Palestra* take this?

Scrib. Gladd to bee rid of such a slavery,
Yet sadly weepinge for her casket's losse,
That which included ample testimony
Bothe of her name and parents.

Clowne. All her ill luck go with it![87]--Heere will be simple newes to bringe to my mayster when hee hears shee hath bene shippwreckt! Il make him beleeve I went a fishinge for her to sea and eather drewe her ashore in my netts, or batinge my hooke strooke her and drewe her upp by the gills with myne angle. Make you hast for I'l staye till you come back.   [*Exit*.

Scrib. But this delaye had allmost putt me from
What I was sent about; yes this is the place.
         [*Knocks*.

Enter Godfrey.

[*Godf.*] Whoes that that offers violens to these gates
That never yet offended? What want you?

Scrib. That which the earthe
Dothe forebidd none, and freely yelds to all,
A little fayre springe water.

Godfr.--One of those giurles
Beelyke this morninge shippwrackt and now scapt?
A dainty peece of maydes fleshe. Such sweete bitts
Are not heare often swallowed, and my mouth
Waters at this fine morsell.

Scrib. Water, frend;
Tis that I crave for heaven's sake.

Godfr. Wee have none
Of guift, unless you by't.

Scrib. Will you sell that
The earthe affourds you gratis, and sett pryse
Of what a foe would yeeld an enemy?

Godfr. Not, pretty lasse, so thou'lt afford mee that,
Freely and without bargen, which not only
One frend will to another but oft tymes
A stranger to a stranger.

Scrib. What's that, prithee?

Godfr. Only a kisse, sweete wensh.

Scrib. Ye are too familiar,
I'l by none at that pryse: or fill my pale
Or I'l returne back empty.

Godfr. Well for once
I will not greatly stand out, yet in hope,
That what att our fyrst meetinge you'l not grant
You'l not denye at partinge; reatch thy pale.

Scrib. Quick as you love mee.

Godfr. As you love mee! right:
Who[88] ever lov'd that lov'd not att fyrst sight?
The poet's excellent sayeinge.

[*Exit*[89] to draw water.

Scrib. What shall I saye or howe shall I excuse
This my longe staye? but nowe I cast myne eyes
Backe on the roughe yet unappeased seas,
I quake to thinke upon our dangers past.
But see the fearefull object of a death
More menacinge and affrightfull, a sea monster
Cast from the deepes to swallow us ashore!
Malevolent fate and black desaster still
Pursues us to all places, but of all
   Enter Myldew and Sarlaboys to her.
This, this the greatest, and to this one compard
All that are past but trifles. Oh that grand maister
Of mechall[90] lusts, that bulke of brothelree,
That stillary of all infectious sinnes,
Hath scapt the wrack, and with his fellowe guest
And partner in corruption makes this waye,
And with no tarde pace. Where shall I hyde mee!
Whether shall I fly to *Palestra* back
And with this sadd relation kill her quite
That's scarce recovered! rather, you hy powers,
Then to prolonge our griefes, shorten our howers.
                  [*Exit.*

Godfr. Where[91] is my daynty damosella? where?
Mee thought the water mett mee the half way
And lept up full three stepps to meete my pale.
This 'tis when as a man goes willingly
About his busines. Howe fresh a kisse will tast
From her whyte lipps! and every part besydes
From head to toe have bin so lately duckt
And rincht in the salt water. Wheres my sweete?

Not heare? no where? why, hoe, my whytinge mopp[92]
Late scapt from feedinge haddocks! ha, what, gone?
Nay then, go thou too that shee sent mee for,
To him that next shall find thee! yet not so:
This learned pale instructs mee by these letters
That it beelonges unto this monastery.
And iff it shoold be lost by my default
I may be chardged with theft or sacriledge.
No, I'l deliver it to the owners suer,[93]
And this the place.

Enter the Bawde Mildewe and Sarlaboyse.

Mild. Hee that woold stoody to bee miserable
Lett him forsake the land and putt to sea.
What widgeing,[94] that hath any voyce at all,
Would trust his safety to a rotten planke
That hath on earthe sounde footinge!

Sarlab. None but madmen.

Mild. Why thou of none, thrifty and well advised,
Stryvest thou to make mee such, where's now the gayne
And proffitt promist? the riche marchandyse
Of lust and whooringe? the greate usury
Got by the sale of wantons? these cursed jewelryes
With all the wealthe and treasure that I had,[95]
All perisht in one bottom, and all, all,
Through thy malicious counsell.

Sarlab. Curse thy selfe.
The trusty bark, ore laden with thy sinnes,
Baudryes, grosse lyes, thy theft and perjuryes

Beesydes the burdene of thy ill gott gooddes,
Not able to indure so greate a weight
Was forct to sinke beneathe them.[96]

Mild. Out, dogge!

Sarl. Out, devill!

Mild. By thee I am made nothinge. Oh my giurles
You sweete and never faylinge marchandyse,
Comodityes in all coasts, worthy coyne,
Christiane or heathen! by whom in distresses
I coold have raysed a fortune! more undoone
That I should loose you thus!

Sarl. I knowe hee had rather
See halfe a hundred of them burnt[97] a land
Then one destroyde by water. But, oh **Neptune**,
I feare I have supt so much of thy salt brothe
Twill bringe mee to a feavour.

Mild. Oh my **Palestra**
And fayre **Scribonia**, weare but you too safe,
Yet som hope weare reserved me.

Sarl. I praye, **Mildewe**,
When you so early to the bottom dyv'd,
For whom weare you a fishinge?

Mild. Marry, for maydens;
Woold I knewe howe to catch them. But my gutts,
Howe they are sweld with sea brine!

Sarl. Tis good phisick
To cure thee of the mangy.

Mild. Wretched man!
That have no more left of a magazine
Then these wett cloathes upon mee, nay the woorst
Of all I had and purposely put on
Only to lyv a shipp-board.

Sarl. Once to-day
Thou wert in wealthe above mee, nowe the seas have
Left us an equall portion.

Mild. In all the wourld
I vowe I am not woorthe a lighted faggott
Or a poore pan of charcoale.

Sarl. Justly punisht
Thou that hast all thy lyfe tyme dealt in fyre-woorks,
Stoves and hott bathes to sweet in, nowe to have
Thy teethe to falter in thy head for could
Nimbler then virginall Jacks.[98]

Mild. Th'art a sweete guest.

Sarl. Too good for such an host, better to have bin
Lodgd in som spittle; or, if possible,
To bee imprisoned in som surgeon's box
That smells of salves and plasters.

Mild. Nowe what sharke
Or wyde-mouth'd whale shall swallowe upp my budgett,
May it at th'instant choake him!

Sarl. Cursedly twas got,
And nowe thy curse goes with it.

Mild. But those giurles!
Nought so much greives mee as to part with them
Before they lost theire maiden-headds. Had they lyvd
Till I had seen them women, and oth' trade,
My tast and care bestowed to bringe them upp
I should have thought well spent, which nowe with them
Is meerely cast away.

   Enter Godfrey.

Sarlab. Peace now your pratinge and heare another spirit.

Godfr.[99] The pale religious, which was the pledge
Of a kisse lascivious, I have given backe,
Ey, and to boote the water; but within
There's such a coyle betwixt the 2 young giurles
Such quakinge, shakinge, quiveringe, shiveringe
Such cryeinge, and such talk of flyinge, then of hyding,
And that there's no abydinge; one cryes out and calls,
The others redy to breake downe the walls;
Then weepinge they whisper together,
And saye they woold roone if they knew whither,
And are indeede putt to such strange affrights
That I was afrayde they weare hunted with sprights,
And therefore cam and left them: lass, poor giurles,
They are in piteous feare.

Mild. Hee talkt of guerles: why may not these bee they,
Escapt as wee? staye, younge man, good frend, staye.

Godf. Too ould drown'd ratts: I'l have som sport with them,
And though I pitty those I'l play with these.

Mild. What gurles weare those thou spakest of?

Sarl. Tell us fyrst
Where wee might finde som comfort.

Godf. Lett us oh lett us bee advys'd
And living still to all men,
So though wee bee but midle sizd
Wee shalbe held no small men.

Mild. Concerning these fayre damosels, speake of that.

Sarl. Which now concernes us most, where may wee meete
With warmth, with foode, and shelter?

Godf. Oh thou that dost demand of mee
Som fyre, som meate and harbor,
I see thou lately hast ben washt,
Hath **Neptune** ben thy barbor?

Sarl. This fellowe mearely flowtes our misery,
And laughs att our distresses.

Mild. But, kind frende,
Concerninge these yonge women, are they fayre?

Godf. Fayre flesh and cleane they bothe appeare
And not lyke gypsies umber'd.

Mild. How many?

Godf. Just as thou and I when wee are
Once but number'd.

Mild. Oh, **Sarleboys**, there's comfort in these woords;
They have allredy warmed my hart within,
Why may not these bee they?

Sarl. Bee they or not,
I had rather see one caudell downe my throate,
To wash downe this salt-water, than bee mayster
Of all the wenshes lyveinge.

Mild. Oh where, where,
Where might I see too such?

Godf. Thou that goest sydewayes lyke a crabb, gapst on mee lyke an oyster,
Followe thy flat nose and smell them there, in th'out part of this cloyster.

Mild. Oh maye this peece of earthe proove happy to mee
As hath the sea bin fatall.

Sarl. I'l followe and coold wish
Boath cloyster and whole villadge weare a fyre
Only to dry my clothes by.

Godf. Marry hange you
You that so late scaped drowning for I take you
For too pestiferous rascalls.

Exeunt.

Explicit Actus 2.

Act 3.

SCENE 1.

Enter the Lady de Averne with a letter in her hand readinge, and with her mayde.

Lady. And howe came you by this?

Mayde. Followinge you to th'chappell
And I protest not thinking anythinge,
Fryar *Jhon* o'th suddeine pluckt mee by the sleeve
And whisperd in myne eare to give that to you,
But privatly, bycause it was a thinge
Only toweard your person.

Lady. Twas well doonne;
But prithee do no more so, for this tyme
Tak't for a warninge.

Mayde. Madam I am skool'd.

Lady. Doo so, or ever loose me. Heeres[100] sweet stuffe!

Can this be in a vowed monastick lyfe
Or to be fownd in churchmen? 'tis a question
Whether to smyle or vex, to laughe or storme,
Bycause in this I finde the cause of boathe.
What might this sawcy fellowe spy in mee
To incorradge such a boldnes? yes this letter
Instructs mee what: he seythe my affability
And modest smiles, still gracinge his salutes,
Moovd him to wryte. Oh what a chary care then
Had womene neede have boathe of lipps and eyes
When every fayre woord's censur'd liberty,
And every kind looke meere licensiousnes!
I have bin hitherto so greate a stranger
To these unus'd temptations that in truthe
I knowe not howe to take this. Sylly fryar!
Madnes or folly, one of these't must bee.
If th'one I pity, at the other laughe,
And so no more reguard it.

Maid. Madam, if ought bee in that letter ill,
Mee thinks 'tis good [that] you can tak't so well.

Lady. Peace you; a braineles weake, besotted fellowe!
But lett mee better recollect myself.
Madnes nor folly, and add lust to them,
Durst not in fury, heate, or Ignorans,
Have tempted my unquestioned chastity
Without a fowrth abetter, jealousy.
The more I ponder that, I more suspect
By that my Lord should have a hand in this,
And,[101] knowinge there's such difference in our yeares,
To proove my feythe might putt this triall on mee.
Else how durst such a poore penurious fryar

Oppose such an unheard of Impudens
Gaynst my incensed fury and revendge?
My best is therefore, as I am innocent,
To stooddy myne owne safety, showe this letter,
Which one [?] my charity woold have conceiled,
And rather give him upp a sacrifice
To my lord's just incensement then indanger
Myne owne unblemisht truthe and loyalty
By incurringe his displeasure; heare hee coms.

   Enter the Lord de Averne with som followers;
  his man Denis

L. Averne. Howe, Lady? reading?

Lady. Yes, a letter, sir.

L. Averne. Imparts it any newes?

Lady. Yes, syr, strange newes,
And scarce to bee beleaved.

Lord Av. Forreyne.

Lady. Nay, domestick,
Tis howsehould busines all.

Lord Av. May I impart it?

Lady. Oh, syr, in any case,
As one it most concernes; but I intreate you,
Reade it with patiens; the simplicity

Of him that writte it will afford you mirthe,
Or else his mallice spleane.--Nowe by his temper
And change of countenance I shall easily find
Whose hand was cheife in this.

Lord Av. All leave the place.

Denis. We shall, syr.

Lord Av. Possible
That this shoold bee in man, nay in man vowed
Unto a strickt abstemious chastity!
From my owne creature and from one I feede,
Nay from a place built in my holiest vowes,
Establisht in my purpose in my lyfe,
Maintayn'd from my revenue, after death
Firm'd and assur'd to all posterityes--
That that shoold breede such vipers!

Lady. Patiens, syr; the fellowe suer is madd.

Lord Av. I can be madd as hee too and I will.
Thus to abuse my goodnes! in a deede
Som woold hold meritorious, att the least
Intended for an act of piety,
To suffer in my zeale! nay to bee mockt
In my devotion, by these empty drones
That feede upon the honey of my hyve!
To invert my good intentements, turne this nest
         [***Ink: paper ready***.
I built for prayer unto a bedd of sinnes!
Which thus I'l punish; this religious place,
Once vowed to sanctity, I'l undermyne

And in one instant blowe the structure upp
With all th'unhallowed covent.

Lady. Praye, no extreames:
Where one offends shall for his heighnous fact
So many suffer? there's no justyce in't.

Lord Av. Som justyce I would showe them heare on earthe
Before they finde it multiplyed in heaven.

Lady. For my sake, syr, do not for one man's error
Destroy a woorke of perpetuity,
By which your name shall lyve. One man offends;
Lett the delinquent suffer.

Lord Av. So't shallbe,
And thou hast well advysed. Som pen and Inke theire!

Lady. What purpose you?

Lord Av. That's soly to my selfe
And in my fyxt thoughts stands irreproovable.

Enter Dennis with pen, inke, and paper.

Syr, heares pen inke and paper.

Lord Av. To his letter
My self will give him answer.   (***writes***)

Denis. Suer all's not well that on the suddane thus
My lord is so distempered.

Lady. I have, I feare,
Styr'd such a heate, that nought save blood will quensh:
But wish my teares might doo't; hee's full of storme,
And that in him will not bee easily calmd.
His rage and troble both pronounce him guiltles
Of this attempt, which makes mee rather doubt
Hee may proove too seveare in his revendge,
Which I with all indevour will prevent
Yet to the most censorious I appeale,
What coold I lesse have doone to save myne honor
From suffringe beneathe skandall?

Lord Av. See, heare's all:
'Tis short and sweete, wryte this in your own hand
Without exchange of the least sillable.
Insert in copiinge no suspitious dash,
No doubtfull comma; then subscribe your name,
Seal't then with your own signet and dispatche it
As I will have dyrected; doo't, I charge you,
Without the least demurre or fallacy.
By dooinge this you shall prevent distrust
Or future breach beetwixt us; you shall further
Expresse a just obediens.

Lady. Syr, I shall,
What ere your concealed purpose bee, I shall.

Lord Av. Provyde mee horses, I will ryde.

Denis. When, syr?

Lord Av. Instantly, after dinner, and gie't out

I am not to returne till three dayes hence,
So spreade it throughe the howse.

Denis. What followers, Syr,
Meane you to take alonge?

Lord Av. Thyself, no more,
For 'tis a private busines, and withall;
Provyde mee,--harke thyne eare.

Denis. A stronge one, Syrr.

Lord Av. One that will howld; withall give pryvate order
At night the guarden gates may bee left open,
By whiche wee may returne unknowne to any.
What I intend lyes heare.

Denis. All wee servants
Are bownd to doo, but not examine what;
That's out of our comission.

Lord Av. 'Twixt us too
I shall resolve thee further.

Denis. I am gone, Syr.

Lord Av. Nowe, sweete ladye, have you doon?

Lady. As you commanded.

Lord Av. Itt wants nothinge nowe
But seale and superscription; I'll see't doone.

And marke mee nowe; at evensonge, passinge through
The cloyster to the chappell, when the fryar
Amongst the rest bowes with his wonted duckes,
Add rather then deminish from your smiles
And wonted favours. Let this shee post then
Conveigh this letter to the fryar's close fist,
Who no dowbt gapes for answer.

Lady. All shall bee
As you instructe; but punishe, syr, with pitty;
Putt him to payne or shame, but deathe, alas,
Is too seveare.

Lord Av. Tush, wyfe, feare not; think'st thou Ile
quale[102] a churchman?
                [*Exeunt.*

SCENE 2.

    Enter after a great noyse within, the Clowne,
    meetinge with Ashburne and Godfrey.

Clowne. If this villadge bee inhabited with men as this place within
is with monsters; if with men that have eyes and can distinguishe bewty,
or that have hartes and therfore saver of pitty; if you bee fathers and
know what belonges to children, or christians and therefore what is ment
by charity; if husbandmen and have hope of your harvest, or marchants of
your trade's increase; if fishermen that would thryve by your labours,
or any of all these that would be knowne by your honesty--

Ashburne. Many of those thou namest have place in us,
Great'st part if not all.

Clowne. Then lend your helpeinge hands to succor, releive, defend, deliver, save, serve, patronadge, abett and mynteyn--

Ashb. Whom, what?

Clowne. Bewty, vertue, purity, syncerity, softnes, sweetenes, innocens, and chastity.

Ashb. Gainst what? gainst whome?

Cl. Oppression, frawde, rudenes, reproch, synn, shame, debate, discourse, theft, rapine, contempt of religion and breach of sanctury, against a magazine of misdemeanors and a whole monopoly of mischeif.

Godf. I knowe the busines, syr, if in that place
These are the too distressed wrecks at sea
We sawe this morninge floatinge, sweeter guerles
I never yet sett ey on, and opprest
By too ill lookeinge raskells that to warme them
Wisht all the towne a bonefire--

Ashb. Miscreant slaves!
For one younge damsell's sake I once cald daughter,
And in the absens of there greater frends,
I'l stand betwixt them and these injuryes.

Clowne. These are they after whome I have been seeking, and my mayster was enquiringe. If you will but secure them heare in the villadge whilst I carry woord to my mayster in the citty, you shall doo me a curtesye and him a most noble offyce.[103]

Ashb. It was no more then promisse, and I shoold
Fayle in my goodnes not to see that doone.
Post to thy mayster, bid him meete us heare:
Mean tyme my menn shall rayse the villagers
Boathe in the reskewe of these innocent maydes
And in defens of holly priveledge.

Clowne. I fly lyke the winds.

Godf. And I'l go call the pesants
To rayse another tempest.

      [Exeunt[104] Clown and Godfrey.

Ashb. Hasten boathe
And till ayde com I'l laye myne eare and listen
To heare what further coyle is kept within:
All's silent on the sudden.
          Musick.

  [***Song within***.]

(1) Helpe, Helpe, oh ayde a wretched mayde
    or els we are undoon then.

(2) And have I caught, and have I caught you?
    in vayne it is to roonne then.

(1) Som reskewe then[105] from gods or men
    redeeme us from these crosses!

(2) Tis all in vayne, since nowe I gaine

part of my former losses.

(1) Oh heaven, defend! what, yet no end
of these our strange desasters?

(2) No favour's knowne, no pittye's showne
to them that fly there maysters.

(1) Why to defame, reproch, and shame
poor innocents thus dragge yee?

(2) With[106] your offens there's no dispence:
away then! wherefore lagge yee?

A tumult within and sudden noyse. Enter at one doore
Godfrey with country fellowes for there reskewe, at the
other Mildewe, Sarlaboys, Palestra, Scribonia.

Palest. Where, in what place shall wee bestowe our selfes
From this injust man's fury?

Scrib. If compeld
And dragg'd from sanctuary by prophane hands,
Where shall we flye to safety?

Ashb. Wheither, if
Not unto us? wee often see the gods
Give and bequeathe there justyce unto men,
Which wee as fythefully [*sic*] will see performed.

All. Downe with these saucy companyons!

Godf. Downe with these sacraligious silsepaereales [?], these unsanctified *Sarlaboyses* that woold make a very seralia of the sanctuary, and are meare renegadoes to all religion!

Mild. Stay, hold, are you bandetty? rovers, theives,
And wayte you heare to robb and pilladge us
The sea so late hathe ryfled? these are myne,
My chattells and my goodes, nor can you cease them
As wrecks; I appeale unto the admirall.

Ash. His power I in his absens will supply,
And cease yee all as forfett; these as goodds
You as superfluous ladinge, till that coort
Shall comprimise betwixt us.

Mild. I'the meanetyme
Lett mee possesse myne owne; these are my slaves
My utensills, my mooveables, and bought
With myne owne private coyne.

Sarl. To which I am witnes.

Mild. And by the heyre I'l dragge them as myne owne,
Wear't from the holly alter.

Pal. Succor!

Scrib. Helpe!

Ashb. Are they not Christians?

Mild. Yes.

Ash. What nation?

Mild. *Englishe*.

Ashb. In myne owne country borne and shall not I
Stand as theire champion then? I tell thee, pesant,
England's, no broode for slaves.

Pal. Oh Syr to you
Wee fly as to a father.

Ashb. And I'l guard you
As weare you myne owne children.

Mild. Gainst there lord,
Owner and mayster?

Ashb. None is lordd with us
But such as are freeborne; our Christian lawes
Do not allowe such to bee bought or sould
For any Bawde or pander to hyre such
To comon prostitution. Heere they stand:
Tutch but a garment, nay a heyre of theres
With thy least finger, thy bald head I'l sinke
Belowe thy gowtye foote.

Mild. I am opprest,
Is theire no lawe in *France*?

Ashb. Yes, Syr, to punish
These chastityes seducers.

Mild. Give me fyar,
I will not leive of all this monastery
Of you or these, of what's combustible,
Naye of my self, one moiety unconsumed.

Godf. His frend before him wisht the towne a fyre,
Now hee would burne the cloyster: too arch-pillers![107]

Ashb. And lyke such
Our purpose is to use them. Dare not, miscreant,
But to give these a menace whom thou calst thyne,
No not by beck or nod; if thou but styer [stir]
To doo unto this howse of sanctity
Damadge or outrage, I will lay thee prostrate
Beneathe these staves and halberts.

Mild. Is this lawe?

Godf. Yes *Staffords*[108] lawe.

Ashb. Naye, feare not, pretty guerles;
The fryars them selfs, weare they not at theire prayers
Wold have doon more than this in just defens
Of theire immunityes; but in theire absens
I stand for them, nor shall you part from hence
Or dare to sqeelche till they themselves be judge.
Of injurye doone to this sacred place,
Or such as I have sent for make appearance
To clayme what thou unjustly calst thyne owne.

Godf. Nay, thou shall stand; wee have too stringes to our Bow.

Ashb. If hee but styer then stryke.

Mild. This ***Stafford*** law,
Which I till nowe heard never nam'd in ***France***,
Is for the present a more fearefull coort
Then chancery or star-chamber. I want motion;
You have made [me] a statue, a meere Imadge.

Godf.[109] Styer and thou diest: weele maule you.

Mild. Iff heare I can have none, lett me depart
To seake elcewhere for justyce.

Sarl. Keepe him prisoner,
And sett mee free to finde some advocate
To pleade in his just cause.

Godf. Neather styrre
In payne of too ***Frensh*** crownes, and they so crack[t]
Never more to passe for currant.

Ashb. That presume.

Mild. Misery of miseryes! I am bound hand and foote,
And yet boath legges and armes at liberty.

Godf. Yes by the lawe cald ***Stafforde***.

   Enter Mr. Raphael, Mr. Treadway and the Clowne.

Raph. Durst then the slave use my ***Palestra*** thus,
And dragge her by the heyre from sanctuary?

Clowne. Most trew, Syr.

Raph. Why did'st not kill him?

Clowne. If I had had but a swoard I had doon't, but I sought the villadge through and cold find neare a cutter.

Raph. Weare there no skattered stones lye in the streete
To have beate his breynes out?

Clowne. Not a stone to throwe att a dogg.

Raph. Had'st thou not heeles

Clowne. Yes to have kickt him lyke a dogge, but I reserved them to roon the more nimbly about your busines.

Pal. I nowe spye a newe sanctuary, his armes,
In which I may pursue security.
My *Raphael*!

Raph. My *Palestra*, art thou safe?
Beefore I give due thankes to this good man,
Which tyme shall paye in all pluralityes,
Oh shewe mee but that monster of mankind
And shame of men on whom to bee revendgd!

Mild. The storme at sea was not more terrible
Then this the land now threatens; againe undoone,
Over and over wretched!

Clowne. See the limbe

Of his ould syre the Devill.

Raph. Perjured slave!
Perfidious, but that I abhore to take
The hangman's office from him, this should open
A doore by which thy black soule should fly out
Unto assured damnation.

Tread. Bee more patient;
Proceede with him after a legal course,
And bee not sweyde by fury.

Raph. Well advys'd:
What can thy false toonge pleide in thy excuse,
Thou volume of all vyces?

Mild. Why, what not?

Raph. Is thy hart sear'd, thy browe made impudent,
And all thy malefactions crownd[110] with lyes
Against just testates and apparent truthes?
When I had payde full ransom for this pryze,
Why didst thou beare her hence?

Mild. I did not doo't,--
These bee my witnes; have I borne her hence
When I have brought her to thee?

Raph. Thy bawdes rhethorick
Shall not excuse thee thus. Frends guarde him safe.

Clowne. We will see his fooles coate guarded,[111] ey and reguarded too from slipping out of our fingers.

Godf.[112] Weel finde amongst us more then ... him; fower elbowes elbowe him off all sydes, gentlemen. It shall appeare beefore hee parts with us that hee hathe shewed him self no better then a coxcomb.

Tread. Beleeve mee nowe, I do not blame my frende
To fishe in trobled streames for such a pearle,
Or digge in black mowled for so ritch a myne;
But to redeeme a chast and inocent sowle
Forthe from the fierye jawes of lust and hell,
Exprest a most comended charitye.
What second bewtyes that ... frend,
That tremblinge flyes from his infectious ills
To patronise her youth and inocence
Beneathe that goode man's goodnes--

Raph. Alyke suffers
With her in all distresses, lyke in years,
In vertue, no way differing of our nation;
Who knowes but neare all yee too?

Tread. I feele somthinge
Growinge on mee, I know not howe to style,
Pitty or love, synce it hath tast of boathe.
And sinne itt weare such parity in all thinges,
Age, mindes, wrecks, bondadge, pursiutes, injuryes
Shoold nowe bee separate; the one be freede
The t'other left in durance, for the want
And pious tender of so smalle a somme.
I somwhat have in purpose.

Raph. Dragge them boathe
Before the magistrate.

Sarlab. Mee? wherefore? why?

Godf. As his abettor and ill counseller:
One would have burnt the villadge, and the other
Threatned to fyar the cloyster.

Raph. Boathe acts capitall
And worthy seveare censure.

Mild. Though thou pleedst interest
In waye of earnest in *Palestra*, yet
Robb mee not quite, give me the tother backe,
My only portion left me by the sea
And stock to sett upp trade by.

Scrib. Rather torture mee
With any violent deathe.

Tread. Leive them in trust
And chardge of this grave reverent gentleman,
Untill you heire the sentence of the coort.

Ashb. I willingly accept theire patronadge:
Heere att my howse they shall have meate and harbour.

Raph. Nobly spoke:
Meane tyme hale these to'th coort.

Mild. My *Palestra*,
What? not one woord of pitye?

Raph. Stopp his mouthe.

Mild. My *Scribonia*,
Wilt thou intreate them neather?

Tread. Tyme's but trifled;
Away with them to justyce!

Mild. Take my skinne then,
Synce nothinge else is left mee.

Clown. That's rotten allredy and will neather
make goodd leather nor parchment ... theire.

           [*Exeunt*.

Ashb. Com, damsalls, followe mee where I shall leade:
I have a cross wyfe at home I tell you that,
But one that I presume will not bee jealous
Of too such harmeles sowles.

Pal. You are to us
A patron and defender.

Scrib. Bounde unto you
Not as an host but father.

           [*Exeunt*.

SCENA 3.

Enter the Lord de Averne, his Lady,
Dennis and the waytinge mayde.

Lord Av. Are all thinges redye as I gave in chardge?

Denys. Redy, syr.

Lord Av. Inoughe; and you deliver'd it
To his owne hands?

Mayde. I did.

Lord Av. Howe did hee tak't?

Mayde. With smiles and seeminge joy.

Lord Av. Sorrowe and shame
I feare will bee the sadd end on't.

Lady Av. Syr, you'r troubled.

Lord Av. I would not have you so; pray, to your rest;
You shall remove mee from all jelosyes
If you betake you to your sowndest sleeps,
And without more inquiry.

Lady Av. Syr, remember
That all offences are not woorthy deathe:
Fellowny, murder, treason and such lyke
Of that grosse nature maye be capitall;
Not folly, error, trespasse.

Lord Av. You advyse well,
Lett mee advyse you lyke-wyse: instantly
Retyre in to your chamber, without noyse
Reply or question, least part of that rage
Is bent gainst him you turne upon your self,
Which is not for your safety.

Lady Av. Syr, good night.   [*Exit*.[113]

Lord Av. How goes the hower?

Denis. Tis almost tenn.

Lord Av. The tyme of our appointment: you attend
Upon his knocks and give him free admittans;
Beinge entred, refer him into this place;
That doon, returne then to your Ladye's chamber
There locke your self fast in.

Mayde. My lorde, I shall.--
Poore fryare, I feare theyl put thee to thy penance
Before they have confest thee.

Lord Av. Come, withdrawe;
The watchwoordes not yet given.

   Enter the Fryar with a letter.

Fr. Jhon. 'Tis her owne pen, I knwe it, synce shee sett
Her hand to establishe our foundation,
And, sweete soule, shee hath writt a second tyme

To build mee upp anewe:--My Lord is ridd
A three dayes jorney, loose not this advantadge
But take tyme by the fore-topp. Yes I will
By the fore-topp and topp-gallant. At the posterne
Shee to whose hand you gave your letter, Fryar,
Attends for your despatch:--my busines
I hope shalbee despatcht then:--Fare you well,
Fayle mee this night and ever. I'l sooner forfett
All pleasures, hopes, preferments, with th'assurance
Of a longe lyfe blest with most happy howers,
Then this one night's contentment.

Mayde. Ha, who's theire?
Fryar *Jhon*?

Fr. Jhon. The same: you, mystresse *Millisent*
My Ladye's gentlewoman?

Mayde. I am the closett
That treasures all her counsells.

Fr. Jhon. Is all cleare?

Mayde. As such a dark night can bee--to one, I feare,
That scarce will looke on daye more.

Fr. Jhon. Where's my lady?

Mayde. Attends you in her chamber.

Fr. Jhon. Guide mee too't,
Nay, quickly guerle:--how I allredy surfett

In this nights expectation!

Mayde. Staye you heare
In this withdraweinge roome, I'l fetch a light
For safeguard of your shinnes.

Denis. Shee might have sayde
For safeguard of his necke.

Mayde. My sceane's doone;
The next act lyes amongst them.   [*Exit*.[114]

Fr. Jhon. My part dothe but beginne nowe and I'l act it
In exquisite cleane linnen; and this capp
Proffred of purpose, least I should smell fryar.
What differ wee i'th darke, save our shaven crowne,
From gentlemen, nay Lords? nature hath araied us
As well as the best layemen: why should lawe
Restreyne from us what is allowed to them?
Lett it curbe fooles and idiots, such as throughe folly
Will not, or nycenes dare not, tast what's sweete,
Alyke made for all pallats.

Lord Av. Howe the slave
Insults in his damnation! cease the wretch,
I can indure no lonnger.

Fr. Jhon. Such as ban
Proffred delights may, if they please, refuse;
What's borne with mee I will make bold to use.

Lord Av. And I what thou weart borne too, that's a halter.
Pull without feare or mercy, strangle him

With all his sinnes about him; t'were not else
A revendge worthe my fury.

[*Fry: strangled.*

Dennis. I dare nowe
Lodge him a whole night by my syster's syde,
Hee's nowe past strompetting.

Lord Av. Tis night with him,
A longe and lastinge night.

Denis. Hee lyes as quiet.
You did well, Fryare, to putt on your cleane linnen;
Twill serve you as a shrowde for a new grave.
Whither shall wee lyft his body?

Lord Av. I am on the suddeine
Growne full of thoughts; the horror of the fact
Breedes strange seditions in mee.

Denis. Hee perhapps
But counterfetts dead sleep. I'l hollowe to him
To see if I can wake him.

Lord Av. Trifle not;
The sinne will proove more serious. To a conscience
Startled with blood and murder, what a terror
Is in the deede, being doone, which bredd before
Boathe a delight and longing! This sadd spectacle
Howe itt affrights mee!

Denis. Letts remove itt then.

Lord Av. The sinne it self, the churches malediction,
As doone to one of a sequestred lyfe
And holly order, the lawes penalty,
Being duble forfeture of lyfe and state,
Reproach, shame, infamy, all these incur'd
Through my inconsiderate rashnes!

Denis. My lyfe, too.
Howe to prevent the danger of all these?

Lord Av. Ey, that will aske much breyne, much project.

Denis. Sir,
Shall we poppe him in som privy?

Lord Av. Duble injurye,
To praye upon the soule and after deathe
Doo to the body such discoortesy;
It neather savours of a generous spyritt
Nor that which wee call manly.

Denis. Anythinge
For a quiett lyfe,[115] but this same wryneckt deathe,
That which still spoyles all drinkinge, 'tis a thinge
I never coold indure; as you are noble
Keepe still my wind pype open.

Lord Av. Out of many
Museings[116] for boath our safetyes I have fownd
One that's above the rest most probable.

Denis. What, what, I praye, Syr?

Lord Av. Interupt mee not:
Staye I should nowe begett a stratagem
To save myne owne lyfe, myne estate and goodds,
Ey, and secure thee too.

Denis. 'Twere excellent, Syr.

Lord Av. I have project for all these, as willingly
To lengthen boathe our lyves, and limitt us
Tyme to repent his deathe.

Denis. But howe, I praye, Syr?

Lord Av. Ey, there's the difficulty; but nowe I hav't.
Betwixt us and the cloyster's but one wall,
And that of no greate height; coold wee in private
Conveighe this fryar into the monastery,
It might be then imadgind som of them
Might bee his deathe's-man; which might seeme more probable
Bycause, as I had late intelligens,
There hathe bin stryfe amongst them.

Denis. Better still.

Lord Av. Now howe can wee incurr the least suspect?
For what should hee doo from the fryary,
Or what seeke heere att this unseasoned hower?

Denis. I apprehende thee; and, to further this,
In the backe yard there is a ladder, Syr:
Mount him upon my back, and I'l conveighe him
Where som, not wee, shall answer for his death.

Lord Av. As desperate wounds still must have desperate cure,
So all rash mischeiffes shuld have suddeine shiftes.
Wee'l putt it to ye venter.

Denis. Mount him then;
I'l once trye if the ventur of a ladder
Can keepe mee from the halter.

[*Exeunt*.[117]

Explicit Actus 3.

Actus 4.

SCENA PRIMA.

Enter the Clowne.

Clowne. I have left a full coort behynde mee, **Mildewe** pleidinge of the one syde, my mayster on the other, and the lawyers fendinge and prooveinge on boathe; there's such yeallinge and ballinge, I know not whether it made any deafe to heare it, but I am suer I was almost sicke to see't. Whyle they are brablinge in the cittye I am sent backe to the villadge to cheire up the too younge mermaydes; for synce theire throates have bin rincht with salt water they singe with no lesse sweatenes. But staye; I spy a fisherman drawinge his nett upp to the shore; I'l slacke som of my speede to see how hee hathe spedd since the last tempest.

Enter the Fisherman.

Fisher. I see hee that nought venters nothinge gaynes;
Hee that will bee awake when others sleepe
May sometymes purchase what may give him rest,
When other loyterers shalbe forct to ryse
Or perish through meare want; as, for example,
Although the tempest frighted hence the fishe,
I have drag'd some thinge without finne or skale
May make mee a good markett. Lett mee better
Surveigh my pryze; 'tis of good weight I feele;
Now should it bee some treasure I weare mayde.

Clowne. Which if it proove I'l half marr you or be half made with you.

Fisher. It must be gold by th'weight.

Clowne. If it bee so heavy 'tis ten to one but I'l do you the curtesye to ease you of part of your burden.

Fisher. None save myself is guilty of this pryze;
'Tis all myne owne, and I'l bee thinke mee best
Howe to beestowe of this ritche magazin.

Clowne. And I am stooddiinge too with what lyne, what angle, what fisguigge[118] what castinge nett I cann share with you in this sea booty.

Fisher. I will dissemble, as most ritche men doo,
Pleade poverty and speake my mayster fayre;
By out my freedom for som little somme,
And, beeinge myne owne man, by lands and howses;

That doon, to sea I'l rigge shipps of myne owne,
And synce the sea hathe made mee upp a stocke
I'l venter it to sea; who knowes but I
In tyme may prove a noble marchant?

Clowne. Yes of eele skinnes.--Staye you, Syrra, ho!

Fisher. I knowe no fish of that name; limpet, mullet, conger, dolphin, sharke I knowe, and place; I woold som body else had thyne; for hearinge I woold thou hadst none, nor codd; for smelt thou art too hott in my nose allredy; but such a fishe cald Syrra never came within the compasse of my nett. What art thou, a shrimpe, a dogg fish or a poore Jhon?[119]

Clowne.[120] I am one that watcht the tyde to know what thou hast caught, and have mony in my pockett to by thy draught.

Fisher. And I am one thou seest that have only an empty wett nett, but not so much as the tale of a spratte at thys tyme to sell for love of mony.

Clowne. I grant this is no Fryday and I at this tyme no cater for the fishmarkett. I only cam to desyre thy judgement and counsell.

Fisher. Go to the bench for judgment and to the lawe courts for counsell, I am free of neather, only one of *Neptunes* poore bastards, a spawne of the sea, and nowe gladly desyres to be rydd of thee aland.

Clowne. Onely one question resolve mee, and I have doone.

Fisher. To bee well ridd of the I care not if I loose so much tyme.

Clowne. But feythefully.

Fisher. As I am honest peeterman.[121]

Clowne. Observe mee then:
I saw a theif, comitting fellony;
I know the mayster of the thing was stolne,
I com unto this theif, as't might bee thee,
And make this covenant; eather give mee half
And make mee sharer or thou forfettest all,
I'l peach thee to the owner; in this case
What may I justly claime?

Fisher. Rather than forfeit all I shoold yeild halfe.

Clowne. Knwe then 'tis thy case, and my case a most playne case, and concernes the booty in that cap-case.[122] I knowe the lord that wants it and the mayster that owes[123] it; boath howe it was lost and where it was lost. Com, unloose, unbuckle, unclaspe, uncase, lett's see then what fortune hathe sente us, and so part it equally beetwixt us.

Fisher. Staye, staye, my frend this my case must not be opend till your case bee better lookt into. Thou knowest who lost it, I who fownd it; thou the lord of it that was, I the owner that nowe is; thou who did possess it, I who doth injoye it; hee had it, I have it; hee might have kept it, I will keepe it; I venter'd for all, I will inherit all; and theres thy pittifull case layde open.

Clowne. First proove this to bee thyne.

Fisher. I can and by the fisherman's rethorick.

Clowne. Proceed sea-gull.

Fisher. Thus land-spaniell; no man can say this is my fishe till hee finde it in his nett.

Clowne. Good.

Fisher. What I catche is myne owne, my lands my goodds my copy-hold, my fee-simple, myne to sell, myne to give, myne to lend, and myne to cast away; no man claimes part, no man share, synce fishinge is free and the sea common.

Clowne.[124] If all bee common that the sea yeelds why then is not that as much mine as thyne?

Fisher. By that lawe, when wee bringe our fishe to the markett, if every one may freely chuse what hee lykes and take where hee lyst, wee shoold have quikly empty dorsers[125] and cleane stalls, but light purses.

Clowne. How can'st thou proove that to bee a fishe that was not bredd in the water, that coold never swimme, that hathe neather roe nor milt, scale nor finne, lyfe nor motion? Did ever man heare of a fishe cald a budgett? What shape, what collor?

Fisher. This shape, this collor, there's nowe within better then the spawne of sturgeon; I must confesse indeed, they are rarely seene, and seldom fownd; for this is the fyrst I ever catcht in all the tyme of my fishinge.

Clowne. All this sea-sophestry will not serve your turne, for where my right is deteind mee by fayre meanes I will have it by force.

Fisher. Of what I caught in the sea?

Clowne. Yes, and what I catch hold on ashore. With what consciens can'st thou denye mee part of the gaine, when the owner heareinge it is in thy custody and within my knowledge, must eather find mee a principall in the theft, or at least accessary to the fellony.

Fisher. I'l showe thee a redy waye to prevent boathe.

Clowne. How's that?

Fisher. Marry, thus: go thou quietly thy way, I'l go peacably myne; betraye thou mee to nobody, as I meane to impart to thee nothinge; seeke thy preferment by land as I have doone myne by sea; bee thou mute, I'l be dumbe; thou silent, I mumbudgett; thou dismisse mee, I'l acquitte thee; so thou art neather theife nor accessary.

Clowne. Syrrah, though you bee owner of the boate I'l steare my course at healme.

Fisher. Hands off, I saye. But hark a noyse within
Letts cease our controversy till wee see   [***Noyse***.
An end of that.

Clowne. Trew, and bee judg'd by the next quiet man wee meete.

Fisher. Content.

   Enter after a noyse or tumult, Ashburne, his wyfe,
   Palestra, Scribonia and Godfrey.

Woman. I'l not beleeve a sillable thou speak'st;
False harts and false toonges go together still,
They boathe are quick in thee.

Ashb. Have patience woman.

Woman. I have ben too longe a grizell. Not content
To have thy hawnts abroad, where there are marts
And places of lewd brothelry inoughe
Wheare thou maiest wast thy body, purse and creditt,
But thou wooldst make thy private howse a stewes!

Ashb. But heare me, wyfe.

Wom. I'l heare none but myselfe.
Are your legges growne so feeble on the suddeine
They feyle when you shoold travell to your whores,
But you must bringe them home and keepe them heere
Under my nose? I am not so past my sences
But at this age can smell your knavery.

Pal. Good woman, heare's none suche.

Woman. Bold baggadge, peace!
'Tis not your turne to prate yet; lust and impudens
I know still goe togeather.[126] Shewes it well
In one thats of thy yeares and gravity,
That ought to bee in lyfe and government
To others an example, nowe to doate
So neere the grave! to walke before his dooer
With a younge payer of strumpetts at his tale!
Naye, make his honest and chast wyfe no better
Then a madam makarell![127]

Godfr. Why, this stormes woorse then that until'd the howse!

Ashb. But understand mee:
Itt is meare pitty and no bad intent,
No unchast thought but my meare charity
In the remembrans of our longe lost child,
To showe som love to these distressed maydens.

Woman. Sweete charity! nay, usury withall!
For one chyld lost, whose goodnes might have blest
And bin an honor to our family,
To bringe mee home a cuple of loose thinges!
I know not what to terme them, but for thee,
Owld fornicator, that jad'st mee at home
And yet can fend [?] a yonge colt's toothe abroad,
Ould as I am myne eyes are not so dimme
But can discerne this without spectacles.
Hence from my gate, you syrens com from sea,
Or as I lyve I'l washe your painteinges off
And with hotte skaldeinge water instantly.
                    [*Exit*.

Godfr. Nay then, sweeteharts, you canott staye, you have had could interteinment.

Pal. The land's to us as dreadfull as the seas,
For wee are heare, as by the billows, tost
From one feare to another.

Ashb. Pretty sowles,
Despyer not you of comfort; I'l not leive you
To the least danger till som newes returne
From him that undertakes your patronadge.
You, syrrah, usher them into the fryary,
Whence none dares force them. I have a cross wyfe you see,

And better you then I take sanctuary.

Scrib. Wee will be sweyde by you as one in whome
Wee yet have fownd all goodnes.

Ashb. Leive them theere
To safety, then returne.

[Ex't. ma: Ashb.[128]

Clown. What say'st thou to this gentleman?

Fisher. No man better.--Now it will go on my syde; this is my owne master, sure hee cannot bee so unatrall to give sentens against his owne natural servant.--Syr, good daye.

Ashb. Gramercyes, I in truth much suffered for thee,
Knowing howe rashly thou exposd thyself
To such a turbulent sea.

Clown. I likewyse, Syr, salute you.

Ashb. Thanks, good frend.

Clown. But, syr, is this your servant.[129]

Ashb. Yes, I acknowledge him;
And thou I thinke belongst to Mr *Raphael*,
Imployde about these women.

Clown. Yes I acknowledge it; but you are sure hee's yours?

Ashb. Once againe I doo confesse him myne.

Clown. Then heare mee speake.

Fisher. Heare mee your servant.[130]

Ashb. I'l heare the stranger fyrst.

Clown. In this you doo but justyce, I pray tell mee[131] ... Sea, is this a fishe or no, or if a fishe what fishe do you call it (peace you).

Ashb. It is no fishe nor fleshe.

Clowne. Nor good redd herringe--fisherman, y'r gone.

Fisher. Thou art deceav'd I am heare still, and may have heare for ought I knowe to by all the redd herringe in Marcell[es].

Clowne. Did you ever heare of a fishe cal'd a budgett?

Ashb. I protest never synce I knew the sea.

Clowne. You are gone againe fisherman.

Fisher. I am heare still; and now, master, heare mee.

Clowne. Lett mee proceede. This bagge, this knapsacke, or this portmanteau hee woold make a fishe bycause tooke in his nett. Nowe, syr, I com to you with this ould proverbe, all's not fishe that com's to nett.--There you are, gone againe.

Fisher. But--

Clowne. No butt, nor turbutt. I suspect this budgett to be the bawde's, in which are the discoveryes of this yonge woman's coontry and parents. Now, syr, for their sakes, for my masters sake, for all our sakes use the authority of a mayster to searche, and showe the power you have over a servant to comand.

Ashb. Will hee or not, hee shall assent to that.

Clowne. A meere trick to undoo mee, ere I knwe
What I am wanting.

Ashb. Call in the damseles,
Intreate them fayrely heather; say wee hope
We shall have good newes for them.

Fisher. I will part with it only on this condition, that if there bee nothinge in it which concernes them, the rest may returne to mee unrifled and untutcht.

Ashb. Did it conteyne the valew of a myne
I clayme no part in it.

Fisher. Nor you?

Clowne. Nor I.

Fisher. By the contents of this budgett.

Clowne. I sweare.

Ashb. I vowe.

Fisher. Then there tak't to you, mayster, and once more
Good lucke on my syde!

Enter Godfrey, usheringe in Palestra and Scribonia.

Palest, You sent to speake with us?

Ashb. I did indeed,
Saye, knowe you this? y'have leave, surveigh it well.

Pal. This? knowe I this? oh, my *Scribonia*, see!
Yes, and by this alone may knowe myself.
Looke well upon't, deare syster; extasy
May dimme myne eyes, it cannot purblind thyne.

Scrib. Itt is the same, *Palestra*.

Fisher. Then sure I shall not bee the same man in the afternoone
that I was in the morninge.

Scrib. In this is a greate masse of wealthe included,
All that the bawde hath by corruption gott
In many a thrifty yeare.

Fisher. Comfort for mee.

Ashb. But tell me is there ought of yours included,
Which you may justly chalendge?

Pal. Of that gould
No not the valewe of one poor deneere:[132]

'Tis all base brokadge boathe of sinne and shame
Of which wee neare weare guilty; yet inclosed
There shall you find a cabinet of myne,
Where boathe my naturall parents you may see
In a small roome intended.

Fisher. An unatrall child thou art to trust thy naturall parents into a leatheren bagge and leave them in the bottom of y'e sea.

Pal. Showe mee the caskett: if before you ope it
I do not name you every parcell in't
Lett it no more bee myne, mak't your own pryse;
But such small trifles as I justly chalenge
And cannot yeeld you the least benefitt,
Of them let mee bee mystresse, synce they are
The somme and crowne of all my future hopes,
But from my tender infancy deteined.
As for the gould and Jewells mak't your spoyle;
Of that I clayme no portione.

Fisher. I accept of the condition.

Ashb. Itt is boathe just and honest; we'll have no juggling,
And, *Gripus*, synce the busines concernes you,
Have you a curious ey too't.

Fisher. Feare not mee, for boathe at sea and land I was ever a goodd marksman.

Ashb. The caskett is nowe open'd: what coms fyrste?

Pal. Above, the clothes in which I fyrst was swathde,
The linnen fyrst worne in myne infancy.

Ashb. These are child's swathinges; whether thyne or no
It is to mee uncertaine. To the rest.

Pal. And next to these is a ritche handkercher,
Where you shall find in golden letters wrought
My place of byrthe, myne and my father's name.

Ashb. Heare's such a handkercher, such letters workt:
Speake them, as I shall reade them.

Pal. Mirable.

Ashb. Right! *Myrable*.

Pal. Daughter of Jhon Ashburne, merchant.

Ashb. Trewe: of *Jhon Ashburne* merchant--Oh my sowle!
--Proceed, prithee proceede.

Pal. And borne in Christ-chyrch, London, Anno--

Ashb. 160(?)0.[133]
Oh you Imortall powers. I stagger yet
Beetwixt despayer and hope, and canott guesse
Which weye my fate will swaye mee; oh speake, speake!
Thy mothers name?

Pal. Reade it in sylver letters pleynly wrought
In the next Imbrodered Linnen.

Ashb. If that fayle not

I have a firme rock to build upon.--
The guift of Isabell to her daughter Mirable.--
Oh frend, oh servant!

Clown. How is't, syr?

Fisher. How now, mayster?

Ashb. I that so many yeares have been despoyl'd,
Neclected, shattered, am made upp againe,
Repaired, and new created.

Pal. Search but further
And there's a golden brooch in it, a diamond,
Upon my byrthday geven mee by my father.

Ashb. I have longe sought and nowe at lengthe have found
That diamond, thee my daughter.

Pal. How, syr?

Ashb. Shee that so late excluded thee my house
And shutt these gates against thee, **Isabell**
Thy mother, these weare her owne handyworkes
Bestowde upon thee in thyne infancy
To make us nowe boathe happy in thy yoouth.
I am **Jhon Ashburne** marchant, **London, Christ Church**;
The yeare, place, tyme agree thee to bee myne,
Oh merher [mirror] of thy sex, my **Myrable**!

Pal. This surplusadge of joy should not bee forged.

Ashb. No more than these noates are infalleble.

Pal. Thus then in all Humility I kneele
To you my acknowledgd father.

Ashb. Ryse, my guerle.

Fisher. Had I not drawne this leeward out of the sea, where had it bin? all drownd by this.

Ashb. No triflinge nowe: post, *Godfrey*, to my wyfe,
Tell her no more then thou hast heard and seene:
Shee's hard of faythe, relate it punctually,
Beare her (oh lett me borrowe them so longe)
These better to confirme her; bid her hast,
And for the truth add these as testimony:--
Nay, art thou heare still?

Godf. Lyke a shadowe vanisht,
But to returne a substance.   [*Exit Godfrey*.[134]

Ashb. Oh my deare doughter!--where's young *Raphael's* man
Beare him of all what thou hast seene a perfect
And trew relation.

Clowne. Ay, syr.

Ashb.[135] Bidd him too,
All business sett apart, make hether.

Clown. Ay, syr.

Ashb. Tell him that his *Palestra* is my *Mirable*.

Clown. Ay, syr.

Ashb. And that shee is my doughter, my lost child.

Clowne. Ay, syr.

Ashb. And that of all this I am most assur'd.

Clown. Ay, syr.

Ashb. Thou wilt not doo all this?

Clown. I will, you lye, syr.

Ashb. Howe, syr.

Cl. Ay, syr.

Ashb. Saye that this daye shee shalbee made his wyfe.

Cl. Ay, syr.

Ashb. Why then add winges unto your heeles and fly, syr.

Cl. Ay syr, but ere I take my flight, for this good servyce You'll mediate with him for my freedom?

Ashb. So.

Cl. And woo your doughter to doo so too?

Ashb. So.

Cl. And, syr, to him I shalbee thankefull.

Ashb. So.

Cl. Your doughters and your servant ever.

Ashb. So.

Cl. To go, roonne, ryde of all your arrants.

Ashb. So.

Cl. In all this you'l bee slack in nothinge?

Ashb. So.

Cl. And you'l heareafter love mee still?

Ashb. So, so.

Cl. Howe, but so, so?

Ashb. Yes, so and so and so.

Cl. Why, then I go, go, goe.   [*Exit Clown*.

Ashb. But one thinge I intreate you, *Mirable*:
This thyrteene yeares, since by rude creditors
Tost and opprest, nay rent out of myne owne,

I have bin forct to seeke my fate abroad,
Howe weare you ravisht thence, or since that tyme
What strange adventures past?

Enter Godfrey, and the wyfe with the handkercher.

Mirable. My mother's presence
Must now prevent my answer.

Wyfe. Where is shee? oh wheare, wheare? for by these tokens,
These of her childhood most unfallid signes,
I knwe her for my doughter.

Mir. I have bene
The longe and wretched owner of that cabinet
With all therein contein'd.

Wyfe. Into thy boosom
Oh lett mee rayne a shower of joyfull teares
To welcom thee, my *Mirable*.

Godf. You threatned her but nowe with skaldinge water; mee thinks you had more neede to comfort her with hott waters, for sure shee canott bee warme synce shee came so late out of the could bathe.

Wyf. Make fyares, bid them make ready wholesom brothes,
Make warme the bedd, and see the sheetes well ayred.
Att length then have I fownd thee?

Ashb. But what's shee
That's in thy fellow-shippe?

Mir. My fellowe sharer
In all misfortunes; and for many yeares
So deere to mee, I canot tast a blessednes
Of which shee's not partaker.

Wyfe. For thy sake
Shee shall bee myne too, and (in her) I'l thinke
The powers above have for my single losse
Given mee at lengthe a duble recompense.

Scrib. For which hee that protects all inocence
Will in good tyme reward you.

Wyfe. Praye, in, in;
This could is prejuditiall to your Healthes.
I'l count you boathe my twinnes.

    [*Ext. Wife, Palestra, and Scribonia*.

Ashb. Strange alteration!
Skoldinge is turn'd to pittye, spleen and mallyce
To mercye and compassion.

Fisher. But your promisse
Tutchinge my budgett?

Ashb. *Godfreye*, beare it in
And lodge it safe; there's no tyme for that;
We'll talke of it herafter.

Godf. Fellow *Gripus*, I am made for this tyme porter. Ladeys, your trusty treasurer.
    [*Ext. Ashbourne and Godfrey*.

Gripus. These are the fishermen and I the fishe catcht in the nett; well my comfort is, thoughe my booty have made me no ritcher then I was, poorer then I am I canott bee. Nowe[136] wherein is the ritche more happy then the poore? I thinke rather lesse blessed and that shall approue by this excellent good ballet, thoughe sett to a scurvy tune.

> Lett ech man speake as he's possest
> I hold the poore man's state most blest.
> For if longe lyfe contentment bredes,
> In that the poore the ritche exceedes;
>
> The ritch man's dayes are short, as spent
> In pleasures and supposed content;
> Whylst to us poore men care and troble
> Makes every hower wee wast seeme duble.
>
> He that hathe ech daye to his backe
> Chandge of gaye suites, whylst wee alacke
> Have but one coate, that coorse and ould,
> Yet it defends us from the could;
>
> As warme too in an equll eye
> As they in all theere purple dye;
> 'Mongst all theere store, they weare, we see,
> But one at once, and so do wee.
>
> The ritche that at his table feasts
> With choyse of dayntyes, sundry guests,
> In all his plenty can but fill
> One belly; so the poore can still
>
> With cheese and onions and disguest[137]

As well with them as th'others feast.
The pesent with his homespoon lasse
As many merry howers may passe

As coortiers with there sattin guerles,
Though ritchly dect in gould and pearles;
And, though but pleyne, to purpose wooe,
Nay ofttymes with lesse danger too.

And yet for all this I have one crotchett left in my fate to bate a new hooke for the gold in the portmanteau.

[*Exit*.

Actus 4to.

SCENA 3A.

Enter Dennis with the Fryar from aboue upon his backe.

Den. Whether a knavishe or a sinneful load,
Or one or bothe I know not; massye it is,
And if no frend will for mee,[138] I'l bee sorry
For myne owne heavinesse. And heare's a place,
Though neather of the secretest nor the best,
To unlade myself of this Iniquity.
When I satt late astryde upon the wall,
To lyft the ladder this waye for descent,
Mee thought the fryar lookt lyke S *George* a horsback

And I his trusty steede. But nowes no triflynge:
Hee's[139] where hee is in Comons, wee discharged,
Boathe of suspect and murther; which lett the covent
To-morrowe morninge answere howe they cann.
I'l backe the waye wee came; what's doon, none sawe
I'th howse nor herde; they answer then the Lawyer.
     [*Exit*.

Enter Fryar Richard.

Fr. R. Of all Infirmityes belonginge to us
I hould those woorst that will not lett a man
Rest in his bedd a-nights. And I of that,
By reason of a late could I have gott,
Am at this instant guilty; which this rushinge
From a warme bedd in these wild frosty nights
Rather augments then helpes; but all necessityes
Must bee obeyde. But soft, there's one before mee:
By this small glimpse of moone light I perceave him
To bee Fryar *Jhon*, my antient adversary.[140]
Why *Jhon*? why *Jhon*? what! not speake! why, then
I see 'tis doon of malyce, and of purpose
Only to shame mee, since hee knowes the rest
Take notyce what a loose man I am growne.
Nay prithee, sweete fryar *Jhon*, I am in hast,
Horrible hast; doo but release mee nowe,
I am thy frend for ever. What! not heare!
Feigne to bee deaf of purpose, and of slight!
Then heare is that shall rouse you. Are you falne?
  [*Eather*[141] *strykes him with a staffe or casts a stone*.
What, and still mute and sylent? nay, not styrr?
I'l rowse you with a vengance! not one limbe
To doo his woonted offyce, foot nor hand?

Not a pulse beatinge, no breathe? what no motion?
Oh mee of all men lyvinge most accurst!
I have doon a fearefull murder, which our former
Inveterate hate will be a thousand testats
That I for that insidiated his lyfe.
The deedes apparant and the offens past pardon.
There's nowe no waye but fly: but fly! which way?
The cloyster gates are all bar'd and fast lockt;
These suddeine mischieffes shuld have suddeine shifts.
About it breyne and in good tyme. I hate![142]
Suspitious rumors have bene lately spread
And more then whispered of th'incontinent love
Fryar *Jhon* boare to the knight's Lady. Had I meanes
Howe to conveighe his body o'er the wall
To any or the least part of the howse,
It might bee thought the knight in jelosy
Had doone this murder in a just revendge.
Let me surveighe th'ascent: happy occation!
To see howe redy still the devill is
To helpe his servants! heare's a ladder left:
Upp, Fryare, my purpose is to admitt you nowe
Of a newe cloyster. I will sett his body
Upright in the knights porche and leave my patron
To answer for the falt, that hath more strength
Then I to tugge with Benches.
      [*Exit. Carry him up*.

Enter the knight, half unredy, his Lady after him.

D'Avern. Ho, *Denis*!

Lady. Give mee reason, I intreate,
Of these unquiet sleepes.

D'Av. You dogg mee, Lady,
Lyke an Ill genius.

Lady. You weare woont to call mee
Your better angel.

D'Av. So I shall doo still,
Would you beetake you to your quiet sleepes
And leave mee to my wakinges.

Lady. There beelonges
Unto one bedd so sweete a sympathy,
I canott rest without you.

D'Av. To your chamber!
There may growe els a woorse antypathy
Beetwixt your love and myne: I tell you, Lady,
Myne is no woman's busines. No reply:
Your least insured presence att this tyme
Will but begett what you would loathe to beare,
Quarrell and harshe unkindnes.

Lady. Ever your lipps
Have bene too mee a lawe.--I suspect more
Then I would apprehend with willingnes;
But though prevention canott helpe what's past,
Conjugall faythe may expresse itself at last.
              [*Exit Lady.*

D'Av. Why, **Denis**, ho! awake and ryse in hast!

Denis. What, is your Lordshipp madd!

D'Av. Knowest thou what's past
And canst thou skape this danger?

Denis. Did I not tell you
That all was safe, the body too disposed
Better then in his grave?

D'Av. Strange thoughts sollicite mee.
Upp and inquire about the cloyster wall
What noyse thou hearest, if any private whisperinge
Or louder uprore 'bout the murder ryse.

Denis. I shall, I shall, Syr.   [*Exit Dennis.*

D'Av. Guilt, thoughe it weare a smooth and peacefull face,
Yet is within full of seditious thoughts
That makes continuall follie.   [*Exit.*

Enter Fryar Richard with Fryar Jhon upon his backe.

Fr. Rich. This is the porch that leades into the hall;
Heare rest for thyne and myne own better ease.
This havinge done, to prevent deathe and shame
By the same stepps I'l back the way I came.

   [*Fryer sett up and left. Exit.*

Enter Denis half unredy.

Denis. This is the penalty belonges to servyce:
Masters still plott to theire owne private ends,

And wee that are theire slaves and ministers
Are cheef still in the troble; they ingrosse
The pleasure and the proffitt, and wee only
The swett and payne. My Lord hath doon a mischeef
And nowe I must not sleepe.--What art thou?
None of the howse sure, I should knwe thy face then:
Beesydes my Lord gives no such lyverye.
Nowe in the name of heaven, what art thou? speake,
Speake if thou beest a man! or if a ghost
Then glyde hence lyke a shadowe! tis the--oh!--
The fryar hathe nimbly skipt back over the wall,
Hath lyke a surly Justyce bensht himself
And sitts heare to accuse uss! where's my Lord?
Helpe, Helpe! his murdered ghost is com from Hell
On earth to cry *Vindicta*![143]

 Enter L. D'Averne.

D'Av. What clamors this?

Denis. Oh Syr--

D'Av. Why, howe is't, ***Denis***?

Denis. Never woorse--the fryar, Syr--

D'Av. What of him?

Denis. The slave that would not leive the place but carried,
Is of himself com back.

D'Av. Whether?

Denis. Looke theere.

D'Av. That which I took to bee meare fantasy
I finde nowe to bee real; murder is
A cryinge sinne, and canot be conceal'd.
Yet his returne is straunge.

Denis, 'Tis most prodigious;
The very thought of it hath put a cricke
Into my necke allredy.

D'Av. One further desperate tryall I will make
And putt it too adventer.

Denis. Pray hows that, Syr?

D'Av. There's in my stable an ould stallion, once
A lusty horse but now past servyce.

Denis. Godd [*sic*], syr.

D'Av. Him I'l have sadled and capparisond.
Heare in the hall a rusty Armor hanges,
Pistolls in rotten cases, an ould sword,
And a cast lance to all these sutable.
I'l have them instantly tooke downe.

Den. And then?

D'Av. In these I'l arme the fryar from head to knee;
Mount him into his saddle, with stronge cords
There bind him fast, and to his gauntlet hand
Fasten his lance; for basses[144] tis no matter,

These his grey skyrts will serve. Thus arm'd, thus mounted,
And thus accoutred, with his beiver upp,
Turne him out of the gates, neither attended
With squire or page, lyke a stronge knight adventures
To seeke a desperate fortune.

Denis. Hee may so if hee please
Ryde post unto the Devill.

D'Av. This I'l see doone,
'Tis a decree determinde.

Denis. Capp a pe
I'l see him arm'd and mounted.

        [*Exeunt*.

Enter Fryar Richard.

Fr. R. This murder canott bee so smothered upp
But I in th'end shall paye for't; but feare still
Is wittye in prevention. Nowe for instance
There's but one refuge left mee, that's to flye:
The gates are shutt upon mee and myself
Am a badd foottman, yet these difficultyes
I can thus helpe; there to this place beelonges
A mare that every second d[a]yes' imployde
To carry corne and fetch meele from the mill,
Distant som half league off; I by this beast
Will fashion myne escape.--What, baker, ho!

Within Baker. What's hee that calls so early?

Fr. R. I, Fryar *Richard*.

Baker. What would you have that you are stirringe thus
An hower before the Dawne.

Fr. Rich. I cannott sleepe
And understandinge there's meale redy ground,
Which thou must fetch this morninge from the mill,
I'l save thee so much pey[n]es. Lend mee the beast,
And lett mee forthe the gate; I'l bringe boathe back
Ere the bell ringe for mattens.

Baker. Marry, Fryar *Richard*,
With all my hart, and thanke yee. I'l but ryse
And halter her, then lett you forthe the gate;
You'l save mee so much labour.

Fr. Rich. This falls out
As I coold wishe, and in a fortunate hower;
For better then to too legges trust to fower.

Explicit Actus 4.

Act 5.

SCENE PRIMA.

Enter Thomas Ashburne the younger brother to John,
a merchant, with one of the Factors.[145]

Thomas. Are all things safe abord?

Factor. As you can wish, sir;
And notwithstandinge this combustious stryfe
Betwixt the winds and Seas, our ship still tight,
No anchor, cable, tackle, sayle or mast
Lost, though much daunger'd; all our damadge is
That where our puerpose was for ***Italy***
We are driven into ***Marcellis***.

Thomas. That's myne unhappines
That beinge come upon a brother's quest
Longe absent from his country, who of late
After confinement, penury, distresse
Hath gained a hopefull fortune, and I travelling
To beare him tydeinges of a blest estate
Am in my voyage thwarted.

Factor. In what province
Resydes hee at this present?

Thomas. His last letters
That I receav'd weare dated from ***Leagahorne***;
Nowe wee by this infortnate storme are driven
Into ***Marcellis*** roads.

Factor. For the small tyme
Of our abode heare what intend you, Sir?

Thomas. To take in victuall and refresh our men,
Provyde us of thinges needefull, then once more

With all the expeditious hast wee can
Sett sayle for *Florens*.

Factor. Please you, Sir,
I'l steward well that busines.

Thomas. I'th meanetyme
I shall find leisure to surveigh the towne,
The keyes, the temples, forts and monuments;
For what's the end of travell but to better us
In judgment and experiens? What are these?
Withdrawe and give them streete-roome.

Enter Raphael, Treadeway and the Clowne.

Raph. Hath my *Palestra* fownd her parents then?

Clowne. As sure as I had lost you.

Raph. And free borne?

Clowne. As any in *Marcellis*.

Raph. *Englishe*, sayst thou?

Clowne. Or *Brittishe*, which you please.

Raph. Her trew name *Mirable*
And *Ashburne's* doughter?

Clowne. Suer as yours is *Raphaels*
And *Tread-wayes* his.

Thomas. *Mirable* and *Ashburne*!

Factor. Names that concerne you, Sir.

Thomas. Peace, listen further.

Raph. Thou with these woords hast extasyde my sowle
And I am all in rapture. Then hee's pleasd
Wee too shalbee contracted?

Clowne. 'Tis his mynd, Sir.

Raph. The moother, too, consents?

Clowne. So you shall finde, Sir.

Raph. And *Mirable* pleasd, too?

Clowne. Shes so inclind, Sir.

Raph. And this the very day?

Clowne. The tyme assignd, Sir.

Raph. Shee shalbee suerly myne.

Clowne. As vowes can bind, Sir.

Raph. Thou sawest all this?

Clowne. I am suer I was not blind, Sir.

Raph. And all this shall bee done?

Clown. Before you have din'd, Sir.

Raph. Oh, frend, eather pertake with mee in Joy
And beare part of this surplus, I shall else
Dye in a pleasinge surfett.

Tread. Frend, I doo
Withall intreate you interceade for mee
To your fayre loves companion, for if all
Th'estate I have in *France* can by her freedom,
Shee shall no longer faynt beneathe the yoake
Of lewdnes and temptation.

Raph. The extent
Of that fyxt love I ever vowde to thee
Thou in this act shall find.

Tread. And it shall seale it,
Beyond all date or limitt.

Raph. Come, hasten, frend, methinks at lengthe I spy
After rough tempests a more open skye.

[Exeunt[146] Raphael and Treadway.

Clowne. And I will after you home, Syr,
Since so merrily blowes the wind, Sir.

Thomas. Staye, frend, I am a stranger in these parts

And woold in one thinge gladly bee resolved.

Clowne. I am in haste.

Thomas. That little leasure thou bestowest on mee
I shalbee gladd to pay for; nay, I will.
Drinke that for my sake.

Clowne. Not this, Syr, as it is; for I can make a shifte to dissolve
hard mettall into a more liquid substance. A cardeq![147] oh Syr, I can
distill this into a quintessence cal'd *Argentum potabile*.[148]

Thomas. I heard you name one *Ashburne*; can you bring mee
To th'sight of such a man?

Clowne. Easily I can, Syr. But for another peice of the same stampe,
I can bringe you to heare him, to feele him, to smell, to tast him, and
to feede upon him your whole fyve senses.

Thomas. There's for thee, though I have no hope at all
To finde in *France* what I in *Florens* seeke.
And though my brother have no child alyve,
As longe synce lost when I was rob'd of myne,
Yet for the namesake, to my other travells
I'l add this little toyle, though purposeles.
I have about mee letters of Import
Dyrected to a merchant of that name
For whose sake (beeinge one to mee intyred)
I only crave to see the gentleman.

Clowne. Beleeve mee Syr I never love to jest, with those that
beforehand deale with me in earnest. Will you follow mee?

Thomas. Prooves hee my brother, and his dowghter found,
Lost by my want of care, (which canott bee
All reasons well considered) and I so happy
To bringe him newes of a recovered state,
Who to his foes so longe hathe been a prey,
I'd count my monthes and years but from this day.

[*Exeunt*.

SCENE 2.

Enter at one door D'Averne, and Dennis with the Fryar armed.
At the other Fryar Richard and the Baker.

D'Averne. So nowe all's fitt, the daylight's not yet broake;
Mount him and lock him in the saddle fast,
Then turn him forthe the gates.

Dennis. Pray, Syr, your hand to rayse him.

D'Av. Nowe lett him post, whether his fate shall guide him.

[*Exeunt*.

Ent. Rich. and Baker.

Baker. The mare's ready.

Fr. R. Only the key to ope the cloyster gate,

Then all is as it shoold be.

Baker. Tak't, there tis.
But make hast, good Fryar **Richard**; you will else
Have no new bredd to dinner.

Fr. R. Feare not, baker;
I'l proove her mettall. Thus I back one mare
Least I shoold ryde another.   [*Exit*.

Baker. It is the kindest novyce of my consciens
That ere woare hood or coole.

[*A noyse within. Trampling of Horses*.

What noyse is that? now by the Abbot's leave
I will looke out and see.
                        [*Clere*.

Enter Averne and Dennis.

D'Av. Howe nowe? the newes?
The cause of that strange uprore?

Den. Strange indeed,
But what th'event will bee, I cannott guesse.

D'Av. Howe is it, speake.

Den. I had no sooner, as your Lordshipp badd,
Putt him upon his voyadge, turn'd him out,
But the ould resty stallion snuft and neighd,

And smelt, I thinke, som mare, backt (I perceavd
By the moone light) by a Fryar, in whose pursuite
Our new made horseman with his threatninge lance,
Pistolles, and rotten armor made such noyse
That th'other, frighted, clamours throughe the streetes
Nothinge but deathe and murder.

D'Av. But the sequell?--
The clamour still increasethe.   [*Noyse.*

   Enter the Baker rooninge.

Baker. Oh never, never,
Was seene such open mallyce!

Den. What's the busines?

Baker. Give mee but leave to breath--Oh especially in a cloyster!

Den. Out wee't, man.

Baker. The novyce ***Richard***, to save mee a labour,
Borrowed my mare to fetch meale for the mill.
I knowe not howe the devill Fryar ***Jhon*** knew't,
But all in armor watch't him gooinge out
And after spurrs to chardge him, beeinge unarmd,
0 suer if hee cannott reatch him with his lance
Hee'l speede him with his pistolls.

Denis. All's well yet.
              [*Noyse.*

Baker. This noyse hath cal'd much people from there bedds,
And troobled the whole villadge.

Fr. R. (*within*). Hold, hold, I do confesse the murder.

Baker. Suer hee hath slayne him, for murder is confest.

D'Av. Tis better still.

    Enter Ashburne, Godfrey, &c.

Godf. Was never knowne the lyke!

Baker. Is *Ritchard* slayne?
I sawe Fryar *Jhon*, arm'd dreadfully with weapons
Not to be worne in peace, pursue his lyfe;
All which I'l tell the abbott.
        [*Exit Baker*.

Ashb. Most strange it is that the pursude is fownd
To bee the murderer, the pursuer slayne.
Howe was it, *Godfrey*? thou wast upp beefore mee
And canst discoorse it best.

Godfr. Thus, Syr: at noyse of murder, with the tramplinge
Of horse and ratlinge armor in the streetes,
The villadgers weare wakend from there sleepes;
Som gap't out of there windowes, others venter'd
Out of theere doores; amongst which I was one
That was the foremost, and saw *Ritchard* stopt
At a turninge lane, then overtooke by *Jhon*;
Who not him self alone, but even his horse

Backing the tother's beast, seemd with his feete
To pawe him from his saddle; att this assault
Friar **Richard** cryes, hold, hold and haunt mee not
For I confesse the murder! folke came in
Fownd th'one i'th sadle dead, the t'other sprallinge
Upon the earthe alyve, still crynge out
That hee had doun the murder.

D'Av. Exellent still; withdrawe, for wee are saffe.

   Enter the Abbott, the baker, Fryar Richard, prisoner
   and guarded, &c.[149]--

Abbott. These mischeefes I foretould; what's mallyce elsse
Than murder halff comitted? though th'event
Bee allmost above apprehension strange,
Yet synce thyne owne confession pleades thee guilty
Thou shalt have leagall tryall.

Fr. Rich. I confess
I was the malefactor and deserve
Th'extremity of Lawe; but woonder much
Howe hee in such a short tyme after death
Should purchase horse and weapons.

Abbot. Murder's a sinne
Which often is myraculously reveal'd.
Lett justyce question that; beare him to prison,
The t'other to his grave.

Baker. Beeinge so valiant after deathe mee thinkes hee deserves the honor to bee buried lyke a knight in his compleate armor.

Abbot. These thinges shoold not bee trifled. Honest frendes,
Retyre you to your homes; these are our chardge.
Wee will acquaint our patron with this sadd
And dyre desaster; fyrst his counsell use,
Next as wee maye our Innocens excuse.

[*Exeunt*.

SCENA 3, ET ULTIMA.

Enter Mildewe and Sarleboyes.[150]

Mild. May the disease of **Naples** now turn'd **Frensh**
Take bothe the Judge and Jurors! they have doomd
The fayre **Palestra** from mee.

Sarl. So they had
Scribonia too, and mulcted us beesydes,
But that in part they did comiserate
Our so greate losse by sea.

Mild. This is the curse
Belonges to all us bawdes: gentle and noble,
Even th'ouldest fornicator, will in private
Make happy use of us with hugges and brybes;
But let them take us at the publick bench,
Gainst consciens they will spitt at us and doome us
Unto the post and cart. Oh the coruptnes
Of these dissemblinge letchers!

Sarlab. 'Tis well yet
You have reserved one virgin left for sale;
Of her make your best proffitt.

Mild.[151] A small stocke
To rayse a second fortune; yet com, frend,
Wee will go seeke her out.

Enter Gripus the Fisherman.

Fisher. No budgett to bee com by; my ould mayster,
Hee stands on consciens to deliver it
To the trew owner, but I thinke in consciens
To cheate mee and to keepe it to him selfe;
Which hee shall never doo, to prevent which
I'l openly proclayme it.
       [***Oh yes***!
  If any userer or base exacter,
  Any noble marchant or marchant's factor,
  Bee't marchant venterer or marchant Taylor
  Bee hee Mr. Pilot, botswyne or saylor--

Enter Godfrey to them.

Godf. Hist, ***Gripus***, hyst!

Fish. Peace, fellowe ***Godfrey***. I'l now play the blabber.--
If eather passinger owner or swabber[152]
That in the sea hathe lost a leather budgett
And to the Dolphins, whales or sharkes, doth grudge itt--

Godf. Wilt thou betraye all? I'l go tell my mayster.

Fish. Yes, **Godfrey**, goe and tell him all and spare not,
I am growne desperate; if thou dost I care not.

Mild. Hee talkt of a leatheren budgett lost at sea;
More of that newes would please mee.

Fish. Bee hee a Cristian or beleeve in **Mawmett**[153]
I such a one this night tooke in my drawnett.

Mild. My soone, my child, nay rather, thou young man,
I'l take thee for my father, for in this
Sure thou hast new begott mee.

Fish. Blessing on thee!
But shood I have a thousand children more,
I almost durst presume I never should have
Another more hard favored.

Mild. Thou art any thinge.
But hast thou such a budgett?

Fisher. Syr, I have
And new tooke from the sea. What woldst thou give
And have it safe?

Mild. I'l give a hundred crownes.

Fish. Tush, offer me a sowse[154] but not in th'eare;
I will barr that afore hand.

Mild. And all safe,
I'l give thee then too hondred.

Fish. Offer me a cardeq!

Mild. Three hondred, 4, nay fyve
So nothinge bee diminisht.

Fish. I will have
A thousand crowns or nothinge.

Mild. That growes deepe.

Fish. Not so deepe as the sea was.

Mild. Make all safe,
And I will give a thousand.

Fish. Tis a match,
But thou wilt sweare to this.

Mild. Give mee myne othe.

Fish. If, when first I shall beehold
    My leatheren bagge that's stuft with gould,
    At sight thereof I paye not downe
    To *Gripus* every promist crowne--
        Now say after mee.
May *Mildewe* I in my best age.

Mild. May *Mildewe* I in my best age.

Fish. Dy in some spittle, stocks or cage.[155]

Mild. Dy in some spittle stocks or cage.

Fish. I'l keepe my promisse, fayle not thou thine oathe.
So inn and tell my mayster.   [*Exit Fisherman*.

Mild. Yes, bawdes keepe oaths! t'must bee in leap-yeare then,
Not now; what wee sweare weel forsweare agen.

Enter Ashburne, Godfrey, and Gripus, to 'em.

Ashb. And hee in that did well, for Heaven defend
I shoold inritche mee with what's none of myne.
Where is the man that claymes it?

Grip. Heare's my sworne soon, that but even now acknowledgd mee to bee his father.

Ashb. Knowest thou this?

Mild. Yes for myne owne. I had thought, lyke one forlorne,
All fortune had forsooke mee, but I see
My best dayes are to com. Welcom my lyfe!
Nay if there bee in any bawde a sowle
This nowe hath mett the body.

Ashb. All's theire safe
Unrifled, naye untutcht, save a small caskett
With som few trifles of no valewe in't,
Yet to mee pretious, synce by them I have fownd
My one and only doughter.

Mild. Howes that, pray?

Ashb. Thus; thy **Palestra** is my **Mirable**.

Mild. Now may you to your comfort keepe the guerle,
Synce of my wealthe I am once againe possest.
I heare acquitt you of all chardges past
Due for her education.

Ashb. You speake well.

Grip. It seemes you are possest, and this your owne.

Mild. Which I'l knowe howe I part with.

Grip. Com quickly and untrusse.

Mild. Untrusse, Syr? what?

Grip. Nay if you stand on poynts,[156] my crowns, my crowns:
Com tell them out, a thousand.

Mild. Thousand deathes
I will indure fyrst! synce I neather owe thee
Nor will I paye thee any thinge.

Grip. Didst thou not sweare?

Mild. I did, and will againe
If it bee to my profit, but oathes made
Unto our hurt wee are not bound to keepe.

Ashb. What's that you chalendge, **Gripus**.

Grip. Not a sowse lesse
Then a full thousand crownes.

Ashb. On what condition?

Grip. So much hee vowed and swore to paye mee downe
At sight of this his budgett; a deneere
I will not bate; downe with my dust, thou perjurer.

Ashb. But did hee sweare?

Mild. Suppose it, saye I did.

Ashb. Then thus I saye, oathes ta'ne advisedly
Ought to bee kept; and this I'l see performed,
What's forfett to my man is due to mee;
I claime it as my right; these your bawdes fallacyes
In this shall no weye helpe you, you shall answer it
Now as a subject and beefore the judge.

Mild. If I appeare in coort I am lost againe;
Better to part with that then hazard all.
These bagges conteine fyve hundred pownds apeece,
Tak't and the pox to boot.

Grip. And all these myne?

Godf. Would I might have a share in't.

Ashb. Nowe tell mee, *Mildewe*, howe thou ratest the freedome
Of th'other virgin yonge *Scribonia*,
Companion with my dowghter?

Mild. I am weary
Of this lewde trade; give mee fyve hundred crownes
And take her; I'l gie't over now in tyme
Ere it bringe mee to the gallowes.

Ashb. There's for her ransom; she's from henceforthe free.

Grip. Howe, Syr?

Ashb. These other, **Gripus**, still belonge to thee
Towards the manumission.

    Enter at one doore Palestra, Scribonia; at the other
    Raphael, Treadway, Thomas Ashburne and the Clowne.

Raph. If all bee trewe my man related to mee
I have no end of Joy.

Ash. This is my **Mirable**,
My doughter and freeborne; and if you still
Persist the same man you profest your self,
Beehold shee is your wyfe.

Raph. You crowne my hopes.

Mir. This very day hathe made mee full amends
For many yeares of crosses.

Tread. Nowe my suite.

Raph. Nor are my expectations yet at heighte

Before my frend bee equally made blest
In this fayer damsell's love.

Tread. To accomplishe which
If all the wealth that I injoye by land,
Or what at Sea's in ventur, will but purchase
With her release a tye of love to mee,
This hower it shalbe tenderd.

Ashb. Offer'd fayrely;
But knwe, syr, could you winne her to your wishes,
She shall not lyke a bondemaide come to ye;
Fyve hundred crownes are tenderd downe all redy
(Unknowne to her) for her free liberty.

Scrib. This is a Juberly, a yeare of Joy,
For chastity and spotles Inocens.

Tread. Shall I intreate you to receive them backe?
Lett it bee made my woorke of charity.

Ashb. I knowe you woorthy, but that must not bee;
Yet proove her, court her, with my free consent
And use the best love's rethorick you can:
If with the motion shee rest satisfied,
And you pleas'd to accept her, it shall never
Bee sayde you tooke a captyve to your bedd
But a free woman.

Tread. Nobly have you spoake.

Raph. Fayre *Mirable*, the fyrst thinge I intreate you
In which to expresse your love, speake for my frend.

Mir. And with my best of Oratory.

Raph.[157] Weel be all
Assistants in the motion.

Ashb. If you prevayle,
I in the absens of som nearer frend
Have vowed to stand her father.

Clowne. Now, Sir, I have showed him you, but are you ever the wyser?

Thom. Ash. Peace, I am somwhat trobled. Oh tis hee,
My brother; and those rude and violent gusts
That to this strange Road thrust my shipp per force,
And I but late for new disasters curst,
Have with there light winges mounted mee aloft,
And for a haven in heaven new harbord mee.
Yet they but feede upon theire knowne delights;
Anon I'l make them surfett.

Scrib. If to this frendly fayer society,
I, a poore desolate virgin, so much bownd,
Should putt you off with delatory trifles
When you importune answer, t'would appeare
In mee strange incivility: I am yours
And, beeinge so, therefore consequently his.

Ashb. A match then! but, ere further you proceede,
Resolve mee one thinge, *Mildewe*,--not as thou art
Thyself, but as thou once weart made a Christian,--
Knowest thou this made's descent, and parentadge?

Mild. I will resolve you lyke a convertite,[158]
Not as the man I was: I knew there byrthes,
But for myne owne gayne kept them still conceal'd.

Ashb. Now as thou hop'st of grace--

Mild. The nurse late dead
That had these too in chardge, betrayde a shipboord
And ravisht from her coontry, ere she expyr'd
Nam'd her the doughter of *Jhon Ashburne*, marchant.
Her I *Palestra* cal'd, shee *Mirable*;
That, *Winefryde*, doughter to *Thomas Ashburne*
Brother to the sayde *Jhon*, I cal'd *Scribonia*.
They too are coosin germans.

Ashb. This our neece?

Thom. My doughter?

Pal. Partners in sorrowe, and so neere allyde,
And wee till nowe neare knewe it!

Scrib. My deere coosin.

Ashb. Nay, I'l bee my woords mayster; reache your hands,
And thoughe no nearer then an Unkle, once
I'l playe the father's part.

Thom. Praye hold your hand, Syr;
Heares one that will doo't for you.

Ash. Brother *Thomas*!

Thom. Peruse that letter, whilst I breathe these Joys,
Impartinge these a most unlimitted love
In equall distribution, doughter, neece,
Brother, and frends; lett mee devyde amongst you
A fathers, brothers, and a kinsman's yoake
With all th'unmeasured pleasures and delights
That thought of man can wishe you.

Ashb. Spare reply.
These tell mee, that those bloodhounds who pursude
My fall, my oppressinge creditors I meane,
Are gone before to answer for my wronges,
And in there deathes with due acknowledgment
Of all theire violens doon mee; peace with them!
That lykewyse by the deathe of a ritche alderman,
My unkle, I am left a fayer estate
In land, eight hundred by the yeare, in coyne
Twenty fyve thousand pound. Make mee, oh heaven,
For this greate blessinge gratefull! and not least
To you my Indeer'd brother.

Thom. One thinge woonders mee
That I should fynd you neare *Marcellis* heare,
When I was aym'd for *Florens*; where your letters
Inform'd mee you were planted.

Ashb. But even thither
Those crewell men dog'd mee with such pursuit
That theire I fownd no safety, but was forct
To fly thence with that little I had left
And to retyre mee to this obscure place;
Where by the trade of fishinge I have lyv'd

Till nowe of a contented competens.
Those bates, hookes, lynes and netts for thy good servyce,
Gripus, I nowe make thyne.

Grip. You are my noble mayster, and would I could have fownd more tricks then these in my budgett, they had bin all at your servyce.

Ashb. I purpose nowe for *England*, whether so please
These gentlemen consort us with theire brydes.

Boathe. Most willingly.

Ashb. There you shall see what welcome
Our *London*, so much spoake of heare in *France*,
Can give to woorthy strangers.

Thom. Att my chardge
Your shippinge is provyded, and at anchor
Lyes ready in the roade.

Ashb. Oh happy storme
That ends in such a calme!

   Enter Godfreye in haste.

Godf. Staye, gentlemen, and see a dolefull sight;
One ledd to execution for a murder
The lyke hath scarce bin heard of.

Ash. Of the Fryar?
In part we weare ey witness of the fact,
Nor is our hast so great but wee maye staye

To viewe his tragick end, whom the strickt lawe
Hathe made a Just example.

Enter the Abbott, Fryar Richard, Shreeve and officers.

Abb. Upon thy trewe confession I have given thee
Such absolution as the churche allowes.
What hast thou else to saye ere thou art made
To all men heare a wofull spectacle?

Fr. R. This only, that betwixt Fryar *Jhon* and mee
Was ever hate and mallyce; and althoughe
With no entent of murder, this my hand
This most unfortnate hand, beereft his lyff,
For which vile deede I mercy begge of Heaven,
Next of the woorld, whom I offended too,
Pardon and pitty. More to saye I have not:
Heaven of my sowle take chardge, and of my body
Dispose thou, honest hangeman.

Clown. Lasse, poore Fryar, and yet there's great hope of his sowle,
for I canot spye one heyre betwixt him and heaven.

Fisher. And yet I dowbt hee will make but a bald reckninge of it.

Enter the Lord De Averne and his man Dennis.

Av. Staye the execution.

Abb. Our noble fownder out of his greate charity
And woonted goodnes begg'd him a reprieve!

Av. Brought a reprieve I have: lett go the Fryar,

And take from mee your warrant; I dischardge him.

Sherif. And yet, my Lord, 'tis fitt for our dischardge
That the Kinge's hand bee seene.

Av. If not my woord
Will passe for currant, take my person then,
Or if you thinke unequall the exchaunge
I tender my man's too to valewe his.
Meanetyme dismisse him as one Innocent
Of what hee is condemde.

Abb. By his owne mouthe
Hee stands accus'd.

Av. And wetnes all of you,
As frely I acquitt him.

Sher. Honored Syr,
Praye bee more playne, wee understand you not.

Av. I'l make it playne then.

Cl. Now if thou bee'st wyse drawe thy neck out of the collar, doo,
Slipp-stringe, doo.

Rich. Marry, with all my hart and thanke him too.

Av. Attend mee, reverend father, and you all
Of this assembly: for som spleene conceiv'd
Against the Fryar deceast, I strangled him;
The cause why no man heare importun mee:
For many reasons to my self best knowne

I hold fitt to conceale it, but I murdered him
In myne owne howse.

Abb. But by your Honor's favour
How can that bee when **Richard** heere confest
Hee slewe him in our cloyster?

Av. Heare me outt.
At fyrst, untutcht with horror of the fact,
My purpose was to laye the guilt elswhear
And for that purpose caus'd my man to mount him
Over the cloyster wall.

Denis. Which soone I did
By th'helpe of a short ladder, sett him theire
In a close-place and thoughe not of the sweetest
Yet as I thought the safest; left him there.

Fr. R. Just in that place I found him, and imadgining
He satt of purpose theire to despight mee,
I hitt him with a stone, hee fell withall
And I thought I had slayne him.

Dennis. But howe the Devill
Gott hee into our porch? that woonders mee.

Fr. R. I fownd a ladder theire.

Den. The same I left.

Fr. R. Gott him upon my shoolders and by that
Conveighd him back and left him in that porch,
Wheare, as it seemes, you fownd him.

Av. This troblinge us, it drove us to newe plotts.
We arm'd the Fryar, accoutred as you sawe,
Mounted him on a stallion, lock't him fast
Into the saddle, turn'd him forthe the gates
To trye a second fortune.

Fr. R. Just at the tyme
When, I beeinge mounted on the baker's mare,
The gates weare sett wyde ope for mee to fly.

Abb. So that it seemes one beast pursuide the tother,
And not the dead Fryar ***Richard***.

Av. Howsoever,
As one repentant for my rashnes past,
And loathe to Imbrewe mee in more Innocent blood,
I fyrst confesse my servant's guilt and myne,
Acquitt the Fryar, and yeeld our persons upp
To the full satisfaction of the lawe.

Enter the Lady Averne and her maid Mellesent.

Lady. Which, noble Sir, the Kinge thus mittigates:
See, I have heare your pardon. In the tyme
That you weare ceas'd with this deepe melancholly
And inward sorrowe for a sinne so fowle,
My self in person posted to the Kinge
(In progresse not farr off), to him related
The passadge of your busines, neather rose I
From off my knees till hee had signd to this.

Av. Th'hast doon the offyce of a noble wyfe.

His grace I'l not despyse, nor thy great love
Ever forgett, and iff way may bee fownd
To make least satisfaction to the dead,
I'l doo't in vowed repentance.

Abb. Which our prayers
In all our best devotions shall assist.

Ashb. All ours, great Syr, to boote.

Av. Wee knowe you well and thanke you.

Ashb. But must nowe
Forsake this place, which wee shall ever blesse
For the greate good that wee have fownd therein,
And hence remoove for *England*.

Av. Not beefore
All your successfull Joyes wee heare related
To comfort our late sorrowes; to which purpose
Wee invite you and your frends to feast with us.
That granted, we will see you safe aboord:
And as wee heare rejoyce in your affayers,
Forget not us in *England* in your prayers.

[*Exeunt*.

FINIS.

INTRODUCTION TO THE COSTLIE WHORE.

The Costlie Whore, though not of the highest rarity, is a scarce play. It has never been reprinted, and thoroughly deserves on its own merits a place in the present collection. The conduct of the story is simple and straight-forward; the interest is well sustained; and the poetry has all the freshness and glow of youth.

The play bears some indications of having been written in 1613. In I. 2, where the Duke's brothers are devising schemes for enriching themselves at the state's expense, occurs the following passage:--

"*Al*. I have a commission drawne for making glasse.
Now if the Duke come, as I thinke he will,
Twill be an excellent meanes to lavish wood;
And then the cold will kill them, had they bread.

Hat. The yron Mills are excellent for that.
I have a pattent drawne to that effect;
If they goe up, downe goes the goodly trees;
Ile make them search the earth to find new fire."

The mention of the "yron Mills" appears to refer to the patent granted to Clement Daubigny for cutting iron into rods. On 13th March,[159] 1612-13, the Commissioners of Suits forwarded to the Lord Mayor a petition from Daubigny for the renewal of letters patent. They enclosed petitions from nailmakers and other smiths, shipmasters, shipowners, and shipwrights, from which it would appear that the iron imported from foreign parts was brittle and useless; and being themselves unable to judge accurately of the quality of iron, they directed the Lord Mayor to take the evidence of the Master and some of the Wardens of the Blacksmiths', Ironmongers', and Carpenters' Companies, of the Master and some of the Brethren of the Trinity House, and of any others that he might think fit to consult: after hearing the evidence, he was to draw up a statement of his own views and return Daubigny's petition. On 31st March the Lord Mayor addressed a letter to the Lords of the Council, in which he stated that from the evidence of the various witnesses he had been convinced that the patent would raise the price of iron, hinder the king in his customs, and further the decay of woods; and he added that the Flemish iron was for the most part good and tough. It will be observed that one of the objections raised by the Lord Mayor to the granting of the patent--namely that a great consumption of wood (as fuel for smelting the ore) would follow--is specially put forward by the dramatist. The mention in Alfred's speech of a scheme for glassmaking seems also to suggest 1613 as the date of authorship; for on 17th November of that year Sir Jerome Bowes and Sir Edward Zouch procured patents for making glass.[160]

There are other allusions that point to 1613. In II. 4, we find--"Make us for want coyn brasse and passe it current." The first patent for the coining of brass farthing-tokens was granted on 10th April, 1613, to John Stanhope, Lord Harrington; and the grant caused general dissatisfaction.[161] Again: in the same scene there is a reference to the exportation of broad cloth:--"I, an't please your honour, have a commoditie of good broad cloth, not past two hundred; may I shippe them over? and theres a hundred poundes." When we turn to the State Papers we discover that numerous complaints were made in 1613 about the exportation of undressed broadcloth. On 3rd March, 1612-13, the King forwarded to the Lords of the Council a petition from the clothworkers and dyers that the statutes against the exportation of undressed and undyed goods should be strictly enforced. I am inclined to think that these passages, taken collectively, afford strong proof that The Costlie Whore was written in 1613--twenty years before the date of publication.

In I. 2, we have the story of Bishop Hatto and the Rats told briefly but effectively. Mr. Baring-Gould in his **Curious Myths of the Middle Ages** has investigated the sources of the legend with much fulness. He refers us specially to Wolfius's **Lect. Memorab**., Lavingae, 1600, tom. i. p. 343. From the Stationers' Registers it appears that a ballad of The Wrathfull Judgement of God upon Bishop Hatto was licensed to H. Carre on 15th August, 1586. The dramatist has invested the story with the glamour of that poetical strangeness which is the very salt of such narrations:--

"***Alf.*** He did proclaime reliefe unto the poore;
Assembled them unto a private Barne,
And, having lockt the doore, set it on fire,
Saying hee'de rid the countrie of such Mice:
And Mice and Rats have rid him from the World.

* * * * *

Duke. Could not this palace, seated in the **Rheine**
In midst of the great River, (to the which
No bridge, nor convay, other then by boats
Was to be had) free him from vermine Rats?

Alf. Against their kind the land Rats took the water
And swomme in little armies to the house,
And, though we drownd and killed innumerable,
Their numbers were like **Hydra's** heads increasing;
Ruine bred more untill our brother died.

Duke. The house is execrable; Ile not enter.

Hat. You need not feare, my Lord; the house is free
From all resort of Rats; for at his death,
As if a trumpet sounded a retreat,
They made a kind of murmure and departed."

THE COSTLIE WHORE.

A COMICALL HISTORIE,

Acted by the companie of *the Revels*.

LONDON Printed by *Augustine Mathewes*, for WILLIAM SHEARES, and HVGH
PERRIE, and are to be sold at their shoppe, in *Brittaines Burse*. 1633.

The Actors Names.

Duke of Saxonie.
Fredericke his sonne.
Hatto, | Brothers to the Duke.
Al[f]rid, |
Montano, kinsman to the Duke.
Euphrata, daughter to the Duke.
Constantine, a lover of *Euphrata*.

Otho, a friend to *Constantine*.
Alberto, | Two Lords.
Reynaldo, |
Vandermas, a Pander.
Valentia, the Costly *Whore*.
Julia, a Gentlewoman to *Euphrata*.
Two Maides.
Petitioners.
Beggers.
Servants.

THE COSTLY **WHORE**.

[*Act the First.*]

[SCENE 1.]

    Enter Constantine and Otho.

Constantine. How do'st thou like the lovely *Euphrata*?

Otho. I did not marke her.

Const. Then thou didst not marke
The fairest *Saxon* Lady in mine eye
That ever breath'd a maid.

Otho. Your minde now knowne,

Ile say shee is the fairest in the world,
Were she the foulest.

Con. Then thou canst dissemble.

Otho. You know I cannot; but, deare **Constantine**,
I prethee tell me first, what is that Ladie,
That wonder of her sexe, cal'd ***Euphrata***?
Whose daughter is she?

Const. I cannot blame thee, ***Otho***,
Though thou be ignorant of her high worth,
Since here in ***Saxon*** we are strangers both;
But if thou cal'st to minde why we left ***Meath***,
Reade the trice[162] reason in that Ladies eye,
Daughter unto the Duke of ***Saxonie***,
Shee unto whom so many worthy Lords
Vail'd Bonnet when she past the Triangle,
Making the pavement Ivory where she trode.

Otho. She that so lightly toucht the marble path
That leadeth from the Temple to the presence?

Const. The same.

Otho. Why, that was white before,
White Marble, ***Constantine***, whiter by odds
Then that which lovers terme the Ivory hand,
Nay then the Lillie whitenesse of her face.

Con. Come, thou art a cavilling companion:
Because thou seest my heart is drown'd in love,

Thou wilt drowne me too. I say the Ladie's faire;
I say I love her, and in that more faire;
I say she loves me, and in that most faire;
Love doth attribute in Hyperbolies
Unto his Mistris the creation
Of every excellence, because in her
His eies do dreame of perfect excellence.--
And here she comes; observe her, gentle friend.

[*Enter Euphrata*.

Euph. Welcome, sweet *Constantine*.

Con. My *Euphrata*.

Euph. Thy *Euphrata*, be thou my *Constantine*.
But what is he? a stranger, or thy friend?

Con. My second selfe, my second *Euphrata*.
If thou beest mine, salute her, gentle *Otho*.

Otho. An humble and a true devoted heart
I tender to you in a mindes chast kisse.

Euph. Welcome to me, since welcome to my friend.

Otho.--A beautiful, an admirable Ladie!
I thinke 'tis fatall unto every friend
Never to love, untill his friend first love,
And then his choice; but sooner will I teare
Out of this brest mine affection with my heart.

Euph. Hearing, sweet *Constantine*, thou wert so nere me,
I came as I were winged to gaze on thee.

Con. And would to heaven there were no bar in time
To hinder me from thy desired sight,
But thousand sutors eyes, do watch my steps;
And harke, I heare some trampling. How now, *Julia*?

   Enter Julia.

Juli. Madam, the Lord Montano, spying you
To leave the presence and to enter here,
Hath ever since waited your comming foorth.
And will not be denied untill he see you.

Euph. Of all my sutors, most importunate.

Con. What is he, love?

Euph. Of very noble birth,
But my affection is not tyed to birth.
I must dispense with this kind conference
For some small time, untill I rid him hence.
Therefore within my closet hide thy selfe;
Your friend shall *Julia* guide into the garden,
Where through a private doore, but seldome us'd,
He may at pleasure leave us and returne.
Deny me not I prethee, *Constantine*;
Thou hast my heart, and would thy birth were such
I need not feare t'avouch thee for my Love.

Otho. Madam, I take my leave.   [*Exit Otho*.

Con. Farewell, deare friend,
Returne as soone as may be; farewell Love.   [*Exit*.

Euph. Now guide *Montano* hither.

   Enter Montano.

Mon. Gracious Madam,
I have seene the noble Palsgrave, the Prince
Of *Milleine*, and the Palatine of the *Rheine*,
With divers other honorable sutors,
Mounted to ride unto their severall places.

Euph. Of me they took their farewell yesternight.

Mon. What meanes your grace to be so unkind to all?
You drive away good fortune by disdaine.

Euph. Why are you grieving too?

Mon. I am your subject,
The meanest that did humbly seeke your love,
Yet not the meanest in affection;
And I am come to take my farewell too.

Euph. Why, then farewell.

Mon. So short with them that love you?

Euph. Your journey may be great, for ought I know;
And 'tis an argument of little love

To be the hinderer of a traveller.

Mon. My journey, Madame, is unto my house,
Scarce halfe a league hence, there to pine and die,
Because I love such beauteous crueltie.

Euph. God speede you, sir.

Mon. Nay then I will not leave you.
Madam, 'tis thought, and that upon good ground,
You have shrin'd your affection in the heart
Of some (whatere he be) noble or base,
And thats the cause you lightlie censure[163] all.

Euph. Who thinkes it?

Mon. I doe, Madame, and your father.

Euph. It is upon my vowed chastitie.

Mon. What devill made you sweare to chastitie,
Or have you tane that oath onely for a terme?

Euph. A terme, what terme?

Mon. A terme of some seven yeeres,
Or peradventure halfe the number more.

Euph. For terme of life.

Mon. You have sworne, to be forsworne:
He was no well disposed friend of yours

That gave you consaile [*sic*] to forsweare such beautie.
Why, 'tis as if some traveiler had found
A mine of gold, and made no use of it.
For terme of life! Why, then die presently;
So shall your debt to nature be farre lesse,
Your tyranny over man's yeelding heart
Be lesse condemned. Oh, you were made for man,
And living without man to murder men.
If any creature be so fortunate
That lives in grace of your all gracious selfe,
Though I am well perswaded 'tis not I,
I vow by all the rites of vertuous love,
Be he ignoble, of the basest sort,
To please you, Madame, Ile renounce my suite
And be a speciall meane unto your father
To grant your hearts affection, though I die.

Euph. Now, Lord **Montano**, you come neere my heart,
And were I sure that you would keepe your word,
As I am sure you love me by your deedes,
I might perchance deliver you my thoughts.

Mon. By heaven and by your beauteous selfe I will.

Euph. Then, **Constantine**, come forth; behold thy friend.

   Enter Constantine.

Con. Madame, what meane you, to reveale our love?

Mon. This is a very stubborne Gentleman.
A Gentleman? a pesant! **Saxonie**,
Affords not one more base.

Con. He does me wrong,
That termes me meaner then a gentleman.

Mon. I tearme thee so.

Euph. Why, how now, Lord *Montano*?
You do forget your oath.

Mont. And you your selfe,
Your Princely father, and the Dukedomes honour,
To chaine your liking to a groome so base.

Con. He lies that calles me groome.

   Enter Julia.

Ju. O God, forbeare:
His Excellence your father's comming hither.

Mon. He comes in happie time, to know the cause
Why such great Princes have bin made your scorne.

Euph. What, will you tell him?

Mon. Will I? let me die
Contemn'd of heaven, in publique obloquie,
If I reveale not this lascivious course.

Ju. We are undone.

Con. Hence with this prating Maide.

If thou hast any anger in thy brest
Towards this Lady, turne it all on me.
She is a woman, timerous by her kinde;
I, man-like borne, and beare a man-like minde.

Mon. Ile trie your courage.   [*Draw*.[164]

Euph. As thou fear'st my frowne,
As thou hast hope to thrive in thy new choice,
As thou respect'st the favour of the gods,
Welfare in any action thou intends,
Doe not reveale unto my fretfull father
This humble choice that my high birth hath made.

Mon. Why, then forsweare him.

Euph. Sooner set thy feet
Upon my breast, and tread me to the ground.

Ju. As thou art any thing more then a beast,
Doe not procure my Ladie such disgrace.

Mon. Peace, bawde, Ile have no conference with you.

Euph. He cannot hurt me, 'tis my Love I feare.
Although my father be as sterne as warre,
Inexorable like consuming fire,
As jealous of his honour as his crowne,
To me his anger is like *Zephires* breath
Cast on a banke of sommer violets,
But to my Love like whirlewinde to a boate
Taken in midst of a tumultuous sea.

Enter Duke of Saxonie and Fredericke.

Alas, he comes! Montano, prethee, peace.
Courage, sweete Love.

Con. I see our love must cease.

Euph. Not if my wit can helpe; it shall goe hard
But Ile prevent the traitor.

Mon. Heare me, my Lord.

Euph. Heare me, my gracious father.

Mon. Heare me, my liege: ther's treason in your Court,
I have found a peasant in the Princesse closet;
And this is he that steales away her honour.

Euph. This villaine, gracious father, 'tis that seekes
To rob me of mine honor, you your daughter.

Mon. Now, as you are a right heroike Prince,
Be deafe unto your daughters faire[165] words.

Euph. Be deafe to him, as you regard your selfe.

Duke. What strange confusion's this that cloyes our hearing?

Fred. Speake, beauteous sister, who hath done thee wrong?

Mon. Her self.

Euph. This traitor.

Fre. Lord *Montano*?

Euph. Hee.

Fred. Villaine, thou dyest.

Mon. Stay, she meanes *Constantine*,
He that I found infolded in her closet,
Reaping the honour which a thousand Lords
Have fail'd in seeking in a lawful course.

Con. He does me wrong, my gracious soveraigne.

Ju. He wrongs my Ladie, an't please your grace.

Mon. Ile tell the trueth.

Euph. Or rather let me tell it.

Mon. Lacivious love is ever full of sleights.

Euph. Villaines, that seeke by treason their desires,
Want no suggestion to beguile a trueth.

Mon. I say, I found this peasant in her closet
Kissing, imbracing, and dishonouring her.

Euph. I say, an't please your gracious Excellence,
I found this Gentleman within my closet,
There set by subornation of this Lord,

And here appointed to dishonor me.
Speake, is't not true?

Con. True, if it please your grace.

Duke. What say you, strumpet?

Ju. Since my Ladie saies so,
I say and't please your Excellence--

Duke. Speake, woman.

Ju. 'Tis very true.

Mon. O monstrous forgerie!

Fre. O more then falshood to become so smooth
In such a dangerous action!

Duke. This is strange;
Montano seeke the ruine of my daughter!

Euph. Because I would not yeeld unto his suite,
Which he in rapefull manner oft hath sought,
Hee set this Gentleman to doe me shame
Intending by exclaimes[166] to raise the Court,
But that repentance in my waiting Maide
And of his sorrowfull selfe reveal'd the plot.

Mon. O ye gods, how am I over-reacht!

Duke. I know the yong man to be well discended,

Of civill carriage and approved faith,
How ere seduced to this enterprise.

Con. My conscience, would not propagate that plot.

Ju. Nor mine, my Lord, though gold corrupted me.

Mon.--Cleane from the byas! wit, by heaven rare wit!
Ile tell another tale, if they have done.

Duke. What canst thou speake, vild[167] traitor?
Thou seest thou art prevented in thy plot
And therefore desperately coin'st any thing,
But I am deafe to all such stratagems.

Mon. Will you not heare me?

Duke. Forgeries and lies.
My daughters honour is of that high prize
That I preferre it 'fore a traitors braine.
Let it suffice, we know she hath deni'd thee
And some denied (like devills) turne their love
Into excrutiation of themselves
And of the parties whom they have belov'd.
Revenge begins where flatteries doe end;
Being not her husband, thou wilt be no friend.
Thus is thy policy by heaven prevented:
Therefore henceforth we banish thee our Court;
Our Court? our territorie, every place
Wherein we beare the state of Royaltie.
Urge no replie, the fact is plainely prov'd,
And thou art hatefull where thou wert belov'd.

Mon. My gracious Lord--

Duke. We can afford no grace:
Stay here, and reade thy ruine in my face.

Mon. I goe contented with this heavy doome;
'Twas mine owne seeking. Faire and wise, adiew;
Deceit hath kil'd conceit, you know tis true.
              [*Exit*.[168]

Fre. An upright sentence of an act so vilde.

Duk. Remove this waiting virgin from your chamber,
But let this gentleman attend on me.
The best may be deceiv'd by trecherie.

Euph. Then so, my gracious father, may this maid.

Duke. Then let her keep her place; beware of gold,
Honour's too precious to be baselie sold.--
Now to our dying friend, his grace of **Meath**.
Daughter, prepare you; you shall ride along,
For to that end we came; come, sonne, to horse:
Ere we come there, our friend may prove a coarse.

Euph.--Twas well done both, this action rarely fell;
Where women trie their wits, bad plots prove well.

            [*Exeunt omnes*.

[SCENE 2.]

Enter three Beggers.

1. Come away, fellow louse, thou art ever eating.

2. Have I not neede, that must feede so many *Cannibals* as will waite on me whether I will or no?

3. Heres one in my necke, I would 'twere on thy shoulder.

1. Keepe it your selfe, I have retainers enow of mine owne.

2. But whether are you going now?

1. Why, are you our King, and doe not know that?

2. Your King? I am a very roguish King and I hav a companie of lowsie subjects.

Enter Hatto and Alfrid conferring.

2. But looke about my ragged subjects, here comes somebody.

1. O the devills; shall we aske them an almes?

2. Why not? now the rats have eaten up their brother Bishop they will be more charitable; your vocation, you slaves.

3. For the Lord sake, be pittifull to a companie of poore men.

Hatto. What cry is this? beggars so neere the doore

Of our deceased brother? whip them hence
Or bring the Mastiffe foorth [to] worry them.
They are lazie drones, 'tis pittie such should live.

1. I told you, my Lord, how we should find them; whip us! leade the way, soveraigne, weele none of your whipping.

Hat. Hence with these dogs! what make they neere this house?

2. He will be eaten with rats too, he looks like a piece of cheese alreadie.

Hat. You Rogues.

Alf. Good brother, stay your self from wrath;
Thinke on the Bishop and his odious death.

Hat. What odious death, I pray?

Alf. Eaten with Rats,
Whilest he was living, for the wrong he did
Unto the poore, the branches of our God.

Hat. Tis true, and therefore, call the poore againe.
Come hither, friends, I did forget my selfe.
Pray for me, ther's some silver for thy wants.

2. Now the Lord blesse you and keep your good face[169] from being Mouse-eaten; wee came thinking wee should have some dole at the Bishops funerall, but now this shall serve our turne, wee will pray for you night and day.

Hat. Goe to the backe-gate, and you shall have dole.

Om. O the Lord save thee.
> [***Exeunt Beggers.***

Hat. These Beggers pray and curse both in a breath.
Oh wherefore should we fawne upon such curres,
The mice of mankind, and the scorne of earth?

Alf. So said our brother.

Hat. And he was a Bishop,
Had read the Scripture and knew what he said.

Alf. But he hath bought[170] that saying with his death,
With such a loathsome and notorious death
As while the World's a World 'twill speake of ***Meath***.

Hat. The Lord Archbishop of ***Meath***, and die by Rats!

Alf. He did proclaime reliefe unto the poore;
Assembled them unto a private Barne
And, having lockt the doore, set it on fire,
Saying hee'de rid the countrie of such Mice;
And Mice and Rats have rid him from the World.

Hat. Well, Ile not hurt the poore so publikely,
But privately I'le grinde their very hearts.
Torture them living, and yet have their prayers,
And by such meanes that few or none shall know it.

Al. In such a course ***Alfred*** would wind with you;
For though I counsail'd you to be more calme,

Twas not in pittie of their povertie
But to avoide their clamour. To give nothing
Will make them curse you: but to threaten them,
Flie in your face, and spit upon your beard.
No devill so fierce as a bread-wanting heart,
Especially being baited with ill tearmes.
But what course can you take to plague these dogges?

Hat. Why, buy up all the corne and make a dearth,
So thousands of them will die under stalles.

Alf. And send it unto forraine nations
To bring in toies to make the wealthy poore.

Hat. Or make our land beare woad[171] instead of wheate.

Al. Inclose the commons and make white meates deare.

Hat. Turne pasture into Park grounds and starve cattle,
Or twentie other honest thriving courses.
The meanest of these will beggar halfe a Kingdome.

Al. I have a commission drawne for making glasse.
Now if the Duke come, as I thinke he will,
Twill be an excellent meanes to lavish wood;
And then the cold will kill them, had they bread.

Hat. The yron Mills are excellent for that.
I have a pattent[172] drawne to that effect;
If they goe up, downe goes the goodly trees;
Ile make them search the earth to find new fire.

Alf. We two are brothers, and the Duke's our brother.

Shall we be brothers in Commission?
And Ile perswade him to authorize thee
His substitute in *Meath*, when he enjoyes it.

Hat. Death, Ile get thee Regent under him
In *Saxonie*, to oppresse as well as I.
And we will share the profits, live like Kings,
And yet seeme liberall in common things.

Al. Content: what, though the Rats devour'd our brother?
Was not a Prophet murdered by a Lyon?
King *Herod* died of Lice, wormes doe eate us all;
The Rats are wormes, then let the Rats eate me.
Is the dead course prepar'd?

Hat. Embalm'd and coffin'd;
The Citie keyes delivered to my hands;
We stay but onely for his Excellence.

Enter Constantine.

Con. The Duke is comming, if it please your honors.

Al. And he is welcome; let the trumpets sound.

[*Second florish*.

Enter Duke of Saxon, Euphrata, and Julia.

Hat. Welcome, thrice welcome, our renowned brother.
Loe, at thy feete the Cittizens of *Meath*,
By us their Agents, do lay downe the keyes,

And[173] by this crownet and sword resign'd
The state Maiestique to your Princely hands,
Discended to you by our brothers death.

Duke. Then with your loves and persons we receive it.--
Is then our brother the Archbishop dead?

Hat. Too true, my Lord.

Euph. I am sorry for my Uncle.

Hat. And of a death so publique by reporte.

Al. Devour'd by Rats, in strange and wonderous sort.

Duke. Could not this palace seated in the *Rheine*,
In midst of the great River, (to the which
No bridge, nor convay, other then by boats
Was to be had,) free him from vermine Rats?

Alf. Against their kind the land Rats took the water
And swomme in little armies to the house;
And, though we drown'd and kild innumerable,
Their numbers were like *Hydra's* heads increasing;
Ruine bred more untill our brother died.

Duke. The house is execrable; Ile not enter.

Hat. You need not feare, my Lord; the house is free
From all resort of Rats; for at his death,
As if a trumpet sounded a retreat,
They made a kind of murmure and departed.

Duke. Sure 'twas the hand of heaven, for his contempt
Of his poore creatures.--But what writs are those?

Hat. Commissions (if it please your grace,) for glasse,
For yron Mines, and other needful things.

Duke. Our selfe invested in the government,
The Cities care shall lie upon your care.

Hat. *Alfred* our brother may awaite your grace
In *Saxony*, so please you to command.

Duke. We are now but three, and lately have bin seven,
We have cause to love each other; for my part,
Betweene you both we give a brothers heart.
Here or at *Saxonie*, command at pleasure;
I weare the corronet, be yours the treasure.

Al. We thanke our brother.

Duke. Where's my sonne *Fredericke*?

  Enter Fredericke with a glove.

Fre. Father, the state of *Meath* desire your grace
To take the paines to passe unto the Senate.

Duke. What glove is that, son *Fred*., in your hand?

Fre. I found it, if it please your Excellence,
Neere to the state-house: the imbroiderie

Is very excellent, and the fashion rare.

Duke. I have not seene a prettier forme of hand.
Daughter, let's see; is't not too bigge for you?

Euph. Sure 'tis some admirable worke of nature,
If it fit any hand that owes[174] this glove,
If all the rest doe parallel the hand.

Duke. Will it not on?

Euph. Not for a diadem;
Ile trie no longer lest I shame my selfe.

Duke. Try, *Julia*.

Ju. My hand's bigger then my Ladies.

Duke. I cannot tell, but in my minde I feele
A wondrous passion of I know not what.

Fre. The imbroidered glove may be some childs, no womans.

Duke. I should mistrust as much, but that this place
Beares greater compasse then a childish hand.
I must command it.

Fre. Willingly, my Lord.

Duke. Then to the state-house, brothers, leade the way:
First our instalement [*sic*], then a funerall day.

[*Exeunt Duke and brothers and Fred.*

Enter Otho.

Otho. Yonder she goes, the mirrour of her sexe.--
Stay, beauteous *Euphrata*.

Euph. Otho! what, *Julia*?

Ju. Here, madam! what's your will?

Euph. Call *Constantine*;
Tell him his deare friend *Otho* is return'd.

Ju. I will.

Otho. Stay, *Julia*.

Euph. Doe as I bid you, goe.   [*Exit Julia.*

Otho. I had rather have a word or twaine with you.

Euph. I have heard him oft enquire for thee his friend,
I have heard him sigh, I have seene him weepe for thee,
Imagining some mischiefe or distresse
Had falne thee since the closets separation.

Otho.--And what a slave am I to wrong this friend!

Enter Constantine and Julia.

Con. Where is he?

Ju. Here.

Con. The welcom'st man alive.
Unkind, how couldst thou stay from me so long?

Otho. I have bin ill at ease, pray pardon me;
But I rejoyce to see my friend so well.

Euph. Some Ladies love hath made him melancholy.

Otho. Shee hath read the letter that I lately sent her
In a pomegranat, by those words I hope.

Con. Why speake you not? is't love or melancholy?

Otho. If upon love my grief is melancholy?

Con. Ile have the best Phisitians here in *Meath*
Assay by art to cure that maladie.

Euph. Gainst mellancholy minds your onely Phisick
Our Saxon doctors hold that principle.
Now I remember you did lately send me
A choice pomegranate; fetch it, *Julia*.
Some of those graines well stir'd in *Gascoine* wine
Is present remedie.

Otho. Madam, Ile none:
Of all fruits, that I hate.

Euph. And commended it

So highly by the messenger that brought it!

Con. Twas well remembred, you shall take a graine.

Otho. You will but vexe me.

Con. So his melancholly
Doth make him froward with his dearest friend.

   Enter Julia with the pomegranate.

Tis well done, ***Julia***, quickely cut it up;
And bring a cup of wine, or let me doo't.

Otho. I see I shall be plagu'd with mine owne wit;
Being asham'd to speake, I writ my minde.--
Were you my friends, you would not martyr me
With needlesse phisicke; fie upon this trash,
The very sight is loathsome.

Con. Take it up:
But let me see, what letter's that that dropt?
Came it from you, or from the ***Spanish*** fruit?

Ju. Tis all the graines that the pomegranate had.

Con. Then theres some trechery within these graines:
Ile breake it up.
And tis directed to my ***Euphrata***.

Euph. What may the tenure be? I pray thee read it.

[*He opens the letter & reads*.

Otho. O fall upon me some wind-shaken turret
To hide me from the anger of my friend,
O from his frowne! because he is my friend.
Were he an enemie, I would be bold;
But kindnes makes this wound. O, this horror!
The words of friends, are stronger then their power.

Con. Withdraw, good *Julia*.
          [*Exit Julia*.

Euph. Pray, what is it, love?

Con. Tis love indeed to thee, but to my heart
Every loose sentence is a killing dart.
I brought this *Gyges*[175] to my hearts delight
And he hath drown'd his senses with the sight.
Except thy selfe, all things to him were free:
Otho, thou hast done me more then injurie;
Well maist thou fixe thy eye upon the earth,
This action sith[176] breedes a prodigious birth:
It is so monstrous, and against all kinde,
That the lights splendor would confound thy minde.

Otho. I have offended, prethee pardon me.

Con. What cause did move thee?

Otho. Her all conquering sight.

Con. Couldst thou usurpe upon my well known right?

Otho. Thinke, I am flesh and blood, and she is faire.

Con. Thinke how I love thee.

Otho. There proceeds my care.

Con. Our amitie hath bin of ancient dayes,
During which time wrong'd I thee any wayes?

Otho. Never.

Con. But rather I have done thee good.

Otho. I grant you have, O rather shed my blood
Then number the kind deedes betweene us past.

[*Con*.] For this unkindnesse, here I love my last.

Euph. He doth repent, and will renounce his suite.

Otho. I doe renounce it.

Con. O thou canst not do't.

Otho. Suffer me stay a while in her faire sight,
'Twill heal my wound and all love banish quite.

Con. The sight of the belov'd makes the desire,
That burnt but slowly, flame like sparkling fire.
As thou dost love me, take thee to some place
Where thou maist nere see her, nor I thy face.

Otho. By what is deere betwixt us, by our selves,
I vow hencefoorth ten thousand deaths to prove
Then be a hinderance to such vertuous love.

Con. Breake heart, tis for thy sake.

Otho. When I am dead
O then forget that I haue injured.

Con. O hell of love!

Otho. Or rather hell of friends!

Con. Firmely till they love.

Otho. Then thus all friendship ends.

        [*Exeunt*.

Actus Secundus.

[SCENE 1.]

   Enter Duke, Fredericke, Hatto, and Alfred.

Hat. Good brother, heare some Musicke, twill delight you.

Al. Ile call the Actors, will you see a play?

Fre. Or, gracious father, see me runne the race
On a light footed horse, swifter then winde.

Duke. I pray forbeare.

Al. This moode will make you mad,
For melancholy ushers franticke thoughts.

Hat. It makes hot wreaking blood turne cold and drie,
And drithe and coldnesse are the signes of death.

Duke. You doe torment me.

Fred. Is it anything
That I have done, offends your grace?

Hat. Or comes this hidden anger from my fault?

Alf. Heres none but gladly would resigne his life
To doe you pleasure, so please you to command.

Duke. Ifaith you are too [*sic*] blame to vexe me thus.

Hat. Then grounds this sorrow on your brothers death?

Fred. Or rather on the glove I lately found.

Duke. A plague upon the glove, whats that to me?
Your prating makes me almost lunatike.
As you respect my welfare, leave me leave me.

The sooner you depart, the sooner *I*
Shall finde some meanes to cure my maladie.

Fred. Our best course is to be obedient.

[*Exeunt all but the Duke*.

Duke. Farewell.
Was ever slave besotted like to me!
That Kings have lov'd those that they never saw
Is nothing strange, since they have heard their praise;
Birds that by painted grapes have bin deceiv'd
Had yet some shadow to excuse their error;
Pigmalion that did love an Ivory Nimph
Had an *Idea* to delight his sence;
The youth that doted on *Minerva's*[177] picture
Had some contentment for his eye;   [*soft Musique*.
But love, or rather an infernall hagge,
Envying *Saxons* greatnes and his joyes,
Hath given me nothing but a trifling glove,
As if by the proportion of the case
Art had the power to know the jewels nature.
Or Nimph, or goddesse, woman, or faire devill,
If anything thou art, within my braine
Draw thine owne picture, let me see thy face:
To doate thus grossely, is a grosse disgrace.   [*Musique within*.
I heare some Musique: O ye Deities,
Send you this heavenly consort[178] from the spheares
To recreate a love-perplexed heart?
The more it sounds, the more it refresheth.
I see no instruments, nor hands that play;
And my deare brothers, durst not be so bold.
'Tis some celestiall rapture of the minde,

No earthlie harmonic is of this kinde.
Now it doth cease: speake, who comes there?

 Enter Fredericke, Alfred, and Hatto.

Fred. Father.

Duke. From whence proceeds the Musicke that I heard?

Fred. The beauteous and the famous Curtezan,
Allyed unto the banished *Montano*,
Admir'd *Valentia*, with a troope of youths
This day doth keepe her yeerely festivall
To all her suters, and this way she past
Unto her Arbor, when the Musique plaide.

Duke. Admir'd *Valentia*! Curtezans are strange
With us in *Germanie*; except her selfe,
Being a *Venetian* borne and priviledg'd,
The state allowes none here.

Fred. Twere good for *Meath*
She were unpriviledgd and sent to *Venice*.

Al. Of all the faces that mine eye beheld
Hers is the brightest.

Duke. Is she then so faire?

Hat. O beyond all comparison of beautie.

Fred. Upon her hand,

Father, I saw the fellow to your glove.

Duke. Then let it be restor'd.
What, should a Prince retaine a strumpets glove?--
O ye eternall powers, am I insnar'd
With the affection of a common trull!--
Wheres your commissions, that you would have sign'd?
'Tis time I had a president in *Saxonie*.
Receive our signet, and impresse them straight;
Ile remaine here, in *Meath*, some little time.
Brother, have care my Dukedome be well rul'd;
Here I put over my affaires to you.
My sonne I leave unto the joyes of youth;
Tis pittie that his minde should be opprest
So soone with care of governments.
Goe to your pleasures, seeke your sister foorth,
Send *Constantine* to us; so leave me all,
I am best accompanied with none at all.   [*Exeunt*.
            Manet Duke.
Either the Plannets, that did meete together
In the grand consultation of my birth,
Were opposite to every good infusion,
Or onely *Venus* stood as retrograde;
For, but in love of this none-loving trull,
I have beene fortunate even since my birth.
I feele within my breast a searching fire
Which doth ascend the engine of my braine,
And when I seeke by reason to suppresse
The heate it gives, the greaters the excesse.
I loath to looke upon a common lip
Were it as corral as *Aurora's* cheeke
Died with the faire virmillion [of the] sunne.
O but I love her, and they say she is faire.--

Now *Constantine*.

    Enter Constantine.

Con. Your grace did send for me.

Duke. Lend me your habit in exchange of mine,
For I must walk the Citie for a purpose.

Con. With all my heart, my habit and my selfe.

Duke. In any case, watch at the privie chamber.
If any ask for me say I am not well,
And though it be my sonne, let him not enter.

Con. I will.

Duke. Be carefull, gentle *Constantine*.
Now, faire *Valentia, Saxon* to thy bower
Comes like a *Jove* to raine a golden shower.
        [*Exit*.

Con. Prosper, kind Lord, what ere the action be;
Counsailes of Princes should be ever free.

        [*Exit*.

[SCENE 2.]

Enter Valentia and Montano.

Va. Torches and Musique there! the room's too darke.

Mon. Prethee, Neece,
Abandon this lascivious unchaste life;
It is the onely blemish of our house;
Scandall unto our name; a Curtezan!
O what's more odious in the eares of men?

Val. Then why doe men resort to Curtezans,
And the best sort? I scorne inferiour groomes,
Nor will I deign[179] to draw aside my maske
To any meaner then a Noble man.
Come,[180] can you dance? a caper and a kisse:
For every turne Ile fold thee in my armes,
And if thou fal'st, although[181] a-kin we be
That thou maist fall[182] soft, Ile fall under thee.
Oh for the lightnesse of all light heel'd girles,
And I would touch the Ceeling with my lips!
Why art thou sad, *Montano*?

Mon. On just cause,
You know I am banish't from my natiue countrey.

Val. This citie is *Meath*, thou art of *Saxonie*.

Mon. But this belongs unto the *Saxons* Duke,
By the decease of the departed Bishop.

Val. Feare not, thou art as safe within my house
As if perculliz'd in a wall of brasse.
Wheres *Vandermas*?

Enter Vandermas.

Van. Madam, did you call?

Mon. What noble man is that, a sutor to you?

Val. An excellent Pander, a rare doore-keeper.[183]

Mon. I had thought he had bin a gentleman at least.

Val. Because of his attire?

Mon. True.

Val. O the attire
In these corrupted daies is no true signe
To shew the gentleman; peasants now weare robes,
In the habilments of noblemen.
The world's grown naught, such judgement then is base,
For Hares and Asses weare the lion's case.[184]

Mon. 'Tis very costly and exceeding rich.

Val. Ritches to me are like trash to the poore,
I have them in abundance; gold's my slave,
I keep him prisoner in a three-fold chest
And yet his kindred daily visit me.

Mon. Lord, how diligent
Is this rich clothed fellow.

Val. Were he proud
And should but dare to stand still when I call,
I'de run him th[o]rough with a killing frowne.

Mon. Why then belike his service is for love.

Val. Why so are all the servants that attend mee.
They keepe themselves in satin, velvets, gold,
At their owne charges, and are diligent
Daies, moneths, and yeeres, to gaine an amorous smile.
Looke on my face with an indifferent eye,
And thou shalt finde more musicke in my lookes
Then in **Amphions** Lute or **Orpheus** Harpe;
Mine eye consists of numbers like the soule,
And if there be a soule tis in mine ey;
For, of the harmony these bright starres make,
I comprehend the formes of all the world;
The story of the Syrens in my voyce
I onely verified, for Millions stand
Inchanted when I speake, and catch my words
As they were orient pearle to adorn their eares;
Circe is but a fable, I transforme
The vertuous, valiant, and the most precise,
Into what forme of minde my fancie please.
Thou might'st bee proud, great Lord, of my abundance,
For in this beautie I shall more renowne
Our noble progenie then all the pennes
Of the best Poets that ere writ of men.
Unto your health a health! let Musique sound, [**Musick**.
That what I taste in Musique may be drown'd.
So fill more wine, we use to drinke up all;
Wine makes good blood and cheeres the heart withal.

Van. Madam, at such time as I heard you call,
A gentleman, it seemes of good discent,
Humblie did crave accesse unto your honor.

Valen. What did he give?

Van. A brace of bags of gold.

Valen. He shall have libertie to enter straight.
But first inrich the chamber with perfumes;
Burne choice **Arabian** Drugs more deare then
Waters distil'd out of the spirit of Flowers;
And spread our costly Arras to the eye.
Myself sufficiently doe shine in jems;
Where such faire coated Heraulds doe proceed,
It seemes he is honorable and of noble fame.

Mon. Shall I behold this sutor?

Valen. At the full,
At pleasure passe through every spacious Roome.
Be he a Prince, Ile know his high discent
Or proudly scorne to give him his content.
What drum is that?

Van. A Maske, sent by a friend.

Valen. Belike our self must know the mysterie;
Tell them we are prepar'd to see the Maske,
And bid the other noblemen come neere.
Thus am I hourely visited by friends;
Beautie's a counsellor that wants no fee.
They talke of circles and of powerfull spells,

Heeres heavenly art that all blacke art excells.

Mon. Ile walke into the farther gallery.

 Enter Duke.

Valen. Sir, you are welcome what so ere you be;
I guesse your birth great by your bounteous fee.

Duke. Your humble servant, bound by a sweet kisse.

Valen. I give you freedome, gentle Sir, by this.
    [*He whispers her*.
I know your mind; first censure of the sport,
Then you and I will enter *Venus* Court.

Duke. More then immortall, O more then divine,
That such perfection, should turne Concubine.

Mon. That voice is like unto the *Saxon Dukes*.
I feare he hath heard I liv'd here in this place,
And he is come to doe me more disgrace.
Montano, hide thyself till he be gone;
His daughter thirsts for my destruction.
    [*Exit Mont*.

Val. Come sit by me, the Maskers are at hand.

 Enter Maske.

Where are my Maides, to helpe to make the dance?

Enter 2 Maids.

They dance, Valentia with them; they whisper to have her play at dice and stake on the drum.

Valen. What, shall we have a Mumming? heres my Jewell.

[*Play on the drum head*.

Duke. Thou art a jewell most incomparable.--
Malicious heaven, why from so sweete a face
Have you exempt the mind adorning grace?

[*They stake and play*.

She wins, the drum strikes up.

Val. More gold, for this is mine, I thanke yee, dice.

Duke. And so are all that doe behold thy beautie.--
Were she as chaste, as she is outward bright,
Earth would be heaven, and heaven eternal night.
The more I drinke of her delicious eye,
The more I plunge into captivitie.

She wins, strike up.

Valen. Have I wonne all? then take that back agen.
What, scorne my gift? I see you are a gentleman.
No, is't not possible that I may know
Unto whose kindnesse this great debt I owe?
Well, Ile not be importunate, farewell;

Some of your gold let the torch-bearers tell.

Duke. Beautious *Madona*, do you know these galants?

Valen. I guesse them of the Duke of *Saxons* Court.

Duke.--My subjects, and so many my corrivalls
O every slave is grac't before his Prince.

Valen. Are you not well sir, that your colour failes?

Duke. If I be sicke, 'tis onely in the minde:
To see so faire, so common to all kinde;
I am growne jealous now of all the world.--
Lady, how ere you prize me, without pleasure
More then a kisse, I tender you this treasure;
O what's a mint spent in such desire
But like a sparke that makes a greater fire?--
She must be made my Dutches, there it goes;
And marrying her, I marry thousand woes.--
Adiew, kind Mistresse;--the next newes you heare
Is to sit crown'd in an Imperiall chair.[185]

Valen. Either the man dislikes me, or his braine
Is not his owne, to give such gifts in vaine,
But 'tis the custome in this age to cast
Gold upon gold, to encourage men to waste.
Lightly it comes, and it shall lightly flie;
Whilst colours hold, such presents cannot die.

[*Exeunt omnes*.[186]

[SCENE 3.]

Enter Reinaldo, Alfred, and Albert.

Alb. But this is strange, that I should meet your[187] honour
So farre from Court; pray whither were you riding?

Alf. Unto your mannor; heard you not the newes?

Alb. What newes?

Alf. This morning, by the breake of day,
His excellence sent to me by a post
Letters, by which the pillars of the state
Should be assembled to a Parliament,
Which he intends, my Lords, to hold in *Meath*.

Alb. When, if it please your honor?

Alf. Instantly,
With all the haste that winged time can make.

Albert. Sooner the better; tis like the realmes affaires
Are of some weight.

Alb. I will bee there to night,
And so I take my leave.

Reinal. We take our leaves.

[*Exit Albert and Reinaldo*.

Alf. Farewell, my honor'd friend.--
There is within my braine a thousand wiles
How I may heape up riches; O the sight,
Of a gold shining Mountaine doth exceede:
Silver is good, but in respect of gold
Thus I esteeme it.

[*Exit*.

[SCENE 4.]

Enter Hatto, with three petitioners.

Hat. How now, my friends, what are you?

1. Poore petitioners.

Hat. Stand farther then, the poore is as unpleasing
Unto me as the plague.

2. An't please your good Lordship, I am a Merchant, and gladly would convay a thousand quarters of wheate and other graine over the sea; and heres a hundred pounds for a commission.

Hat. Thou art no beggar, thou shalt ha't, my friend;
Give me thy money.

3. I, an't please your honour, have a commoditie of good broad cloth,

not past two hundred; may I shippe them over? and theres a hundred poundes.

Hat. Thou shalt have leave.

1. Although I seeme a poore petitioner,
My Lord, I crave a warrant to transport[188]
A hundred Cannons, fiftie Culverings,
With some slight armours, halberts, and halfe pikes;
And theres as much as any of the rest.

Hat. Away, *Cannibal*! wouldst thou ship ordnance?
What though we send unto the foes our corne
To fatten them, and cloth to keepe them warme,
Lets not be so forgetfull of our selves
As to provide them with knives to cut our throates:
So I should arme a thiefe to take my purse.
Hast thou no other course of Merchandize?
Thou shouldst get gold, twill yeeld thee ten in the hundred
On bare exchange, and raise the price with us;
Make us for want coyn brasse and passe it currant
Untill we find profit to call it in.
There are a thousand waies to make thee thrive
And Ile allow of all, bee it nere so bad,
Excepting guns to batter downe our houses.

1. Letters[189] of Mart I humblie then intreate,
To cease on Rovers that doe secure the seas.

Hat. And on our friends too, if thou canst do't cleanlie.
Spare none, but passe it very closely;
We will be loath to sift thy Piracie,
But open eare to heare what they [thou?] complaine.

Hast thou a Letter?

1. Ready drawne my Lord.
And heres a brace of hundred pounds for you.

Hat. 'Tis very well; I thinke I shall be rich
If dayly tenants pay me rent thus fast.
Give me your licenses, they shall bee seal'd.
About an houre hence, here attend our pleasure.

Omnes. We thanke your Lordship.
                [*Exeunt petiti.*

Hat. O vild catterpillers,
And yet how necassarie for my turne!
I have the Dukes seale for the Citie *Meath*,
With which Ile signe their warrants.
This corne and twentie times as much
Alreadie covertly convai'd to *France*,
And other bordering Kingdomes neere the sea,
Cannot but make a famine in this land;
And then the poore, like dogs, will die apace.
Ile seeme to pittie them, and give them almes
To blind the world; 'tis excellent policie
To rid the land of such, by such device.
A famine to the poore is like a frost
Unto the earth, which kills the paltry wormes
That would destroy the harvest of the spring.
As for the which, I count them painefull men
Worthy to enjoy what they can get:
Beggars are trash, and I esteeme them so;
Starve, hang, or drowne themselves, I am alive;
Loose all the world, so I have wit to thrive.

But I must to the Parliment, and then
Ile have a clause to beggar some rich men.

[*Exit*.

Actus Tertius.

[SCENE 1.]

    Enter Duke, Fredericke, Constantine, Reinaldo,
    Alberto, Alfrid, and amongst them Hatto shuffles in.

Alberto. Princes and pillars of the *Saxon* State.

Duke. You are the elected, speake for the Court.--
Stay, Lord *Alberto*, we usurpe your office:
Who had the charge to fetch *Valentia*?

Con. I, gracious Lord; and when I gave the charge,
A sudden feare, by palenesse, was displai'd
Upon her rosie cheeke; the crimson blood,
That like a robe of state did beautifie
The goodly buildings with a two fold grace,
From either side shrunke downewards to her heart
As if those summons were an adversarie
And had some mighty crime to charge her with.
Millions of thoughts were crowded in her braines:
Her troubled minde her abrupt words describ'd;
She did accuse her selfe without accusers,

And in the terrour of a soule perplext
Cry'd out, 'the Duke intends to cease my goods
Cause I am noted for a Concubine.'
I did replie such comfort as beseemes,
But comfortlesse I brought her to the Court.

Duke. Then she attends our pleasure.

Con. Mightie Lord,
In the next Roome.

Duke. You are careful, **Constantine**.
Conduct her in, and, Lords, give mee your thoughts:
What thinke ye wee intend to **Valentia**?

Alf. Her selfe hath read my sentence in the speech
That **Constantine** delivered to your grace.

Fred. What should my noble father thinke
But that she is a strumpet, and in that
A blemish to the state wherein she lives?

Hat. She is rich in jewells, and hath store of treasure
Got by the slavery of that choice beautie
Which otherwise admires her to the world.

Alb. Confiscate all her goods unto the Crown,
Thereby disburdening many heavie taxes
Impos'd upon the commons of the land.

Hat. Publique example make her to all such;
Offences in that kind are growne too common,

Lesse shamelesse never[190] were the beautious dames
Of *Meath* and *Saxony* then[191] the sufferance
Hath at this instant made them: good my Lord,
Enact some mighty penaltie for lust.

Duke. How wide these Archers shoote of the faire aime
Of my affection! Bring *Valentia* in.

Enter Valentia, usher'd by Constantine.

Valen. The duetie that in generall I doe owe
Unto your excellence and to this Court,
I pay at once upon my bended knee.

Duke. Behold her, Princes, with impartiall eyes,
And tell me, looks she not exceeding faire?

Hat. If that her mind coher'd with her faire face,
Shee were the worthy wonder of this age.

Alfred. I never saw a beautie more divine
Grossely deform'd by her notorious lust.

Fred. Fairnesse and wantonnesse have made a match
To dwell together, and the worst spoyles both.

Albert. Shee is doubly excellent in sin and beauty.

Duke. That they speake truth my conscience speaks,
But that I love her that I speak my self.
Stand up, divine deformitie of nature,
Beautious corruption, heavenly see[m]ing evill,

What's excellent in good and bad, stand up;
And in this Chaire, prepared for a Duke,
Sit, my bright Dutchesse, I command thee, sit.
You looke, I am sure, for some apologie
In this rash action; all that I can say
Is that I love her, and wil marry her.

Fred. How, love a **Lais**, a base **Rodophe**,
Whose body is as common as the sea
In the receipt of every lustfull spring?

Albert. The elements of which these orbes consists,
Fire, ayre, and water, with the ground[192] we tread,
Are not more vulgar, common, popular,
Then her imbracements.

Alberto. To incheyne the thoughts
Unto this semblance[193] of lascivious love
Were to be married to the broad rode[194] way
Which doth receiue the impression of every kind.

Fred. Speech doth want modesty to set her forth
In her true forme, base and contemptible;
The very hindes and peasants of the land
Will bee Corrivals with your excellence
If you espouse such a notorious Trull.

Albert. We shall have lust a virtue in the Court,
The wayes of sinne be furthered by reward,
Panders and Parasites sit in the places
Of the wise Counsellors and hurry all.

Fred. Father, as you are princely in your birth,

Famous in your estate, belov'd of all,
And (which ads greatest glory to your greatnesse,)
Esteemed[195] wise, shew not such open[196] folly
Such palpable, such grosse, such mountaine folly;
Be not the By-word of your neighbour Kings,
The scandall of your Subjects, and the triumph
Of **Lenos, Macrios**,[197] and the hatefull stewes.
Why speake you not, that are his brother friends,
You that doe weare the Liveries of time,
The silver cognizance of gravitie?
Shall none but young me schoole the reverent [*sic*] old?
Birds teach the Dam, stars fill the glorious spheares
Of the all lightning Sunne? speake whilst you may,
Or this rash deede will make a fatall day.

Duke. You have said too much, encourage none to speake
More then have spoke[n]; by my royall blood,
My mind's establisht, not to be withstood.
Those that applaud my choyse give us your hands,
And helpe to tye these sacred nuptiall bands.

Hat. What likes your excellence, likes me well.

Alfred. And I agree to what my Soveraigne please.

Fred. These are no brothers, they are flatterers,
Contrary to themselves in their owne speech.
You that doe love the honour of your Prince,
The care and long life of my father,
The hereditary right deriv'd to me,
Your countries Welfare, and your owne renowne,
Lend me your hands to plucke her from the throne.

Valen. Princes, forbeare, I doe not seeke the match;
It is his highnesse pleasure I sit here,
And if he love me 'tis no fault of mine.
Behoves me to be thankefull to his Grace,
And strive in virtue to deserve this place.

Duke. Thou speak'st too mildly to these hare braind youthes.
He that presumes to plucke her from the chaire
Dyes in the attempt, this sword shall end all care.

Fred. Why, shee's notorious.

Duke. But she will amend.

Fred. 'Tis too farre growne to have a happy end.

Duke. The dangerous the disease, greater's the cure.

Fred. Princes may seeke renowne by wayes more sure,
Shee is dishonest.

Duke. Honestie's unseene;
Shee's faire, and therefore fit to be a Queene.

Fred. But vertue is to be preferd ere lust.

Duke. Those that are once false, shall we ne're trust?

Fred. Wise men approve their actions by the tryall.

Duke. I say she is mine in spight of all deniall;
Bring me the Crowne.

Fred. To set upon her head?
Friends, draw your swords, first strike the strumpet dead.

Duke. My guard, my guard!

Alfred. For shame, put up your swords.

Fred. For shame, great Rulers, leave your flattering words.

Albert. 'Tis madnesse in the King and worse in you.

Hat. Though you prove traytors, we'll not prove untrue.

Fred. Will you dismisse this Strumpet to the stewes,
Or our allegance in this act refuse?

Duke. Doe what you dare, the election still shall stand.

Fred. Woe and destruction then must rule the land.
Come, Lord **Rinaldo**, valiant **Alberto**, come;
We have friends enough to grace a warlike Drum. [*A shout within*.
Hearke how the Commons doe applaud our cause.
Lascivious Duke, farewell, father, oh vilde!
Where Queanes are mothers, **Fredericke** is no child.

[*Exeunt*.

Duke. My guard pursue them, and alive or dead
Cut off the cause by which these cries are bred.
Come, my faire Dutchesse; first unto the Church,
There sollemnize our nuptials; then unto our armes:

A little rough breath overbeares these stormes.

[Exeunt. Manet Alfred & Hatto.

Alfred. The Duke's besotted. Now we are secure;
This match makes well for us; we may command
And on them lay the abuses of the land.

Hat. Excellent good; we are like to have warres indeed,
But in the meane the poore will starve for bread.
Wee must share proffits, howsoere things goe.
Winner or looser, neither is our foe;
For mutually we'll beare our selues in all
Or taking part leane to the strongest wall.

[Exeunt.

[SCENE 2.]

Enter Constantine and Euphrata.

Euph. My father married to a Concubine!
Then he will pardon though I marry thee;
And howsoe'r, about it presently,
The rather for *Montano* is repealde,
Because of his alliance to *Valentia*.

Con. I am ready, gentle love, and glad in mind
That my faire *Euphrata* will prove so kind.

Euph. Come my deare **Constantine**, performe this right [*sic*],
And arme in arme thus will we sleepe to night.

[*Exeunt*.

[SCENE 3.]

Enter Fredericke, Rinaldo, and Alberto, with Drum, Colours, and Souldiers.

Fred. You that are carefull of your countries weale,
Fellow compere, Supporter of the State,
Let us imbrace in steele, our cause is good.
What minde so base that would not shed his blood
To free his countrey from so great an ill
As now raignes in it by lascivious will?
Our[198] friends to warre and, for my part,
Ere lust beare sway, Ile gladly yeeld my heart.

Alberto. I heare the Duke is strong.

Fred. Suppose him so,
And be advis'd strongly to meete the foe.
I had rather, you should think him ten thousand strong
Then find it so to our destruction.
An enemy thought many and found few,
When our first courage failes, gives us a new.

[*Alarum*.

Alberto. That's the Dukes Drum.

Fred. They are welcome to their death,
The ground they tread on covers them with earth.

[*Exeunt*.

Enter Fredericke and Duke severall.

Fred. The enemy sends forth a Champion
To encounter me, I heard him use my name;
The honour of the combate shall be mine.

Duke. Come, boy, retreate not, only I intend
With thy lifes losse this bloody warre to end.

Fred. My naturall father in my blood I feele,
Passion more powerfull then that conquering steele.

Duke. Why dost thou pause, base boy? thy Soveraigne's come,
To inter the life I gave thee in this tombe.

Fred. My father, oh my father! nature, be still
That I may have my fame, or he his will.

Duke. What, dost thou feare thy cause? is't now so evill?

Fred. I am possest with a relenting devill;
Legions of kinde thoughts have supriz'd my sense
And I am too weake to be mine owne defence.

Duke. Thou art a coward.

Fred. And you make me so,
For you come charm'd like a dishonest[199] foe.
You have conferr'd with spirits, and tane their aydes
To make me weake, by them I am betraid,
My strength drawne from me by a slight;
What other meanes could hold me from the fight?

Duke. I have no spells about me.

Fred. 'Tis untrue,
For naturall Magique you have brought with you,
And such an exorcisme in your name
That I forbeare the combate to my shame.
But that I am no coward, from your host
Elect two of the valiantst that dare most;
Double that number, treble it, or more,
I have heart at will t'encounter with a score.
Or had your selfe come in a strange attire,
One of us twaine had lost his living fire.

   Enter[200] Montano, Alfred, Vandermas, Valentia, and others.

Duke. Ile trie your valour; see, audacious boy,
Thou art incompast with a world of foes
Montano, Alfred, Vandermas, and all:
My Dutchesse comes, too, to behold thy fall.
If thou hast spirit enough, now crave her ayd,
Never was poore ventrous souldier worse apayd.
              [*Exit Duke*.

Fred. My[201] desire now from the skie of starres.

Dart all your Deitie, since I am beset,
In honourable wise pay[202] all Natures debt.

 They fight, Fredericke beats them off and courses the Dutchesse over the stage.

Actus Quartus.

[SCENE 1.]

 Enter [at one door] Duke, Montano, Valentia, Hatto, and Alfred.

 Drumme, Colours, and Souldiers. [At another door enter Frederick, Rinaldo, Alberto, with soldiers.]

Duke. Our anger long agoe, renowned Lords,
Is satisfied in faire **Valentias** love.
Behold our proud sonne and these traiterous crew
That dares confront us in the field of **Mars**.

Valen. You have been too patient, my beloved Lord,
In calming these tumultuous jarring spirits.
Scourge them with steele, and make the proudest know
Tis more then death to have their Prince their foe.

Mon. Bloody constraints beseemes where dutie failes,
And, oratory ceasing, force prevailes.

Hat. Peace would doe better, so it pleas'd your sonne.

Fred. In her allurements first [the strife] begun;
Banish her from the land, and Ile resigne.

Duke. Learne thine owne dutie, traitor, I know mine.

Albert. Then there's no banishment?

Duke. None but by death;
Thy head is forfeit for that daring breath.

Alfred. Submit, degenerate and presumptuous Lord.

Albert. When we are ignorant to weild a sword.

Fred. Never shall noble knee bend to this ground,
As long as that vile strumpet liveth crownd.

Duke. I cannot stay to heare my love deprav'd.
In few words is it peace, or shall we fight
Till our deepe wounds shall dampe the heavenly light,
Make the ayre purple with the reaking gore?

Fre. Fight, whilst life serves you, we will nere give ore;
The grasse greene pavement shall be drownd in blood,
And yet Ile wade to kill her in the flood.

Duke. Alarum, Drum! madnesse is on their side,
All vertuous counsell is by them defied.
Upon our part strike Drums, Trumpets proclaime
Death most assur'd to those that love their shame.

Alarum, fight lustily, and drive away the Duke; Fredericke pursues Valentia over the stage and takes her; a Retreate sounded.

Enter at one doore the Duke, Mon., Hatto, and Alfred, with Drum and Colours.--Enter at the other doore Fredericke leading Valentia prisoner, Rinaldo and Alberto with Drum and Colours.

Duke. Why doe traitors sound retreate so soone?

Fred. Behold the cause.

Duke. *Valentia* prisoner?

Fred. The firebrand of this tumultuous warre,
The originall from whence your subjects bloud
Flowes in abundance on[203] this spatious playn.

Valen. And what of all this?

Fred. That thy lifes too meane
To satisfie the unworthiest of the Campe
For the effusion of a loyall drop.

Duke. Meanes *Fredericke* then, to kill his fathers heart In faire *Valentia's* death?

Fred. Not touch your hand,
Other then humble as becomes a sonne;
But she shall suffer for enchanting you.

Valen. I am a Dutchesse, set my ransome downe.

Fred. A Dutchesse! whence proceeds that borowed name?
Of what continuance? scarcely hath the Sunne
Beheld thy pride a day, but doth decline
Shaming to view a crowned Concubine.

Duke. In mine owne honour, *Fredericke*, I command
Thou set a ransome on *Valentia*.

Fred. What honor's that? your Dukedomes interest?
Your princely birth? your honerable fame?
All these are blemisht with a strumpets name.

Mon. Be not so cruell to bereave her life
'Twill draw upon thee a perpetuall scar,--
Thy fathers curse, and a continuall warre.

Duke. Oh doe not threaten; *Fredericke* is so mild
He will not prove such a degenerate child.
I cannot blame him tho' hee rise in armes:
'Twas not in hate to me, but in disdaine
That I should sell my royaltie so vaine;
But did he know the value of the jem,
Hee would not crase[204] it for a Dyadem.
That shee was common her owne words approve,
But many faults are cover'd where men love.
As thou respects my blessing and good dayes,
Restore her, *Fredericke*, and augment her prayse.

Fred. Restore her?

Albert. Never.

Duke. *Albert*, thou wert kind
And I ne're wrong'd thee; doe not change thy minde.

Hat. You doe abase your honour to intreate.

Duke. How can I choose? my affection is so great.

Alfred. Your power is strong, the enemy is but weake.

Duke. In her destruction all my powers will breake.
As thou dost hope of kindnesse in thy choyse
If ere thou love, give eare unto my voice;
Turne not aside thy eye, the feares I feele
Makes me to bow, where tis thy part to kneele.
Loe vassailelike, laying aside command,
I humbly crave this favour at thy hand:
Let me have my beloved, and take my state;
My life I undervalue to that rate.
Crave anything that in my power doth lye,
Tis thine, so faire **Valentia** may not dye.

Fred. My soule is griev'd, and it appals my blood
To see my father pusseld in such mood.
Yet shall shee dye, Ile doe as I have said;
With mine hand Ile chop off the Strumpets head.

Alberto. Kill her, my Lord, or let me have the honour.

Duke. Tigers would save her, if they lookt upon her;
Shee is so beautifull, so heavenly bright,
That she would make them love her for the sight.

Thou art more rude then such if thou proceede
In the execution of so vilde a deede.
Remember one thing, I did never love
Till thou, my *Fredericke*, broughtst that fatall Glove.
That and the Owners name thou didst descry;
Onely for that cause, let not my love dye.

Fred. O gods!

Duke. Cannot my kneeling serve, my teares prevaile,
When all helpes faile mee, yet this will not faile:
Proffer thy weapon to her beautious side,
And with her heart my heart I will divide.
Intreaty Ile urge none more then are past,
And either now relent or heres my last.

Fred. Stay: if I should relent, will you agree
To sign our general pardon presently?

Duke. By heaven I doe, I freely pardon all
And a reward I give in generall.

Fred. Then take her, you deserve her were shee better,
Making your Crown and life to be her Debter.

Duke. Welcome a thousand times, welcome, sweete wife,
Never more deare then now I have saved[205] thy life.

Valen. This more then kindnesse I turne backe to you,
Doubling my chast vow to bee ever true.

Fred. Then here the warres end, here[206] our fightings marde,
Yet by your leave Ile stand upon my Guard.

Duke. Take any course you please, Citie or Towne,
My royall word Ile keepe by this my Crowne.

Fred. Then thus Ile take my leave.

Duke. Since we must part,
Farewell, my Sonne, all farewell with my heart.

[Exeunt Fred, and his [sic].

Mon. Twas well, my Lord, 'twas a good policie,
To gaine your bride: I hope your grace did not meane
To be thus overrulde, by a proud Sonne.

Duke. Why, thinke you he intends some treachery?

Mon. Why not? and did release *Valentia*
To blind your eyes. Hee that could be so proud,
To rise in armes against his naturall Father,
Hath courage to doe more when he sees time.

Duke. But I have pardon'd that offence by oath.

Mon. It were no periury to make him know
Hee is your Sonne, and sonnes a dutie owe.
This sequestration will in time aspire
Unto a flame shall set your Realme on fire;
For[207] when a Subject hath the meanes of will,
'Tis not enough, to say he has no will;
For will is alter'd by the place and time
And hee that's once up knowes the way to clime.
I speake perchance like a prophetique foole,

But these are wise can counsaile with your bride;
Wisedome adviseth timely to provide.

Duke. What thinkes my love of *Frederickes* reconcilment?

Valen. That he has spirit enough, to be a traytor.
But I am beholding to him for a life
And he may brag he gave your grace a wife.
A [O?] good old man, he could not choose but feele
For shame some small remorse to see you kneele.
Pray God he gave me not into your hand
That he might be the ruine of your land.

Duke. Thinkes my love so? but, brothers, what's your censure?

Hat. I am no Polititian.

Alfred. Neither I:
Wee are both content to live quietly.

Duke. Hee may be a villaine tho' he be my Sonne.

Mon. Why not? and worke your ruine like a foe.
Had he meant well, why did he leave you so?
Your noble heart was free from all deceipt,
But hee's retirde to doe some dangerous feate.
When Subjects stand upon their guard, looke to't,
They have some plot in hand, and they will do't.

Duke. What course is readiest to prevent such mischiefe?

Mon. Plucke up the fulsome thistle in the prime:
Young trees bend lightly, but grow strong in time.

Were I the worthiest to advise your honour,
You should pursue him with your spredding bandes
Swifter in march then is the lightning flame,
And take him tardy whilst his plots are tame.
Now to charge on his army, questionlesse
Would drive them all into a great distresse,
If not confound them; having tane your Sonne,
You may be as kind, and doe as hee hath done;
So shall he know himself and be lesse proud.

Valen. The counsailes good.

Duke. And it shall be allowed.
You that doe love me, see the host prepar'd
To scare those traytors that our liues have scarde.
Our armie's many, but their power is few:[208]
Besides, they are traytors, all with us are true.
Sound Drums and trumpets, make the world rebound;
Hearten our friends, and all our foes confound.
    [*Alarum*.

    [*Exeunt*.

[SCENE 2.]

 Enter Montano, with two or three souldiers;
 Vandarmas leading Fredericke bound.

Fred. Base cowards, traytors! how am I surprizde,
[Bound] with these bonds? I am a Prince by birth,

And princely spirits disdaine such clogs of earth.
Let goe, you slaves.

Mon. First know your fathers pleasure.

Fred. You are too bold.

Mon. But you shall keepe a measure.

Fred. Thou blood of common Concubines, must I
Be bound by thee, and heir of *Saxony*?

 Enter Duke and Valen.

Duke. It is our pleasure.

Valen. Have you caught him so?
Now shall you waite the mercy we will shew:
I was too base to be your father's wife.

Duke. But he shall sue to thee to save his life.

Fred. Perjurde, ungratefull, unnaturall,
Is this the pardon given in generall?

Duke. Wee'l talke of that hereafter; make him fast.

Valen. Helpe, *Vandermas*, our self will ayding be
To keepe in awe such sencelesse trechery.

Duke. My helpe and all to prison, there till death
Remaine in duresse.

Fred. Rather stop my breath,
Strangle me with these cords; prison to me
Is twenty deaths, I will have liberty.
Now as you are a father, be more kind;
You did not find me in so sterne a mind.
Are[209] you forgetful of the life I sav'd?
Shall a Duke's Sonne by treason thus be slav'd?
If you suspect my love, grant me the fight;
I dare in single combat any knight,
Any adventurer, any pandorus hinde,
To proue my faith of an unfained mind.

Duke. Away with him.

Fred. I see my death's set downe,
And some adulterous heire must weare that Crowne.
To intreate a *Rodophe*, I had rather dye
Then have my life lodg'd in such infamy:
If all my fortunes on her words depend,
Let her say kill me, and so make an end.

Duke. Why stay you?

Vander. Good my Lord.

Fred. Peace, untaught Groome,
My heart's so great that Ide forerun my doome.
There's no release meant, you have vowed I see
To dam your soules by wilfull periury.
Yet that I am my self, let these words shew:
To die is naturall, tis a death I owe,
And I will pay it, with a mind as free

As I enjoyed in my best libertie.
But this assure your self, when all is done,
They'l kill the father that will kill the sonne. [*Exit*.

Duke. What's to be done now?

Mon. Seale unto his death,
Your warrant nere the sooner takes effect:
'Twill be a meanes to make him penitent.
Seeing his fault, hee'l taste your mercie best,
When now he proudly thinkes he is opprest.

Duke. A Warrant shall be sign'd, and unto thee
I doe commend it; deale not partially;
If he be sorry and in true remorse,
Cancell the Writ, else let it have full force.
Had I ten sonnes, as I have onely this,
They should all die, ere thou depriv'd of blisse.
So great is my affection, my faire wife,
That to save thine Ide frankly give my life.
Come, weele about it strait, all time seemes long,
Where thou hast found slight cause to feare my wrong.

Valen. That writ Ile take, and a conclusion trie:
If he can love he lives, if hate me die.
For howsoere, I seeme to scorne the man,
Hee's somewhat deare in my affection.--
Here comes your brothers.

Enter Alfred, and Hatto.

Alfred. May it please your grace,
By chance entring into Saint *Maries* Church,

This morn by breake of day, I espied
That that I know will vexe your Excellence:
Your daughter *Euphrata* is married
To the ambitious beggar *Constantine*.

Duke. My daughter married to my Chamber-squire?

Mon. Your Excellence did banish me the land
Because I did suspect her with that fellow.

Duke. He shall be tortur'd with th'extreamest plague
For his presumption.--Have you brought them,
That I may kill them with a killing looke?

Hat. Without direction we have ventured
To lay upon them your strict command,
And they attend.

Duke. Bring the presumptuous.

Enter Constantine, and Euphrata, Otho following in disguise.

Euph. Forward, *Constantine*, our Rites are done,
Thou art my husband, doe not feare his eye,
The worst it can import is but to die.

Duke. Base and degenerate.

Euph. He is a Gentleman,
'Twas base of you to wed a Curtizan.

Mon. Her brothers spirit right, bold and audacious.

Euph. When[210] I am no bastard, wherefore should I feare?
The knot is sacred, and I hold it deare;
I am wedded unto virtue, not to will,
Such blessed unions never bring forth ill.
If I offend, in disobedience,
Judge of the power of love by your offence.
Father, you have no reason for this ire;
Frowne whilst you kill us, desire is desire.

Duke. A Curtezan? hath that ambitious boy
Taught you such Rethoricke? you shall taste like joy.
I will not reason with you, words are vaine,
The fault is best discerned in the paine.
Your hastie marriage hath writ downe his death,
And thy proud words shall scale it with thy breath.
By what is dearest to mee, here I sweare,
Both of your heads, shall grace a fatall beere.
Take them to prison, Ile not heare a word,
This is the mercie that we will afford.
Since they are growne so proud, next morn begun,
Let them be both beheaded with my sonne.

Con. Short and sweet: ***Euphrata***, the doome is faire,
We shall be soone in heaven, there ends my care.
I scorne entreatie, and, my deare, I know,
All such slavery thou hatest so,
'Twill be a famous deed for this good man
To kill all's children for a Curtezan.

Euph. Wilt thou die with me?

Const. Would I live in heaven?

Thou art now too high for me, death makes us even.

Euph. Looke to your dukedome: those that hast our fall
Have by their avarice almost hurried all.
There's a whole Register of the poores crie:
Whilst they are reading them, imbrace and die.

[*Flings downe her lap full of Petitions*.

[*Exeunt Euph. and Constant*.

Duke. Beare them away.--And now let's reade these Writes.
What's here? complaints against my worthy brothers
For corne transported, Copper money stampt,[211]
Our subjects goods ceaz'd, and I know not what.
A plague upon this busie-headed rabble!
We will have tortures made to awe the slaves;
Peace makes them ever proud and malapert,
They'l be an Overseer of the State.

Valen. And plead reformation to depose you.

Duk. True, my faire Dutchesse, but Ile cut them short.
Rule still, deare brothers: take these to the fire,
Let me reade somewhat that augments desire,
Authors and golden Poems full of love;
Such the Petitions are that I approve.
So I may live in quiet with my wife,
Let fathers, mothers, children, all lose life.
If thou have issue, in despight of fate
They shall succeed in our Imperiall state.
Come, sweet, to dauncing, then to sport and play,
Till we have ruled all our life away.

[*Exeunt.*

Manet, Otho.

Otho. O pittifull condition of a Realme,
Where the chiefe ruler is ore-rul'd by pleasure!
Seeing my friend supriz'd, in this disguise
I followed him to meete the consequence.
And to my griefe I see his marriage rites
Will cut him short of all this earths delights.
What's that to me? When **Constantine** is dead,
I have some hope to attaine her Nuptiall bed.
But she is doom'd as well as hee to die:
Can the Duke act his daughters Tragedie?
It is impossible; he will relent,
And Ile perswade her freely to repent.
Yet 'tis most likelie that he will agree:
He is so farre spent in vild tyrannie.
The commons hate him for the wrong he hath done
(By his brothers meanes), the Nobles for his sonne.
Famine spreads through the land, the people die;
Yet he lives senselesse of their miserie.
Never were subjects more mislead by any,
Nor ever Soveraigne hated by so many.
But, **Constantine**, to thee I cast an eye;
Shall all our friendship end in enmitie?
Shall I, that ever held thee as my life,
Hasten thy death that I may get thy wife?
Or love or friendship, whether shall exceed,
Ile explaine your vertue in this following deed.

[*Exit.*

[SCENE 3.]

Enter Valentia, Montano, and Vandermas.

Val. Have you the instruments I gave in charge.

Vand. Wee have.

Val. And resolution fitting for the purpose?

Mon. All things are ready, with our faithfull hearts.

Val. And she that undertakes so great an act
As I intend, had need of faithfull hearts
This is the prison, and the jaylor comes
In happy time: where's trayterous **Fredericke**?

Enter Jaylor.

Jaylor. What is your highnesse pleasure with the Prince?

Val. Looke there, if you can reade.

Jai. O heavenly God,
What doe I read? a warrant for his death?

Valen. Resigne your keyes, goe weepe a dirge or twaine
But make no clamour with your lamentation.

Jay. I dare not prophesie what my soule feares,
Yet Ile lament his tragedie in teares.   [*Exit*.

Valen. Oft have I seene a Nobleman arraign'd
By mighty Lords, the pillars of the land,
Some of which number, his inclined friends,
Have wept, yet past the verdict of his death:
So fares it with the Prince. Were I his jaylor,
And so affected unto *Fredericks* life,
The fearfull'st tyrant nor the cruell'st plagues
That ever lighted on tormented soules,
Should make me yeeld my prisoner to their hands.

Mon. Madam, he knowes his duty, and performes it.

Valen. Setting aside all dutie, I would die
Ere like a woman weepe a tragedie;
Tis basenesse, cowardize. Dutie! O slave,
Had I a friend, I'de dye in my friends grave.
But it sorts well for us; Hindes will be Hindes,
And the Ambitious tread upon such mindes.
Waite, whilest I call you, in the jaylors house.

Mon. We will.
         [*Exeunt Van. and Mon*.

Valen. My Lord, Prince *Fredericke*.

   Enter Fred.

Fred. Wofull *Fredericke*

Were a beseeming Epitaph for me,
The other tastes of too much soveraigntie.
What? is it you! the glory of the stewes!

Valen. Thy mother, *Fredericke*.

Fred. I detest that name,
My mother was a Dutches of true fame;
And now I thinke upon her, when she died
I was ordain'd to be indignified.
She never did incense my Princely Father
To the destruction of his loving sonne:
Oh she was vertuous, trulie naturall,
But this step-divell doth promise our fall.

Val. Why doest thou raile on me? I am come
To set thee free from all imprisonment.

Fred. By what true supersedeas but by death?
If it be so, come, strike me to the earth;
Thou needest no other weapon but thine eye;
Tis full of poyson, fixe it, and Ile die.

Val. Uncharitable youth, I am no serpent venom'd,
No basiliske to kill thee with my sight.

Fre. Then thou speak'st death, I am sorry I mistooke;
They both are fatall, theres but little choice;
The first inthral'd my father, the last me,
No deadlier swords ever us'd enemie;
My lot's the best that I dye with the sound,
But he lives dying in a death profound.
I grow too bitter, being so neere my end;

Speake quickly, boldly, what your thoughts intend.

Valen. Behold this warrant, you can reade it well.

Fred. But you the interpretation best can tell:
Speake, beautious ruine, twere great injurie
That he should reade the sentence that must dye.

Val. Then know in briefe 'tis your fathers pleasure.

Fred. His pleasure, what?

Val. That you must loose your life.

Fred. Fatall is his pleasure, 'tis to please his wife.
I prethee, tell me, didst thou ever know
A Father pleased his sonne to murder so?
For what is't else but murder at the best?
The guilt whereof will gnawe him in his brest,
Torment him living, and when I am dead
Curse thee by whose plot I was murdered?
I have seene the like example, but, O base!
Why doe I talke with one of your disgrace?
Where are the officers? I have liv'd too long,
When he that gave me life does me this wrong.

Val. That is thy fathers hand, thou dost not doubt?
And if thou shouldst, I have witnesse to approve it.
Yet tho it be his hand, grant to my request,
Love me and live.

Fred. To live so, I detest. Love thee!

Valen. I, love me, gentle *Fredericke*, love me.

Fred. Incestuous strumpet, cease.

Val. Oh thou dealest ill,
To render so much spleene for my good will.

Fred. Torment farre worse then death.

Valen. Ile follow thee:
Deare *Fredericke*, like thy face, be thy words faire.

Fre. This monstrous dealing doubles my deaths care.

Valen. What shall I call thee to allay this ire?

Fred. Why, call me son and blush at thy desire.

Valen. I never brought thee foorth.

Fred. Art thou not wife
Unto my father?

Val. Thinke upon thy life:
It lyes like mine, onely in gentle breath;
Or that thy father's dead, and after death
'Tis in my choice to marry whom I will.

Fred. Any but me.

Valen. O doe not thinke so ill,
Rather thinke, thou art a stranger, not his sonne;

Then 'tis no incest tho the Act be done.
Nature unto her selfe is too unkind
To buzze such scruples into *Fredericks* minde;
Twas a device of man to avoid selfe love,
Else every pleasure in one stocke should move,
Beautie in grace part never from the kinne.

Fred. If thou persever as thou hast begun,
I shall forget I am my fathers sonne,
I shall forget thou art my fathers wife,
And where 'tis I must die abridge thy life.

Valen. Why did'st not kill me, being thy prisoner then,
But friendly didst deliver me again[212]
Unto thy father, wert not thou didst love me?

Fred. Beyond all sufferance, monster, thou dost move me.
'Twas for my fathers sake, not for thine owne;
That, to thy lifes losse, thou hadst throughly knowne
But that relenting nature playde her part,
To save thy blood whose losse had slaine his heart:
And it repents me not hee doth survive,
But that his fortune was so ill to wive.
Come, kill, for for that you came; shun delayes
Lest living Ile tell this to thy dispraise,
Make him to hate thee, as he hath just cause,
And like a strumpet turne thee to the lawes.

Valen. Good *Fredericke*.

Fred. Tis resolv'd on, I haue said.

Valen. Then fatall Ministers I craue your ayde.

Enter Van. and Mont.

Come, **Vandermas, Montano**, wheres your corde?
Quicklie dispatch, strangle this hatefull Lord.
Or stay: because I love him, he shall chuse
The easiest of three deaths that we may use,
The halter, poyson, or bloodshedding blade.

Fred. Any of them.

Valen. This Aconite's well made, a cup of poyson
Stuft with despatching simples, give him this,
And he shall quickly leave all earthly blisse.
There, take it, **Fredericke**, our last guift of grace;
Since thou must die, Ile have thee die apace.

Fred. O happie meanes, given by a trecherous hand,
To be my true guide to the heavenly land!
Death steales upon me like a silken sleepe;
Through every vaine doe leaden rivers flowe,[213]
The gentlest poyson that I ever knewe,
To work so coldly, yet to be so true.
Like to an infant patiently I goe,
Out of this vaine world, from all worldly woe;
Thankes to the meanes, tho they deserve no thankes,
My soule beginnes t'ore-flow these fleshly bankes.
My death I pardon unto her and you,
My sinnes God pardon; so vaine world adiew.
 [*He falls asleep*.

Valen. Ha, ha, ha.

Mon. Hee's dead, why does your highnesse laugh?

Valen. Why, Lord *Montano*, that I love to see,
He that hath sav'd my life, to die for me.
But theres a riddle in this Princes death,
And Ile explaine it on this floore of earth.
Come, to his sisters execution goe,
We have varietie of joyes in woe.
I am sure, you have heard his Excellence did sweare
Both of their heads should grace a Kingly beare.
Upon a mourning hearse let him be layd;
He shalbe intombed with a wived maid.

[*Exeunt*.

Actus Quintus.

[SCENE 1.]

Enter Duke, Hatto, and Alfred.

Duke. Bring forth the prisoners: wher's my beauteous Dutches
That she may see the ruine of her foes?
She that upbraided her with slanderous wordes,
She that in scorne of due obedience
Hath matcht the honour of the *Saxons* blood
Unto a beggar; let them be brought foorth,
I will not rise from this tribunal seate
Till I have seene their bodies from their heads.

Alfred. Here comes the Dutches with proud *Fredericks* hearse.

> Enter, Valentia, Montano, Vandermas, with others,
> bearing the hearse, with Fredericke on, covered
> with a black robe.

Duke. So, set it downe: why have you honored it
With such a sable coverture? A traytor,
Deserves no cloth of sorrow: set it downe,
And let our other offspring be brought foorth.
My beauteous, lovely, and admired love,
Come, sit by us in an imperiall chayre,
And grace this state throne with a state more fayre.

Valen. My gracious Lord, I hope your Excellence
Will not be so forgetfull of your honour,
Prove so unnaturall to your loving daughter
As to bereave her of her life
Because she hath wedded basely gainst your will.
Though *Fredericke* dyed deservedly, yet shee
May by her loves death clear her indignitie.

Duke. She and her love we have sentenced to die,
Not for her marriage onely, tho that deede
Crownes the contempt with a deserved death,
But chiefly for she raild against thy worth,
Upbraided thee with tearmes so monstrous base
That nought but death can cleare the great disgrace.
How often shall I charge they be brought foorth?
Were my heart guilty of a crime so vilde,
I'de rend it forth, then much more kill my childe.

Val. O, that this love may last! 'tis sprung so hie,
Like flowers at full growth that grow to die.

> Enter Julia, with a vaile over her head, Otho with another, with Officers.

Duke. What means these sable vailes upon their faces?

Val. In signe they sorrow for your high displeasure.
For since the houre they were imprisoned,
They have liv'd like strangers, hood-winkt together.
You may atchieve great fame, victorious Lord,
To save the lives of two such innocents.

Duke. Tis pretty in thee, my soule lov'd Dutchesse,
To make this Princely motion for thy foes.
Let it suffice, the'are traitors to the state,
Confederators with those that sought my life,
A kinne to *Fredericke*, that presumptious boy,
That durst beare armes against his naturall father:
Are they more deare then he? off with their vailes.

Mon. O yet be mercifull unto your daughter.

Duke. You make me mad, headsman; dispatch I say,
They are doom'd to die, and this the latest day.

Otho. Then let him strike, who ever traitors be,
I am sure no treason lives in her or me.

Duke. How now, whats here? *Otho* and *Julia*!
Am I deluded? where is *Euphrata*,

And that audacious traitor *Constantine*?

Otho. Why, fled.

Duke. To whom?

Otho. To safetie, here was none.
I can resolve you of the circumstance:
Betwixt the noble *Constantine* and I,--
Noble I call him for his virtuous minde--
There was a league of love so strongly made
That time wants houres, and occasion cause,
To violate the contract of our hearts.
Yet on my part the breach did first appeare:
He brought me to behold his beauteous love
The faire *Euphrata*; her Angel sight
Begate in me the fire of private love:
I that before did like her for my friend,
Now to deceive him, sought her for my selfe;
But my device was knowne unto my friend,
And worthilie he banisht me his sight.

Duke. Whats this to their destruction? seeke them forth.

Otho. They are far enough from suffering such a death.
I, well considering my unfriendly part,
Bethought me how to reconcile my self
Unto my hearts endeared *Constantine*;
And seeing him carried to the prison, we
Followed, and found meanes for their libertie.

Duke. Are they escapt then?

Otho. Both, in our disguise,
And we stand here to act their tragedies.
If they have done amisse, on us
Impose the Law.

Julia. O let our suites prevaile,
I ask to dye for my deare Ladies sake.

Otho. I for my friend.

Duke. This friendly part doth make
My heart to bleede within me, and my minde
Much perplext that I have beene so unkind.
What second funerall march is that I heare?

> Enter Rainaldo and Alberto, like schollers, grieving
> before the Beare, others following them with bodies of
> Euphrata and Constantine covered with blacke.

Alberto. Health to this presence, though the newes
Impairing health I bring unto this presence;
The bodies of the drowned *Constantine*
And the faire *Euphrata*, behold them both.

Duke. Of drowned *Constantine* and *Euphrata*!
Declare the manner, and with killing words
Temper thy words, that it may wound my life.

Albert. Passing the *Rhine*, bordering upon the tower,
From whence, it seemes they lately had escapt,
By an unskilfull Guide their gundelet[214]
Encountred with an other, and the shocke

Drown'd both the vessayles, and their haplesse lives.
Their bodies hardly were recovered;[215]
But, knowne, we brought them to your excellence
As to a father, that should mourne for them.

Duke. Unto a tyrant, doe not call me father,
For I have beene no father to their lives.
The barbarous Canniball, that never knew
The naturall touch of humane beauty,
Would have beene farre more mercifull then I.
Oh tyrannie, the overthrow of Crownes,
Kingdomes subversion, and the deaths of Kings!
Loe here a piteous object so compleate
With thy intestine and destroying fruite,
That it will strike thee dead! oh *Euphrata*,
Oh princely *Fredericke*, never deare to me
Till now, in you I see my misery.
My sonne, my daughter, vertuous *Constantine*!

Hat. What meanes this griefe, my Lord? these are the traytors
That you in justice sentenced to dye.

Alfred. A trecherous sonne and a rebellious daughter.

Valen. Those that did seeke to take away your life.

Mon. Bereave you of your Crownes prerogative.

Duke. Hence from my sight, blood-thirsty Counsellors!
They never sought my life, but you have sought it.
Vertuous *Alberto* and *Rinaldo*,
Had I given eare to them and to my sonne,

My joyes had flourished, that now are done.

Valen. Yet for my sake allay this discontent.

Duke. Tis for thy sake, thou vilde notorious woman,
That I have past the limits of a man,
The bonds of nature.
'Twas thy bewitching eye, thy Syrens voice,
That throwes me upon millions of disgrace,
Ile have thee tortur'd on the Racke,
Plucke out those basiliske enchaunting eyes,
Teare thee to death with Pincers burning hot,
Except thou giue me the departed lives
Of my deare childeren.

Valen. What, am I a Goddesse
That I should fetch their flying soules from heaven
And breath them once more in their clay cold bodies?

Duke. Thou art a witch, a damn'd sorceresse,
No goddesse, but the goddesse of blacke hell,
And all those devils thy followers.
What makes thou, on the earth, to murder men?
Will not my sonnes and daughters timelesse[216] lives,
Taken away in prime of their fresh youth,
Serve to suffice thee?

Valen. O, you are mad, my Lord.

Duke. How can I choose,
And such a foule ***Erynnis*** gase on me,
Such furious legions circle me about,
And my slaine Sonne and Daughters fire brands

Lying so neere me, to torment my soule?
Extremitie of all extremities:
Take pitty on the wandering sense of mine
Or it will breake the prison of my soule
And like to wild fire fly about the world,
Till they have no abiding in the world.
I faint, I dye, my sorrowes are so great,
Oh mortalitie, renounce thy seate.   [*He fals down*.

Valen. The Duke, I feare, is slaine with extreame griefe.
I that had power, to kill him, will assay henceforth
My utmost industry to save his life.
Looke up my Lord, 'tis not *Valentias* voice,
That Courtezan that hath betray'd thy honour,
Murder'd thy childeren, and almost slaine thee:
I am thy sonne, I am Prince *Fredericke*;
If thou hast any liking for that name,
Looke on my face, I come to comfort thee.

Duke. The name of *Fredericke* is like Hermes wande
Able to charme and uncharme sorrowfull men.
Who nam'd *Fredericke*?

Valen. I pronounc't his name,
That have the power to give thee thy lost Sonne,
Had I like virtue to restore the other.
Behold my Lord, behold thy headlesse Sonne
Blest with a head, the late deceased living;
As yet not fully waken'd from the sleepe,
My drowsie potion kindled in his braine,
But much about this houre the power should cease;
And see, he wakes.

Duke. O happinesse, tis hee.

Valen. Imbrace him then, but ne're more imbrace me.

Fred. Where am I, in what dungeon, wheres my grave?
Was I not dead, or dreamt I was dead?
This am I sure, that I was poisoned.[217]

Duke. Thou art deceiv'd, my Sonne, but this deceit
Is worth commendations; thanke my Dutchesse,
Her discretion reedified thy life,
But she hath prov'd her selfe a gracious wife.

Fred. She tempt[ed] me to lust; wast in my grave?

Valen. 'Twas but to try thy faith unto thy father:
Let it suffice, his hand was at thy death
But twas my mercie that proclaim'd thy breath.

Fred. To heaven and you, I render worthy thankes.

Duke. O liv'd my *Euphrata* and *Constantine*,
How gladly would I all my griefe resigne.

Albert. On that condition, and with this besides,
That you be pleas'd to pardon us and them,
We doe referre our persons to your mercie.

Duke. My daughter, my deare sonne in law,
Vertuous *Alberto*? then, my friend,
My joyes are at the highest, make this plaine
How these sav'd drownd, as *Fredericke* has bin slaine.

Albert. Presuming on the example of these friends,
And know we are all actors in this plot
Boldly presented your presence, with this minde,
If pardoning them your grace would pardon us;
If otherwise, this was the joy of either,
That death's lesse painefull when friends die together.

Duke. We doe receive you all into our favour,
And my faire Dutchesse; my unkind divorce
Shall be confounded with a second marriage,
I here receive thee once more as my wife.

Val. You have your childeren, I have paid that debt,
You have divorc'd me, therefore I am free,
And henceforth I will be at libertie.

Duke. Theres no divorce can part thee from thy Lord.

Valen. Like to unkindnesse there is no divorce,
I will no more be won unto your bed,
But take some course to lament my life mislead.

Duke. Canst thou live better then in sacred wedlock?

Valen. Wedlocke to me is unpleasing, since my Lord
Hath broke the band of marriage with unkindnesse.

Duke. Intreate her, children, **Fredericke, Euphrata**,
Let me not loose the essence of my soule.

Fred. Divine **Valentia**, mirrour of thy sexe,
The pride of true reclaim'd incontinence,

Honour of the dishonoring, yeeld I pray,
And be mercifull, pitty my fathers smart,
Since thy last thraldome hath neare cleft his heart.

Euph. 'Twas for his children that his spleene did rise,
Anger a torture haunting the most wise.

Valen. O no I am a murderesse, an ***Erinnis***,
A fury sent from ***Limbo*** to affright
Legions of people with my horrid sight.

Hat. What doe you meane? be won by their intreaties.

Alfred. 'Tis madnesse in you to be thus perverse.

Val. Who ever speaks, base wretches, be you dumb;
You are the catterpillers of the state,
By your bad dealings he is unfortunate.
Thou, honorable, true, beloved Lord,
Hearken to me, and by thy antient love,
I charge thee, banish these realme-sucking slaves,
That build their pallace upon poore mens graves.
O those are they that have wrong'd both you and me,
Made this blest land a land of miserie;
And since, by too much loving, your grace hath falne
Into a generall hating of your subjects,
Redeeme your lost estate with better dayes;
So shall you merit never dying praise,
So shall you gaine lives quietnesse on earth,
And after death a new celestiall birth.

Duke. Unto thy wisedome I referre their doomes,
My selfe, my Dukedome, and my crowne.

Oh were there anything of higher rate,
That unto [t]hee I'de wholly consecrate.

Val. This kind surrender shewes you are a Prince,
Worthy to be an Angell in the world
Of immortalitie,
Which these cursed creatures never can attaine.
But that this world may know how much I hate
This cruell, base oppression of the poore,
First, I enjoyne you for the wrongs you have done,
Make restitution; and because your goods
Are not sufficient so to satisfie,
I doe condemn your bodies to the Mynes,
Where live like golden drudges all your lives,
In digging of the mettall you best love:
Death is your due, but for your noble race
This gentle sentence I impose on you:
The Duke succeeding shall behold it done.

Duke. Who's that, my love?

Valen. Kind ***Fredericke***, your sonne:
The interest that your grace hath given to me,
I freely doe impart.

Duke. We doe agree,
To what my Dutchesse please.

Valen. The state is thine,
Thy Uncles sentence, ***Fredericke***, shall be mine.

Fred. Beare them away, what you have said shall stand,
Whilst I have interest in this new given land.

Hat. We doe receive our judgements, with a curse.

Valen. Learne to pray better, or it shall be worse:
Lords, see those wormes of kingdomes be destroyed.
And now, to give a period to my speeche
I doe intreate your grace, if that your love
Be not growne colde, but that your heart desires
The true societie of a chaste wife,
Be pleas'd to undergoe a further doome.
Wee haue liv'd too lightly, we have spent our dayes,
Which should be dedicated to our God,
In soule destroying pleasure, and our sloth
Hath drawne upon the Realme a world of plagues.[218]
Therefore hereafter let us live together
In some removed cell or hermitage,
Unto the which poore travellers mislead
May have direction and reliefe of wants.

Duke. A hermetary life is better then a kingdome,
So my *Valentia* beare me company.

Valen. If my dread Lord will for my sake endure
So strickt a calling, my bewitching haires
Shall be made napkins to dry up the teares
That true repentance wringeth from our hearts;
Our sinnes we'l number with a thousand sighes,
Fasting shall be the Steward of our Feast,
Continuall prayer in stead of costly cates,
And the remainder of our life a schoole
To learne new lessons for the land of heaven.
The will, where power is wanting, is good payment;
Grace doth reject no thought, tho' nere so small,

So it be good; our God is kind to all.
Come, my deare Lord, this is a course more kind;
No life like us that have a heavenly mind.

Mon. O let me be a servant in that life.

Valen. With all my heart, a Partner let him be
There's small ambition in humility.

Duke. *Fredericke*, farewell, deare *Euphrata*, adue;
Remember us in prayer, as we will you.

    [*Exeunt D. & D*

Fred. A happy change: would all that step awry
Would take like course in seeking pietie.

Otho. Two humble suites I crave of my best friend:
First, pardon for my rashnesse in your love,
Next this most loyall Virgin for my wife.

Con. With all my heart, if *Julia* be pleas'd.

Julia. I have no power to disobey your grant.

Con. Then she is yours.

Fred. Alberto,
The offices belonging to our Uncles
We doe derive to you for your good service
In our late warres, and in our sisters love.
And now set forwards: Lords, let us be gone

To solemnize two mariages in one.

The Epilogue.

Encouragement unto the valiant
Is like a golden spurre upon the heele
Of a young Knight, like to a wreath of Bay
To a good Poet; like a sparkeling Crowne,
Unto a Kings Son. Honour and renowne
Is the efficient and persevering cause
Of every well deserved action.
Take away some recorde, encouragement,
And the World's like a *Chaos,* all delight
Buried unborne in everlasting night.
Even so it fares with us, and with the rest
Of the same facultie, all meerely nothing:
Without your favour every labour dyes,
Save such whose second springs comes from your eyes.
Extend your beames of love to us at full,
As the Sunne does unto the Easterne clime,
And England may bring forth like India
As costly spice, as orientall Jems.
The earth's all one, the heate refines the moulde,
And favour makes the poorest ground yielde gold.

FINIS.

INTRODUCTION TO EVERIE WOMAN IN HER HUMOR.

This old "comical satire" has come down in a very corrupt state. A sadly tattered appearance is presented by the metrical passages. I have ventured to patch only a few of the many rents in the old coat of 1609.

The anonymous playwright owes much more than the title of the play to Ben Jonson. Acutus, overflowing with bitter and tedious moralising, is evidently modelled on Macilente in *Every Man Out of His Humour*. The very dog--Getica's dog--was suggested by Puntarvolo's dog. Indeed, throughout the play we are constantly reminded of Every Man Out of His Humour; but the unknown writer had some inventiveness of his own, and was not a mere copyist. The jolly fat host, with his cheery cry "merry hearts live long," is pleasant company; and his wife, the hard-working hostess, constantly repining at her lot, yet seemingly not dissatisfied at heart, has the appearance of being a faithful transcript from life. Cornutus (the hen-pecked citizen) and his gadding wife are familiar figures, but not the less welcome on that account. Getica's anxiety at the loss of her dog is amusingly depicted. In fact, the whole play would be tolerable, if the moralising were cut out and the text were free from corruptions.

EVERIE Woman in her Humor.

LONDON Printed by E.A. for *Thomas Archer*, and are to be solde at his shop in the *Popes-head-Pallace*, neere the Royall Exchange. 1609.

Everie Woman in her
   Humor.

Enter Flavia as a Prologue.

Gentles of both sexes and all sortes, I am sent to bid yee welcome; I am but instead of a Prologue, for a she-prologue[219] is as rare as an Usurers Almes, **non reperitur in usu**; and the rather I come woman because men are apt to take kindelye any kinde thing at a womans hand; and wee poore foules are but too kinde if wee be kindely intreated, marry otherwise, there I make my *Aposiopesis*. The Author hath indeede made me an honest merrye wench one of his humorists, yet I am so much beholding to him, I cannot get mee a husband in his play that's worthe the having, unlesse I be better halfe of the sutor my selfe; and having imposed this audacity on me, he sends me hither first for exercise. I come among ye all, these are the Contentes: that you would heare with patience, judge with lenity, and correct with smiles; for the which our endeavour[220] shall shew it selfe, like a tall fellow in action; if we shall joyne hands, a bargaine.

   As a lowely earnest, I give this curtesie before,
   And in conceite I give ye twenty more.

[ACT THE FIRST.

Scene 1.]

Enter Accutus and Graccus.

Gra. Nay but, ***Accutus***, prethee what mis-shapen vizard of Melancholly hast thou mask't thy selfe in? Thou lookst as thou wer't changing thy religion; what? is there a breach in thy Faith? come declare, and let me set thy [my?] wits on worke to amend it.

Acut. Ha, ha, ha!

Gra. Prettie; a man's well advisd to offer good counsell, and be laught at for his labour: we shall shortly have no counsellors, but Physitians; I spend my breath to thee, and thou answerest me some half an houre after in a sem[i]breve, or like to a Sexton, with a Sobeit or Amen.

Acu. Condemn my Stars then!

Grac. I should wrong am then, as thou dost with a false inditment. I know it took not beeing at thy birth: thou hast been merrie, thou hast sounded hoopes, swallowed whiffes, walkt late, worn favours, seene whoresons; thou canst feele and understand, come thou hast bene a sinner, unloade, discharge, untune, confesse, is ***Venus*** dominatrix? art not in love?

Acut. Yes, I love God and my neighbors.

Grac. Then either for God's sake or thy Neighbors, or both, be smothe, and participate; ist not some underlayer, some she Cammell, that will beare as much of her belly as three beastes on their backes? some Lanthorne-maker? Ile holde thy head; come, up with't!

Acut. Prethee, I hate none, but heaven hate me if I be in love with any.

Grac. Off with these clogs; then break prison and get out of this melancholly Gaole. Harke how the generall noise doth welcome from the *Parthian* wars; each spirit's jocund, fraught with glee, then wrong not thine with this dull meditation.

Accut. Oh! how doe they then wrong my meditation! my thoughts are with themselues at a counsell; til with noise, and thou with continuall talke, hast driven them to a *nonplus*.

Gra. Then make me of thy counsell, and take my advice, for ile take no denyall; Ile not leave thee til the next new Almanackes be out of date; let him threaten the sharpest weather he can in Saint *Swithin* week, or it snow on our Ladies face, ile not budge, ile be thy mid-wife til thou beest delivered of this passion.

Accut. Partake then, and give me the beleefe; thinkst thou or knowst thou any of this opinion, that that mooving marish element, that swels and swages as it please the Moone, to be in bignes equall to that solid lump that brings us up?

Gra. I was sure that thou wer't beyond the *Antipodes*; faith, I am of that faith I was brought up in, I have heard my Father say, and i'me sure, his Recordes came from his Father, that Land and Sea are in nature thus much alike; the owne [*sic*] growes by the Sunne, the other by the Moone, both by God's blessing, and the Sea rather the greater; and so thinke I.

Acut. Good; there we have a farther scope, and holde the sea can (as a looking glasse) answer with a meere simile[221] any mooving shape uppon the earth.

Gra. Nay, that's most certaine, I have heard of Sea-horses, Sea-calves, and Sea-monsters.

Acut. Oh, they are monstrous, madde, merrie, wenches, and they are monsters.

Grac.[222] They call them Sea-maides, or Mermaides, singing sweetelye, but none dares trust them; and are verie like our Land-wenches, devouring Serpents, from the middle downeward.

Acut. Thou hast even given me satisfaction, but hast thou this by proofe?

Grac. Not by my travels (so God helpe me): marrie, ile bring ye fortie Saylers, will sweare they have seene them.

Acut. In truth!

Grac. In truth or otherwise.

Acut. Faith they are not unlike our land-monsters, else why should this *Maximilian* Lord, for whom these shoots [*sic*] and noises befits thus, forsake his honours to sing a Lullabye?
These seeming Saints, alluring evils,
That make earth *Erebus*, and mortals devils--

Gra. Come, thou art Sea-sicke, and will not be well at ease, til thou hast tane a vomit: up with 't.

Acu. Why, ifaith, I must; I can not soothe the World
With velvet words and oyly flatteries,
And kiss the sweatie feet of magnitude
To purchace smiles or a deade mans office;
I cannot holde to see a rib of man,
A moytie of it selfe, commaund the whole;
Bafful and bend to muliebritie.
O[223] female scandal! observe, doe but observe:
Heere one walks ore-growne with weeds of pride,
The earth wants shape to apply a simile,
A body prisoned up with walles of wyer,
With bones of whales; somewhat allyed to fish,
But from the wast declining, more loose doth hang
Then her wanton dangling lascivious locke
Thats whirld and blowne with everie lustfull breath;
Her necke in chaines, all naked lyes her brest,
Her body lighter than the feathered Crest.
Another powtes, and scoules, and hangs the lip,
Even as the banckrout[224] credit of her husband
Cannot equal her with honors liverie.
What does she care if, for to deck her brave,
Hee's carryed from the Gate-house to his grave!
Another in a rayling pulppet key,
Drawes through her nose the accent of her voice,
And in the presence of her good-man Goate
Cries 'fye, now fye, uppon these wicked men
That use such beastly and inhumane talke,'
When being in private all her studies warne
To make him enter into *Capricorn*.
Another as she goes treads a *Canarie*[225] pace,
Jets it so fine and minces so demure
As mistris Bride upon her marriage day;
Her heels are Corke, her body Atlas,

Her Beautie bought, her soule an Atomus.
Another, with a spleene-devoured face,
Her eies as hollow as Anatomy,[226]
Her tung more venome then a Serpents sting,
Which when it wagges within her chap-faln jawes
Is noise more horrid then a cry of hounds
With open mouths pursuing of their game.
Wants she but ritch attire or costly dyet,
With her the Devill can nere live in quiet.
Yet these are weaker vessels, heaven doth knowe;
Lay on them ought but ease, you doe them wrong;
They are as weake as water and indeede as strong,
And then, like mightie ships when pellets sincke,
To them lay more men, sheele never shrinke.

[Enter[227] Getica and Boss, with a dog.]

Boss. Mistris, that face wants a fresh Glosse.

Gent. Prethee, dib it in well, *Bos*.

Acut. *Pigmaleon, Pigmaleon*, I coniure thee appeare; to worke, to worke, make more Marble Ingles. Nature thou art a foole, Art is above thee; *Belzebub*, paint thy face there's some will love thee.

Boss. Rare, Mistris, heeres a cheeke like a Camelion or a blasing Star, you shall heere me blaze it; heere's two saucers sanguine in a sable field pomegranet, a pure pendat ready to drop out of the stable, a pin and web argent in hayre de Roy.

Grac. And a fooles head in the Crest.

Bos. In the Crest? oh sweete Vermilion mistris, tis pittie the

Vermilion Wormes shoulde eate thee, ile set it with pretious stones and ye will.

Gent. Enough, sweete *Bosse*, throwe a little water to spurt's face and lets away.

Bo. Hold up; so, sir, now away. Oh Mistris, your scantling, most sweete mistriss, most derydent starre.

Acut. Then most rydent starre, faire fall ye.

Grac. Nay tis the Moone her self, for there's her man and her Dogge before.

Bosse. I, sir, but the man is not in the moone, and my bush is before me, *ergo*, not at my backe, *et ergo*, not moone sir.

Gent. What's your will sir?

Acut. That you would leave us.

Boss. Leave you! zounds, sir! we scorne their companies, come they are still, doe not open to them, we have no Conies to catch.

[Exeunt[228] Getica and Boss, with the dog.

Acut. Away, keepe no distance, even both together,
for wit ye may be Coacht together.
What sleeke-browde Saint can see this Idiotisme,
The shape and workmanship of omnipotency
To be so blinde with drugs of beastlinesse,
That will not bend the browe and bite the lippe,

Trouble his quiet soule with venome spleene
And feare least the all over-seeer
Can without vengeance see these ignomies?

Grac. Why, therfore are they belooved like Sargeants
and entertained like Beggers;
Think'st thou but any honorable Gate,
But will be shut against these Butterflies?

Acut. Oh *Graccus*! thou beguil'st opinion:
The Gates of great men stand more wide
To entertaine a foole then *Cresus* armes
To hug the Golden God; and faster bard
Against necessitie then *Dives* entrance
At *Olympus* gate.

   Enter Servulus,[229] Scillicet, Philautus and boy.

Servu.[230] Fa, la, sol, lasol; Boy, a Glasse.

Boy. Tis but one and all, sir.

Acut. Angels protect us, what have we heare?

Boy. Ye haue a good memorie, Sir, for they are five minutes ere windefall of your Glasse.

Ser. Sir, be credible, tis ballanst to be superlative politicke custome in these houres to dwell in shallowe accoutrements, as a defence for the abilitie of his pursse from the infringed Oath of some impudent face, that will borrowe a gentlemans revenewes if he be vestally adornd: Ile tell you sir by this bright Horrison--

Scil. A word, I pray yee, sir, ere ye go any further: Boy, my Tables.

Boy. Your Tables are ready, Sir, and all the men ye keep which is indeede halfe a Boy, **Scillicet Videlicet**.

Scil. I pray ye let me request that oath of you.

Serv. A graceful enquirie, and well observ'd: Sir, my company shall make ye copious of novelties, let your Tables befriend your memorie: write, 'by this bright Horrison.'

Phy. 'Here's[231] none but only I' [*sing*]; Boy, how likest thou my head of hayre?

Boy. Your Glasse may flatter ye, but truely I will not; your head is not a hayre better than it should be.

Phy. Is there any scarcitie of haire, Boy?

Boy. Somewhat thin and yet there is more hayre than wit.[232]

Phy. How, Boy?

Boy. Then wit of man can number sir, take it i'th right sence, I pray yee.

Phy. Most ingenious!

Acu. O muffle muffle, good **Graccus**, do not taint thy sence
With sight of these infectious animalles,
'Less[233] reason in thee have the upper hand

To governe sence, to see and shun the sight.
Here's new discovered sins, past all the rest;
Men strive to practice how to sweare the best.'

Scil. I have quoted it, sir; by this bright Hore, Horeson, pronounce ye, sir?

Serv. Horison!

Scil. Horison:--the Widowes mite, sir.

Serv. Not for the Soldans crown, sir.

Scil. Indeede yee shall, by this bright horison ye shall; beleeve me, if I sweare, I think myself beholding for I know it to be no common oath.

Serv. Were it common it past not these doores; Sir, I shift my oathes, as I wash my hands, twice in the artificial day; for in dialoguising, tis to be observ'd, your sentences, must ironically, metaphorically, and altogether figuratively, [be] mixt with your morning oathes.

Scil. Faith, tis verie true.

Accu. That he neither knowes what he saies nor thou understandest.

Serv. As for example, by this illuminate welkin.

Scil. Oh excellent! it shall be downe to.

Accut. There's another Ducket. He utters his oathes apace.
Sure this Villaine has no soule, and for gold

Heele damn his body too, hee's at peace with hell
And brings his Merchandise from thence to sell.

Boy. I have heere two Mistresses, but if the best were chosen out, if *Poliphemus* tother eye were out his choice might be as good as *Argus* broade waking, so difficult is the difference.

Phy. Boy, sleepe wayward thoughts?

Boy. Sir.

Phy. Is it not now most amyable and faire?

Boy. Yes sir, God be praised.

Phy. What meanst thou, Boy?

Boy. The weather, sir.

Phy. I meane my haire and face, Boy.

Boy. Twere amiable if it would not alter.

Phy. Wherfore I often repaire it.

Boy. Me thinkes that should weare it the sooner.

Phy. Not so Boy, for to trimme the Hayer well is a rare qualitie; to bee rarelye quallified is to be wise; apply, Boy.

Boy. That you are wise in trimming your hayre, Maister?

Phy. Right, to be wise is to be rare, for it is rare to see a wise man.

Boy. True, Maister, but if youle see a foole, looke in your Glasse, maister!

Phy. Goe to, I must correct you, Boy.

Boy. You can correct no more then is your own; I am but halfe yours to commaund, if you steale away any parte that is not your owne you are so farre in daunger as the striking of an other mans servant.

Scil.[234] By this illuminate welkin! most sincere and singular: as a small remembrance.

Serv. Not for to winne the faire *Angelica*.

Scillicet. By this illuminate Welkin ye shall now.[235] Sir, I doe not bestowe it, for that I thinke you have neede of it; for if you had, by this bright Horizon, I would not give it, for I know tis no credit to give to the poore. By this illuminate welkin I have (since I tooke upon me this fleshie desire of a Gentleman) throwne out of a window, for a hunts-up, when I had as leef have heard the grinding of a Mustard-Mill; for those are thinges are heere too day, and gone to morrowe; this will sticke by a man, and doe him credit where ere hee goes.

Acut. I, when the foole is clad in clay,
It will sticke sore unto thy soule for aye.

Phy. Signior *Scillicet*, I assure you I have discovered the most queint and new-found device for the encounter of the Ladies at the interview; tis in pricke-song.

Scil. That's excellent and rare.

Phi. I, for prick-song to Ladies is most pleasant and delightfull: as thus for your congie, All hayle to my belooved; then for your departure, sad dispaire doth drive me hence: for all must be to effect.

Grac. Nay, prethee raise no quarrels.

Acut. I can holde no longer: heare you, sir, are not you a foole? and you an Asse? and you a knave?

Phy. Zoundes! an Asse?

Scil. A Foole?

Ser. A Knave, without respect?

Acut. I, for an Asse can beare, a Foole abide, and a Knave deserve.

Omn. Helpe, Helpe!

Gra. Prethee let's away.

Acut. Fooles often brings wise men to trouble,
Farewell, another time ile pay ye double.
               [*Exit*.

   Enter Host, Hostesse, and Prentises.

Host. Bring your Clubs out of doores. There goe in, my fine hostes, Ile talke to the proudest; what, knaves are i'th streete, my dore is my dore, my house is my castell, goe in dame *Helena*, let thine Host alon with this; he that knocks at my hobby, while I have Ale in my house, shall pay for a Surgeon: the honest shall come in, the knaves shall go by; bring Clubs, I say.

Scil. Nay, sir, the heate is past, they that did it have tooke them to their heeles, for indeed heere are of us--

Host. Away with your Clubs then; welcome, my brave Bullies, my Guests shall take no wrong; but welcome, my Bullies.

Scil. Indeede sir, I am a man of few words, I have put up a little bloodshed; marrie, I hope it shall be no stain to my manhoode, if I keepe it out of my clothes.

Host. He shall pay for the blood-shed, my guestes shall take no wrong; mine Host will spend his Cruse as franke as an Emperor; welcome, my brave bullies.

Ser. Sir, be pacificall, the fellowe was possest with some critique frenzie, and wee impute it to his madnes.

Scil. Madde! by Gods slid, if he were as madde as a weaver, I can hardly put it up; for my blow, I care not so much, but he cald me foole; slid, if I live till I dye, the one of us shall prove it.

Host. Some prophane Villaine, ile warrant him.

Scil. Doe you thinke I may not have an action against him?

Host. There's so many swaggerers; but alasse, how fel ye out?

Scil. By the welkin, I gave him not a foule word; first he calles me foole, then he makes a full blowe at my body, and if, by good chance, I had not warded it with my head, he might have spoild me.

Enter Prentices.

Host. There, there my fine fil-pots; give the word as you passe; anon, anon, sir anon; heere and there in the twinckling, looke well at the barre, there again my little Mercuries, froath them up to the brimme, and fill as tis needeful; if their Pates be full of Wine let your Pottles be three quarters; trip and goe, here and there; now, my brave Lad, wash thy woundes with good Wine; bidde am welcom, my little Sybil; put sugar in his hole there, I must in to my guests; sleepe soundly till morning; Canarie is a Jewell, and a Figge for Browne-bastard.[236]
[*Exit*.

Hostes. Gentlemen, ye are welcom, though my husband be a little talkative, yet truly he is an unreasonable honest man, yee shall finde his words and his sayings all one.

Scil. I thinke no less, yet I would desire to enter as time and place shall serve.

Hostes. Ile lead the way forsooth.

Phy. Nay, pray ye, Hostesse, a word. I say little, but i'me sure I have sustained the most wrong; by this light, I had rather he had broke my head in three places; I pray you lend me a brush, hee has put my hat quite out of fashion.

Host. That shall ye sir, a brush there, hoe!

Enter[237] Boss, with the dog.

Bos. Salve, sis salvus. I pray yee which of you five is Hostis of this house?

Boy. That's easily discernd, for foure weare breeches.

Bos. Nere the sooner for that, my diminitive youth, for women now adaies weare breeches as well as men; mary, the difference lies in the bawble.

Hostis. Well, sir, to open the truth, I am the Hostesse.

Bos. The fruit is known, by the Tree at the first view, as the Author writes, learnedly; come ***basilus manus***.[238]

Scil. This kissing becomes a Gentleman, ile use it sure.[239]

Bos. Secondly, Mistris Hostesse, I would know what lodging ye have for my Lady and her traine.

Hostis. What will serve your turne, sir?

Bos. Ile call my selfe to account and specifie thus: my Lady and her Dogge, that's two visible; then there's the Dogge and my Lady, thats four invisible; then there's my Ladies dogge and I, quoth the dogge, that's six; then theres sequence of three, viz., the Dogge, and I, and my Lady; then there's a pair of Knaves, viz., the Dogge & my selfe & my Lady turnd up; viz., my Lady sequence of three, a paire of Knaves and my Lady, turn'd up to play upon:--we can have no less than five beds.

Hostis. Truely you must lye close together (the Servants I meane), for I am so thrust with Guest I [c]an hardly spare so many.

Bos. Faith, weele lie together as close as we can; there's my Lady and her dogge lye al together and I at the bed's feete, and theres all our family of Love.[240]

Hostis. How farre is your mistris behinde?

Bos. The truth is the fatall sisters have cut the thred of her Cork-shoe, & shee's stept aside in to a Coblers shop to take a true stitch, whether I mean to send myself as a Court of Guard to conduct her, but see, oh inconstant fortune! see where she comes, *solus*.

   Enter[241] Getica.

Gent. *Bos*, you serve me well, to let me wait upon my selfe.

Bos. Of two evils, the least is to be chosen, I had a care of your puppie being less then your selfe.

Scil. Gentlewoman, you have an excellent Ch: [sic] I have an appetite as a man would say.

Gent. Whats your will, sir?

Scil. Truth will to light, and the truth is I have an appetite to kisse you.

Phil. This point would become a Gentleman, sure; I pray, who trim'd it so?

Gent. My man, forsooth.

Phy. Sir, I desire your acquaintance; tis excellent, rare.

Gent. You would have said so, had you seene it an houre since.

Ser. Heeres game for me! I hunt for fooles and have sprung a covey.

Hostis. Gentles, please you, draw neere? lead the way into the chambers.

Bos. *Bos* is the name of a thing may be seene, felt, heard, or understood, and the nominative case goes before my Mistris the Verbe; my mistris requires an accusative case to follow, as usus feminae proptus facit.
   [*Exeunt al but Hostis*.

Hostis. Oh fye upont, who would be an hostis, & could do otherwise? [A] Ladie [h]as the most lascivious life, conges and kisses, the tyre, the hood, the rebato, the loose bodyed Gowne, the pin in the haire, and everie day change, when an Hostis must come and go at everye mans pleasure. And what's a Lady more then another body? Wee have legs, and hands, rowling eyes and hanging lips, sleek browes, and cherie cheeks & other things as Ladies have, but the fashion carries it away.

   Prentices passe over. [Re-enter[242] Host.]

Host. There, there, my little Lacky boies, againe, again, my fine fil-pots! where is my fine Hostis? come, come, my little *Dido*, set your corks on a creaking, my knaves are unthrifty; dance not your Canaries heere up & down, looke about to my Guests I say.

Hostis. I, I have much joy, an Hostesse!

Host. What, abides my *Penelope*? heere stand[s] thy *Ulisses*, ile tarry with thee still, thou shall want for no cost. Ile buy thee a brave wistle; looke about to my Guestes, I say.

Hostis. I, Hostesses will bee knowne shortelye as their Signes; still in one weather-beaten suite, as though none weare hoodes but Monkes and Ladies, and feathers but fore-horses and Waiting Gentlewomen, or chaines but prisoners and Courtiers; no Perywigges but Players and Pictures: but the weakest must to the wall still.

Host. Tush, tush, these are toies; ile none of these Flipflaps, ile have no soping, no puffs, nor no Cobwebs, no busks, nor bumbarrels;[243] thou shalt weare thine own haire & fine cloath of Sheep-skins, thy colour shall be Dowlas as white as a Lillie, ile kisse these chop-cheries; thou shalt goe Gossip at Shrovetide; look about to my Guests then.   [*Exit*.

Hostis. I, twas my hard fortune to be an Hostesse; time was I might have done other wise.

   Enter Cittizens Wife.

City W. Why how now, woman, a'th olde disease still? will it never be better? cannot a Woman finde one kinde man amongst twentie? Ah the daies I have seen, when a Womans will was a lawe: If I had a mind to such a thing, or such a thing, I could have had it, but twa's never better since men were Purse-bearers.

Hosty. Mine is een the unnaturallist man to his Wife.

Citie wi. Truely, and commonly are all such fat men: ile tell thee, Gossip, I have buried sixe, I, sixe husbands, but if I should live to have as many more, as I know not what may happen, but sure Ide never have such a fatte man: they be the most unweldey men; that woman[244] shall not want a sore stomack, that's troubled with them I warrant her.

Hosty. And hee maintaines me heare like I knowe not what.

City wi. I, and what say, they are their wives head; well if he be the head, shee's the body, and the body is to beare the head, and the body is to beare the pursse.

Hostis. They cannot misse us, yet they regard us not.

Citty wife. Misse us! no faith, but would all women were of my minde, they call us weaker vessels, they should finde vessels of us, but no weake vessels, I warrant them.

   Enter[245] Prentice.

Pren. Mistris, my Maister cals for ye.

Hostis. Goe, ile come anon, hees not so hastie to give me what I want, I warrant ye.

      [Exit[245] Prentice.

City w. No, would he were; little thinkes the husband what goes through the wives hand, washing, wringing, and rubbing, up early, down late, & a thousand things they looke not too.

Hostis. And yet they must have the government of all.

City w. And great reason they have for it, but a wise man will put in a Woman's hand: what sheele save that hee spends.

Hostis. You have a pretty Ruffe, how deepe is it?

City w. Nay, this is but shallowe, marrie I have a Ruffe is a quarter deepe, measured by the yard.

Hostis. Indeede, by the yard.

City w. By the standard: you have a pretty set too, how big is the steele you set it with?

Hostis. As bigge as a reasonable sufficient--

Enter Prentice.

Pren. Mistris, my Maister would desire you to come in.

Citty w. What? she shall not come yet: if you lay down the bucklers, you lose the victorie.

Hostis. By my troth, I must goe, we shall have such a coyle else.

Cittie w. A coyle! why, have you not a tongue in your head? faith if ye win not all at that weapon, yee are not worthy to be a woman. You heare not the news abroade?

Hostis. No: what newes?

City W. No, I warrant ye, you never come abroad; this is to be troubled with a fatte man, he never comes abroad himself nor suffers his wife out of his sight: yee shall ever have a fatte Host either on his bench at the dore or in his chair at the chimney; & there he spits and spaules a roome like twentie Tobacco-takers. Oh! fye on them, beasts!

Hostis. I prethee, what newes?

Citty w. Oh! woman, the most hardfavoured newes, and without all conscience: they say theres a statute made, any woman that buries her husband is not to marrie againe of two monthes after.

Hostis. A tedious time, by Lady; a month were enough.

Cittie w. I, halfe a month; winter nights are long and colde. Ile tell ye, I have buried sixe, and thank my good fortune I ever knewe the next ere the other was in his winding sheete.

Pre. Mistris, my maister is angrie, and the Guests cal for their Hostesse.

Hostis. Goe, I come: Gossip, when shall I see you agen?

Citty w. Nay, when shall I see you abroad? sildome, i'me sure.

Hostis. I must needes away; God buy you, Gossip.

Cittie w. God buy ye; Gods so, I have forgot wherefore I came: a word ere you goe, the party yee wott on commends him unto ye, he that met the other party in the white felt, the yellow scarf, and the round *Venetian*,[246] when the other party kis't you, and I broake the jest on him, when hee said kisses kindeles Coules and love searches.

Hostis. Oh! I remember him, yes faith, hee's prettie well set; hee ha's the right trick with the tongue in his kisse, and hee dances reasonably comely, but he fals heavie.

Citty w. He savours of a kinde of Gallant, but not of a Courtyer.

Hostis. Well weele have a night out, god be with ye, Gossip.

Cittie wife. God buy ye.

[*Exeunt*.

[ACT THE SECOND.

Scene 1.]

    Enter Lentulus and Tulley.

Lentu. Not yours nor her owne, ***Terentia***.--Yours in modestie, ***Flavia***.
See, ***Tulley***, what an active passive love hath plaide;
I love and am again beloved, but at the shrine
Where I do offer up my Cordiall sacrifice,
I am returnd with peremptorie scorne;
And where I stand but as a gazer, viewing
All alike, I am pursude
With violent passions, a speaking eye
Bindes favours and now discovering lines.[247]
Thy counsell now, deere friend; for at thy direction
Stands my thrall or freedome.

Tul. Oh my Lord, affection is unlimited,
Daring all dangers, having no tipe nor figure,
Beyond all arte.
Then tye not that (Great Lord,) to ***Tullies*** awe;

Fancy forswears all reason, love all lawe.

Lent. How well thy power can shun that which
I followe with obedience. Too true yfaith;
Thou mightst as well put out the eie of day,
Or cover sinne from heaven, or to erect
A towre of sand on the uncertain surge,
Or any thing that were more inficient,
Then to remoove one doting thought of mine
From her disdain. Thy aide, deere *Tulley*,
Be thou an Orratour for *Lentulus*,
My tongue stands tun[e]d to a harsher method;
Breath in her eares, those Organs of receite,
A quintessence distild of honny words,
And charme with a beguiling lullabye
Her free consent to thine and my request:
Which done, thats done which is my sole delight,
Which done, thats done that I can never quite.

Tull. All which to me are problematique mines,
Obscurde inigmaes, and to my studies
Incognite Language; yet, if my powers
Have power to cloath my tongue in love,
Ile be a Lover and in love so pleade
As if that *Tully* loved *Terentia*.

Lent. Thanks, sweete *Cicero*;
This day we dine with olde *Flaminius*,
The forward Father of my Aukeward love.
His willing minde doth strive to make the peace
Betwixt our discord thoughts; his free consent
Is given to *Lentulus*; there, *Tulley*, take on holde,
And, when a Sunne of thy intent shines fayre,

Onset loves fort with polliticke assaults
And conquer; conquest in obtaining that
Where victors are repulsed. But see! our talke
Hath over-tane our way; see, olde *Flaminius*
Comes to welcome us.
With him a looke like[248] the bright orient verge
At the uprising of *Auroraes* shine.

Enter Flaminius, Terentia, and Flavia.

Flam. And, my good Lorde, y'are happily met. Heartily welcome; young *Tullie*, welcome to; yee come wel to ease my charge, these Ladies find fault with their Guardian, I goe too softly for them: old blood is stiffe, & young Ladies will not beare with age; I resigne, I resigne, to you that followe.

Lent. If they admit us for their Guardian,
Weele dare dangers ere we part from them.

Flam. Why well saide, my Lords, Soldiers will not flye indeede; I have seene the day, I could have crackt a tree of yew, made my bowstring whisper in mine eare in[249] the twang, tost my pike lustilye. Tis since the siedge of *Parthia*: bith-'mas a great while; I was lustie then at the service was done there, yet I love the discourse. Come my Lord, I chuse your companye, leave *Tulley* to the Ladies; he can tell them tales of *Venus* and *Adonis* and that best pleaseth them. Now I must heere of raps and blowes, and Bils and Guns, and swords and bucklers. I loved it once; come, our Cookes are backeward, discourse will beget stomacks; y'are like to tarrie long for leane Cates.   [*Exit*.

Lent. Now, gentle *Tulley*, advocate my suite;
Her fore-amazing person makes me mute.

Cicero. He beare these Ladies company if they
Shall deeme acceptance.   [*Exit*.

Teren. With interest of thankes to Cicero.

Flav. Faith, I like not this ods of female, an equallitie were better: yet of both twere fitter the woman should undergoe the oddes. I had rather a said three men to one woman, then two women to one man. Heeres *Tulley* addrest to *Terentia, Terentia* drawing neere to *Tulley*; her's smal comfot [*sic*] left for *Flavia*. Wel, gentles, ile leave ye to the Goddesse. So ho! my Lords, take me with ye.

Teren. Nay stay, good *Flavia*. Youle not loose the sight of *Lentulus*.

Fla. Nor you of *Tulley*; come, if you tel, ile blab.

Cice. But, sweete Lady, *Tulley* is not heere.

Fla. But *Cicero* is, his neere friend, thats as good.

Cice. He was, Lady, till hee changed his habit by putting on the office of an unskillful Servingman, intending to garde *Terentia* to her father's house.

Fla. Then *Flavia* must gard her self; wel use good words and good action, and stalke well before your Ladie; she's kinde, yfaith, and a little thing will please her.

Ter. Will it please *Flavia* to partake?

Fla. Oh fye! twere an injurie I could [not] brook myself, therefore ile leave ye; but be breefe, stand not on pointes, cut them all first; & if ye fall to kissing, kisse not too long for feare ye kisse the post.

Teren. Goe to, youle still be a wagge, *Flavia*.
But what saies *Tulley* to *Terentia*?

[*Exit*[250] *Flavia*.

Cicero. Lady I must maintain my former argument.
Tullie's not heere but heere is *Tullies* friend;
For, ere I speake, I must intreate you wil
Transforme poore *Tulley* into *Lentulus*.

Teren. I have no power of Metamorphosing;
If *Tulley* be not heere, you must concede,[251]
I cannot make of *Tulley Lentulus*.

Cice. Nor can the world make *Cicero* so worthy.
Yet for an houre['s] discourse a Pesant's shape
May represent the person of a king;
Then in the person of the great *Lentulus*
I doe salute Sunne-bright *Terentia*.
Lady, vouchsafe a Saint-like smile on him
(From that angell forme) whose honord minde
Lies prostrate lowly at *Terentia's* feete;
Who hath put off a Golden victors honour
And left the *Parthyan* spoyle to *Lepido*;
Whome many Ladies have bedecked with favours
Of rich esteeme, oh proud he deignd to weare them,
Yet guiftes and givers hee did slight esteeme;
For why? the purpose of his thoughts were bent

To seek the love of faire *Terentia*.
The cho[i]ce is such as choiser cannot bee
Even with a nimble eye; his vertues through
His smile is like the Meridian Sol
Discern'd a dauncing in the burbling brook;
His frowne out-dares the Austerest face
Of warre or Tyranny to sease upon;
His shape might force the Virgine huntresse
With him for ever live a vestall life;
His minde is virtues over-matcht, yet this
And more shall dye if this and more want force
To win the love of faire *Terentia*.
Then, gentle Lady, give a gentle do[o]me;
Never was brest the Land-lord to a heart
More loving, faithful, or more loyall then is
The brest of noble--

Teren. *Tullie*!

Tul. *Lentulus*!

Ter. And why not *Tullie*?

Tul. It stands not aptly.

Tere. I wants a sillible.

Tul. It doth.

Tere. Then noble *Cicero*.

Tul. Thats too deere.

Tere. Gentle is as good:
Then say the best of gentle ***Cicero***.

Tul. Good Lady, wrong not your honour so
To seate unworthy ***Tully*** with your worth.
Oh looke upon the worth of ***Lentulus***,
Let your faire hand be beame unto the ballance
And with a stedded peyze lift up that beame.
In th'one[252] scale put the worth of ***Lentulus***,
His state, his honors, and his revenewes;
Against that heavy waite put povertie,
The poore and naked name of ***Cicero***,
A partner of unregarded Orators;
Then shall you see with what celeritie
One title of his worth will soone pull up
Poore ***Tullies*** dignitie.

Tere. Just to the height of ***Terentias*** heart
Where I will keepe and Character that name,
And to that name my heart shall adde that love
That shall wey downe the worth of ***Lentulus***.

Tul. Deare Madam.

Tere. Speake still, if thou wilt, but not for him;
The more thou speak'st the more augments my love,
If that thou can'st adde more to infinite;
The more thou speakest the more decreaseth his,
If thou canst take away ought from nothing;
Thinke, ***Tulley***, if ***Lentulus*** can love me,
So much and more ***Terentia*** doth love thee.

Tull. Oh Madam,
Tulley is poore, and poore is counted base.

Ter. Vertue is ritch and blots a poore disgrace.

Tul. *Lentulus* is great, his frowne's my woe,
And of a friend he will become my foe.

Ter. As he is friend, we will intreate his love;
As he is great, his threatenings shall not make me love.

Tul. Your fathers graunt makes *Lentulus* your Lord.

Teren. But if thereto his daughter not accord,
That graunt is cancel'd; fathers may commaund
Life before love, for life to true love's paund.

Tul. How will *Flaminius* brooke my povertie?

Ter. Well, when *Flaminius* see's no remedie.
Lord how woman-like are men when they are woe'd!
Tully, weigh me not light, nere did immodest blush
Colour these cheeckes, but ardent.

Tully. Silence, sweet Lady, heere comes *Flavia*.

   Enter[253] *Flavia*.

Fla. Fie, Fie, how tedius ye are; yonders great looking for *Tulley*, the old senate has put on his spectacles, and *Lentulus* and he are turning the leaves of a dog-hay [?], leaves of a worm-eaten Chronicle, and they want *Tullies* judgment.

Tul. About what, sweet Lady?

Fla. To know what yeare it was the showers of raine fell in Aprill.

Tul. I can resolve it by rote, Lady, twas that yeare the Cuckoo sung in May: another token Lady; there raigned in Rome a great Tyrant that yeare, and many Maides lost their heads for using flesh on Fish-daies.

Fla. And some were sacrificed as a burnt offering to the Gods of Hospitallitie, were they not?

Tul. Y'are a wag, *Flavia*, but talk and you must needes have a parting blowe.

Flav. No matter so we stand out and close not.

Tull. Or part faire at the close and too't again.

Flav. Nay, if we should too't againe, *Terentia* would growe jealous.

Tul. Ladies, I take my leave
And my love.

Ter. Take heede ye sigh not, nor looke red at the table, *Tully*.

[Exit [Tully].

Flav. Your shoe wrings you, Lady.

Ter. Goe to, ye are a wanton, *Flavia*.

Fla. How now *Terentia*, in your nine Muses?
Theres none must pleade in your case but an Orator.

Ter. I want one indeede Wench, but thou hast two, and the gentle destinies may send thee three; neere blush, for smoke and the fire of a womans love cannot bee hid. Oh a fine tongue dipt in *Helicon*! a comedian tongue is the onely perswasive ornament to win a Lady; why his discourse is as pleasant--

Fla. As how, I prethee?

Ter. And keepes as good decorum; his prologue with obedience to the skirt; a rough Sceane of ciuill Warres and a clapping conclusion; perhappes a Jigge;[254] if not, the Tragicomicall tale of *Mars* and *Venus*; then must she take the Tale by the end, where he defending *Mars*, & she *Venus*, must fall from billing to byting, from byting to blowes, to get the supremacie.

Fla. A good policie to praise *Cicero*,
For feare I rob you of your *Lentulus*.

Ter. Faith, a Souldier is not for thy[255] humor; now I crie a Warrier; he fights stoutly in a field-bed, discharges his work sure, under his Curtaines would I fight. But come, our Lovers melt while we meditate; thou for thy Scholler, I for my soldier; and if we can not please them so, weele shake off this loose habit and turn Pages to suit their humors.

[*Exeunt*.

[Scene 2.]

Enter Accutus and Graccus.

Grac. Come, **Accutus**, discharge your follower; lets leave rubbing a while, since the byas runs so much the wrong way. Sirra! these bowles which we roule and turn in our lower sypher are by use made wodden worldlings right, for every one strives who shall lye neerest the mistris.[256]

Ac. They post indeed, as their nature is, in an even way, but they are cowards, theile abide no danger, they rub at everie mole-hil; if they tyre in going up a hill, they retire and come back againe.

Grac. Well let them alley, bet all, then to rest away, begone.

Acut.[257] S'foote **Graccus**, heeres a couple of our old gamsters. Oh! for quick conceite to beget a jest! heeres two, that either a man must be aquainted or quarrell with, & of two evils ile chose the latter; I hope I make it the lesser. If I should be acquainted, the foole will haunt me, if I quarrell I may be so blest, as to be rid of a foole.

Grac. I have a womans wit for a suddaine stratageme.

Enter Scil. and Servulis.[258]

Scil. No, by my troth, by this bright horrison--

Accut. An excellent Cuckoo, hee keepes his note in Winter.

Scil. I haue no appetite at all to live in the countrie any more; now, as they say, I have got a smacke on the Cittie. Slid, I thinke (as the proverbe goes) I was wrapt in my mother's smocke the day I was begotten, I thank the Goddesse *Cupid* for it. I am so favourd of the Women, my hostes loves me execrably.

Accut. Good reason, fooles make good sport.

Grac. Sever, sever, ere wee bee discovered.

Ser. Sir, the respective regard of your well governed partes do challenge a mellifluous species of enduement or contumelious estimation.

Grac. Gentles, God save ye, well over-taken Gallants.

Scil. Welcome, by the welkin.

Grac. This is verie pleasant weather.

Ser. Sir the ayre is frugall.

Grac. Is that Gentleman of your Company?

Scil. Our company sir, no, we are no companions for lame Souldiers.

Grac. Propper man, pittie he is so regardles. A good legge, it seemes he has some greefe in it.

Scil. Nay, and he be lame, ile talke to him; there's so many lustie knaves walkes now a daies will not sticke to give a man hard words, if he be not disposed to charitie. Harke ye sir, I understand ye are a propper man, and that you have a good legge.

Accut. And what of that, Sir?

Scil. What of that! slid, he answers me like a sturdie beggar alreadie! by the five elements, or sences, I aske ye for no hurt, ile bestowe my charitie as franke as--

Acut. Stoope and looke out, zounds a Gentleman cannot come by a misfortune in service or so, but everie foole wil ride him. Take that.
[*Exit*.

Gra. Sirra, stay, ile combat thee in his defence.

Serv. Sir, be pacifical, the impotent must be lightly regarded.

Grac. Give me leave Gentlemen, ile follow him.

Scil. Nay, I pray you be malcontented, I have no great hurt, but in revenge hee's a rascall for using me so; he may thank God, discretion governed me, tis wel known I have always bene a man of peace; ile not strike yee the least mouse in anger, nor hurt the poorest Conney that goes in the street, for I know of fighting comes quarrelling, of quarrelling comes brawling, and of brawling growes hard words, and as the learned *puerelis*[259] writes, tis good sleeping in a whole skin.

Grac. Sir, your discretion shall governe me at this time. Your name, I pray ye sir?

Scil. My name is signior *Scillicet*.

Grac. Even so sir? nay, sir, I doe not forget your Argument.

Enter Accutus.

Acut. Save ye, sir, saw ye not a Gentleman come this way even now, somewhat hurt in one of his Legges?

Scil. He went by even now, sir; is he a friend of yours?

Acu. A deare friend, and a propper Gentleman, sir.

Scil. By the horison hee's a propper man indeede, he gave me the time of day as he went by, I have a gallon of wine for him at any time. If ye see anything in me worth Commendations, I pray ye commend me to him.

Acut. I will sir;--twere best you gave me good words, but ile trie ye farther yet;--fare ye well, sir.

Scil. I pray you remember me to him.--You see my anger is over already.   [Exit[260] Acutus.

Grac. Would ye not strike him? lets followe.

Scil. Indeede ye shall not, I hate it.

Ser. I will not be barren of my armorie, in my future perambulation for the lower element.

Grac. You are too patient in wrongs, sir.--Zoundes I know not how to picke a quarrell.

Serv. Sir, the grievous youth is inwardlye possest of a supple spirit, he can brooke impugnying, but tis adverse to my spirit if I were armed.

   Enter Accutus.

Accut. Save ye, gallants, sawe ye not a fellowe come halting this way of late?

Scil. Hath he done any hurt, or is hee a friend of yours?

Acut. Hee's a Rascall and ile maintaine him so.

Scil. Hee's a verie Rascall indeede, and he used mee like a knave: if ere I meete him, I shall hardly put it up; I have it in blacke and blue to shew heere.

Serv. Say, I breath defyance to his front.

Acut. Challenge him the field.

Scil. Doos't thinke heele answere me? I'l challenge him at the pich-fork, or the Flaile, or ile wrastle a fall with him for a bloody nose; anye weapon I have bene brought up in ile--

Accut. What will ye? heere he is, you minime, that will be friend with friends and foe with foes; and you that will defie *Hercules*, and out-brave *Mars* and feares not the Devil; passe, bladder, ile make ye swell.

Scil. By Gods-lid, if I had knowne it had bene you, I would not have said so to your face.
    [*Exeunt.*

Accut. Away, with your Champion, goe.

Grac. This was excellentlye performed, ifaith a better breathing then a game at bowles.

Accut. Theile give you the good salve at any time this month, for I am sure they have salving enough for so long.

Grac. I pittie the foole yfaith, but the tother Horseleach I wish his blowes trebled. I converst with him, but a Rogue so stuft with the lybrary of new minted[261] words, so tearing the sence, I never met with.

Accut. But now we have spoilde our determinate dinner at my hostesse of the Hobbye; we shall nowe bee knowne.

Grac. That holds well still, I am taken for a prooved friend, and thou shalt be disguised, till, I have wrought a league by vertue of a pottle of Canarie.

Acut. Content, mine Host shall be accessarie and ile be a serviter to observe myracles.

Grac. They are good subjects for idle houres:--but soft, what second course is entring heere?

   Enter Phy., Bos, and Boy.

Phy. **For I did but kisse her;** *Bos*, how lik'st thou my relish?

Bos. Oh sir, relish but your licour, as you doe your song, you may goe drunke to bed any day in the weeke.

Phy. **Sister**,[262] **awake, close not, &c**. Does my face hold colour still?

Bos. I, and you would but scaviage the pavilion of your nose.

Gra. I, marrie, *Accutus*, how lik'st thou this Gentlewoman Gallant?

Accut. A good states-man, for common-wealth of Brownists; the Rogue hates a Church like the Counter.

Gra. I, and if my Ladie Argentile were dead, he wold rather live upon almes then fall to worke.

Accut. So he might have tolleration.--What, shal's close with them?

Gra. In any case, but in some mild imbrace, for if we should continue thus rough, we should be shunned like an Appoplex.

Accut. Gallants, the fortune of the day runs with ye: what all at mumchance?[263] how is't? how is't?

Phy. Sir, I think twas you bestowed some abuse of me tother day.

Accu. Which I would wipe out of your memorie
With satisfaction of a double courtesie.

Phy. I accept it ifaith, sir, I am not prone to anger, I assure ye the following night knew not my anger. Your acquaintance, Signior.

Gra. Fye, without ceremony lets yoake this triplicity as we did in the daies of olde, with mirth and melody.

Phy. I, say you? so then *Coll*[264] her and clip her and kisse her, too, &c.

Bos. The triplicitie! heere's those has supt at an ordinarie.

Accu. This gallant humors.

Gra. But the other walkes aloofe.

Bos. The triplicite! heere's those has crackt glasses and drawn blood of a Tapster.

Gra. The visitation of your hand, sir.

Bos. The Triplicitie! will colours change?

Acut. Sir, take no offence, I beseech ye, we gave onlye satisfaction for an olde injurie, but in the degree of amitie your selfe sits in the superlative.

Bos. No sir, but in respect.

Gra. What kinde is your Dogge of, sir?

Bos. Verie kinde to anything but his meat, that hee devours with great alacritie.

Grac. Where was he bred?

Bos. In a Bitch.

Gra. What Countrie?

Bos. A kind of Mungrill, he will carrie but not fetch, marrie hee is to be put to a dauncing schoole for instruction.

Acut. The tricke of the rope were excellent in him, & that ile teach him, if I misse not my mark. Come, Gallants, we waste time, the first Taverne we arrive at weel see the race of an houre-glasse.

Phy. Can ye a part in a Song?

Gra. Verie tollerably.

Phy. Weele have a catch then, if with sol, sol, la: Gentlemen have you any good herbe? you have match, boy.

Boy. Your pipe shall want no fire sir.

Acut. Oh, without ceremony: now, *Graccus*, if we can but pawne their senses in Sack and Sugar, let mee alone to pursue the sequell.

Gra. Follow it away.

[*Exeunt*.

[*Scene* 3.]

Enter Hostis, Cittizens wife, Servulus, and Scillicet.

Hostis. Come, come, bring them out of the ayre: alas good hearts, what rogorous villaine would commit with him? ile tell ye Gosip, hee's eene as kinde an animall, he would not wrong them y'faith.

Citty wife. Tush, feare nothing woman, I hope to make him so again. Alacke, alacke, how fell you out all a head?[265] Oh Butcher! are ye hurt in another place?

Hostis. Did he not throw you against the stones? If he did, doe not conceale, I dare say you gave them not a foule word.

Scil. By the illuminate welkin not a word till my mouth was full of blood, and so made my words foule.

Citty wife. Is not this Gentleman hurt too?

Serv. Onelye the extravagant Artire[266] of my arme is brused.

Cittie wi. See, see, the extravagant of his arme is brused to. Alas, how could ye quarrell so?

Serv. I will demonstrate: in the defence of the generous youth I did appugne my adverse, let violently flie.

Cittie wife. Ah good hearts! would I had stood between you, when he let flie so violently.

Ser. We voide of hostile armes.

Hostis. I, if they had had horses, they had sav'd their armes.

Serv. Be capable, I meane, void of armorie.

Citty-wife. Untill ye had armor on.

Serv. Had I bene accompanied, with my Toledo or morglay.[267]

Cittie wife. I, your Dogge or Bitch.

Serv. Continue, I beseech, I meane my sword, sole lye my sword.

Cittie wife. Or solely your sword, better a bad toole then none at all.

Serv. In the concourse--

Cittie w. Nay, the concourse will light on him for it, I warrant.

Serv. I, for the tuition of my Capitall, did mount my Semisphere, three degrees, that as a strong, & stony guard did defend my Capitall.

Citty w. Twas well ye kept him out, for if he had entered on your stony Guard, he would have spoilede your Capitall.

Serv. In fine, being mortally assaild, he did preambulate [*sic*] or walk off.

Scil. Yes, faith, he did preambulate, and walke mee finely.

Cittie w. Good heartes, how many were there of them?

Serv. About the number of seaven.

Scil. I, there was seaven.

Serv. Or eight.

Scil. Or eight.

Serv. Rather more.

Citty w. I, more at least, I warrant ye.

Hostis. Alasse ye cannot chuse but be more hurt, but ile search you throughly, be assured.

Citty w. And if she cannot helpe ye fewe can; shee knowes what belongs to a Tent,[268] or a bruse, and experience is good in those cases.

Serv. I have a concupiscent forme of trust in your skil, it will malladise.

Citty wi. I, feare not, put both your concupisences in me for that matter.

Serv. The generous will disburse coynage for satisfaction of your metaphisicall endevour.

Scil. Yes, yes, I will discharge all.

Cittie wife. Wee make no doubt of that; come into a chamber, ye shall lye downe awhile; perhaps youle bee stiffe anon, then you shall use your legges, the more you strive with it the better. Alas, good hearts!

[*Exeunt*.

Phy. Sol, sol, la! Tapster, give attendance! Gentlemen, I hope all we are friends, the welkin is skie colour still, and men must grow by degrees; you must pardon me, I must sp--speak my minde.

Grac. The uttermost of your minde at this time cannot be offensive.

Phy. *The fryer was in the*--sol, sol, draw the tother quart. I hope you are not angrie gallants; and ye come to my lodging, ye shall be welcome; my Hostes shall bid you welcome, shee's a good wench; if I say the word, she wil fa--fullfill it.

Acut. Sirra drawer, for the other thats a sleepe; let him so remaine; for the Dog, let him be bound to a post for his appearance, till I take order for his undooing.

Draw. The foole and the Dogge shall both take rest at your commaund, Sir.

Phy. Gentlemen, I hope we are all friends: sol, sol, shal's have a catch?

Grac. I, come, come, everie one catch a part.   [*Sing*.

Phy. Hey good boies ifaith, now a three man's song, or the olde downe a downe; well things must be as they may, fils the other quart; muskadine,[269] with an egg is fine, there's a time for all things. **Bonos nocthus**.[270]   [*Sleepe*.

Grac. Good night to you sirs.

Accut. So now, *Graccus*, see what a polluted lumpe,
A deformed *Chaos* of unsteddy earth
Man is, being in this ill kinde unmand seeming somthing
Bestial man, brutish animall. Well tis thus decreede,
He shall be what he seemes, that's deade.

For what in him shows life but a breathing ayre?
Which by a free constraint it self ingenders
In things without life, as twixt a pair of bellowes
We feele a forcible aire, having of it self
Force and being, no more is this breathing block
But for his use in kinde.--Give out in some bursse or congregation
Among the multitude *Philautus*[271] death.
Let all the customarie rights of funerall,
His knell or what else, be solemnly observed.
Ile take order for his winding sheete,
And further, to furnish it with further suertie,
Ile have a potion that for twentie houres
Shall quench the motion of his breath. Goe, spread,
Let me alone to effect it.

Gra. Ile sow it, I warrant thee; thou talkst of bursse,--I have a way worth ten on't, ile first give it out in my Barbers shop, then at my ordinarie, and that's as good as abroad; and as I cross *Tiber* my waterman shall attach it, heele send it away with the tide, then let it come out to an Oyster wenches eare, and sheele crie it up and down the streetes.

Acut. Let's first secure him from eyes, and at night he shall be portered to our chamber; so, now away.

Grac. Oh a couple that would spred rarely,[272] lets give it for loves sake.

   Enter Hostis and Cittizens wife.

Acut. Call, call.

Grac. Hem, hem.

Citty wife. A pox on your hemmings, do you think we care for your hemmings?

Hostis. Tis some stinking troublesome knave, I warrant ye.

Citty wife. Hang him, regard him not; theres hemming indeede, like a Cat, God blesse us, with a burre in her throate.
                                        [*Exeunt*

Grac. S'hart, how we are ript up for this?

Ac. Oh man, this hemming is the most hatefulst thing, theres not the most publique punck,[273] nor worm-eaten bawd that can abide it, and honestie would run madde to heare it. But come we waste time, tis now about the mid of day; we must sowe arithmatike by the houres, that at[274] the morrowes highth ***Philautus*** awake again, at which time he shall be on his Hearse, and all the Guestes of the Hobbye invited to accompany his ghost, when being awake, himselfe and all shall see if drunkenesse be not mad misterie.

Grac. But I prethee, practise some milder behaviour at the ordinarie, be not al madman.

Acut. Push,[275] ile bee all observative, and yet ifaith I grieve to see this double garded[276] age, all side-coate, all foole. Fye thou keepest the sports from the marke; away, and returne. What newes is now in progresse.

Grac. I have the newest. ***Terentia***, Daughter to the olde Senate, thogh ***Lentulus*** left the field to come to her, yet she hath forsaken him in the open field, and shee's for our young Oratour, ***Tully***; she has vowd by *Venus* legge and the little God of Love, he shall be her captaine; sheele serve under him, till death us depart,[277] and thereto, I plight thee my troth.

Acut. More Ladies *Terentias*, I crie still,
That prise a saint before a Silken foole.
She that loves true learning and pomp disdaines
Treads on *Tartarus* and *Olimpus* gaines.

Grac. I, marrie, but then would learning be in colours, proud, proud; then would not foure nobles purchase a benefice, two Sermons in a yeare.

Accut. I, *Graccus,* now thou hitst the finger right
Upon the shoulder of Ingratitude.
Thou hast clapt an action of flat felony;
Now, ill betide that partiall judgement
That doomes a farmers rich adultus
To the supremacie of a Deanrie,
When needie, yet true grounded Discipline,
Is govern'd with a threed bare Vycarage.

Grac. I, thou speakst well of their sides that are liberally overseene in the sciences. I take no hold on't, but were all men of thy minde, then would everie Schoole-maister bee a Senate, and there would never come Cobler to be Constable againe.

Accut. Ynough, ynough, *Graccus*, let silence seale up our secret thoughts and libertie say,

   Virtus sola summa gloria,
     Quae format homines vero honore.

[ACT THE THIRD.

Scene 1.]

Enter Flaminius and Tully.

Flam. Goe to, I say, urge no more, tis Taverne talke, for Taverners
Table talke for all the vomit of rumor. What newes, saies one? none so
new as this: *Tully* shall be married to *Terentia*. What newes says
another? the same, the same. Whose consent have ye? not mine, I deny it.
I must know of it, ile have a hand; goe to, no more.

Tul. Gentle Sir,
Lay not a leaden loade of foule reproach
Upon so weake a prop; what's done is past recal.
If ought is done, unfitting to be done,
The worst is done, my life must answer it.

Flam. I, you shall answer it in the Senate house, the Emperor shall
knowe it. If she be my childe, I will rule her, ile bridle her, ile
curbe her, ile raine her; if she will not, let her goe, starve, begge,
hang, drawe, sinke, swimme, she gets not a doit, a deneire, ile not owne
her.

Tul. Reverend Sir, be more patient.

Flam. I am impatient, I am troubled, I am vext, I am scoft, I am
pointed at, ile not endure it, ile not abide it, ile be revenged, I wil,
of her, of you both, proud boy, wanton giglot,[278] aspyring, hautie.
Knowe your equals, shee's not for ye, if ye persist, by my holy maker,

you shall answer it, looke to it, you shall, you shall indeede.
[*Exit*[279] *Flaminus*.

Tull. I shall, I must, I will, I will indeede,
Even to the greatest I will answere it;
If great mens eares be ope to inocency,
If greatnesse be not partial with greatenesse,
Even to the greatest I will answere it.
Perhaps, some shallow censurer will say,
The Orator was proud, he would climbe too hie;
But heaven and truth will say the contrarie.
My greatest grief is, I have my friend betraide;
The treasons done, I, and the Traitor's free,
Yet innocent Treason needes not to flee.
His loyaltie bids me abide his frowne,
And he hath power to raise or hurle me downe.

Enter[280] *Terentia*.

Tere. What ailes my *Tully*? wherefore look'st thou sad?
What discontent hath stopped the crimson current
Which ran so cheerefully within that brow,
And makes it sullen like a standing poole?
Tell me who ist hath wrong[d] my *Cicero*?
[Say,[281] is it *Lentulus*?]

Tul. Oh wrong him not.

Tere. Who is it then, that wrongs my *Tully* so?
What, hath *Terentia* ought offended thee?
Doost thou recall my former promises?
Dost thou repent thee of--

Tul. Oh wrong me not.

Tere. What, hath my father done this injurie?
There, there, my thoughts accord to say tis so.
I will deny him then, hee's not my father;
Hee's not my friend will envie *Cicero*.

Tul. Wrong not thy self.

Teren. What heavie string doost thou devide[282] upon?
Wrong not him, wrong not me, wrong not thy selfe.
Where didst thou learne that dolefull mandrake's note
To kill the hearers? *Tully*, canst thou not
Indure a little danger for my love,
The fierie spleene of an angrie Father,
Who like a storme will soon consume it self?
I have indurde a thousand jarring houres
Since first he did mistrust my fancies aime,
And will indure a thousand thousand more
If life or discord either live so long.

Tul. The like will I for sweete *Terentia*.
Feare not, I have approoved armour on,
Will bide the brunt of popular reproach
Or whatsoever.

Tere. Enough, *Tully,* we are discovered.

   Enter[283] *Flavia*.

Fla. Yfaith,[284] are ye at it? what, is there never a loving teare shed on either side? nor you? nor you? *Tullies* [eyes] are red, come,

come, ye fooles, be more breefe. I would have buried three husbands, before youle be married.

Tul. Why lives *Flavia* a Virgin still?

Fla. Because, I haue vow'd virginitie til I can get a husband.

Teren. Why, *Flavia*, you haue many suitors.

Flav. Oh, I am loaden with suitors; for indeede I am faine to beare with any of them, I have a dumbe-shewe of all their pictures, each has sent in his severall shadow, and I swear I had rather have them then the substance of any of them.

Tul. Can you not describe them in action?

Flav. Yes, and their action; I have one honest man of the age of fortie five, or there about, that traverses his ground three mile everie morning to speake to mee, and when hee is come, after the saluting ceremony, of 'how do you, Lady,' he falles to calculating the nativitie of the Moone, prognosticating what faire weather will follow, if it either snow or raine; sometime with a gentle pinche by the fingar intermixed with the volley[285] of sighes, hee falles to discoursing of the prise of pease, and that is as pleasing to me as a stinking breath.

Tul. A good description.

Fla. Another brings Letters of commendation from the Constable of the Parish, or the Church-warden, of his good behaviour and bringing up, how he could write and reade written hand; further desiring that his Father would request my Father that his Fathers Sonne might marrie my Fathers Daughter and heele make her a joynter of a hundred pound a yeare, and beget three or foure fooles to boote.

Teren. Better and better.

Tul.[286] Usus promptus [sic] facit; Faemina[e] ludificantur viros; well, forward.

Flav.[287] I have another that I prise derer then the rest, a most sweete youth, and if the wind stand with him I can smell him half a mile ere hee come at me, indeede hee weares a Musk-cat--what call ye it?--about him.

Tul. What doe you call it?

Flav. What ye will, but he smels better then burnt Rosemarie, as well as a perfuming pan, and everie night after his first sleepe writes lovesicke sonnets, railing against left handed fortune his foe,[288] that suffers his sweet heart to frowne on him so.

Tul. Then it seemes you graunt him no favour.

Flav. Faith, I dare not venture on him, for feare he should be rotten; give me nature, not arte.

Tere. Here comes Lord **Lentulus**.

Tul. Swift danger, now ride poaste through this passage.

   Enter[289] **Lentulus**.

Health to your honour.

Len. And happines to you.

Tul. In[290] heaven, deere Lord, but--

Lent. Tush, tush, on earth; come, come, I know your suite, tis graunted sure, what ere it be.

Tul. My sute craves death, for treason to my friend.

Teren. The Traitor lives while I have breath to spend,
Then let me die to satisfie your will.

Lent. Neither, yfaith, kneele not, rise, rise, I pray;
You both confesse you have offended me?

Both. We doe, we have.

Lent. Then for this offence, be this your doome:
Tulley must die, but not till fates decree
To cut your vital threed, or *Terentia*
Finde in her heart to be your Deathes-man.

Flav. Faith the Fates may doe as they may, but *Terentia* will never finde in her heart to kill him, sheele first burie him quick.

Len. The like is doomde to faire *Terentia*.
How say you both, are yee content?

Teren. My thoughts are plung'd in admiration.

Tul. But can your honour burie such a wrong?

Len. I can, I can; heere, *Tulley*, take *Terentia*,

Live many happie yeares in faithfull love.
This is no more then friendships lawes allow;
Thinke me thy self, another *Cicero*.

Flav. Twere better, my Lord, you did perswade her to think you another *Cicero*, so you might claim some interest in her now and then.

Lent. That I would claim with you, faire Ladie;
Hark in your eare, nay, I must conclude with you.

Flau. Y'oule not bite, my Lord?

Len. No, of my faith, my Lady.

Tere. Thus far, my love, our hopes have good successe;
One storme more past, my griefes were much the less.

Tul. Friendship itself hath beene more prodigal
Then a bolde face could begge upon a friend.

Lent. Why, then theres a bargaine.

Flav. Strike hands upon the same, I am yours to commaund.
Ile love with ye, ile lie with ye, ile love with all my heart,
With all my strength, with all my power and virtue:
Seald and delivered in the presence of us--

Lent. *Marcus Tullius Cicero*.
Then you deliver this as your act and deede?

Flav. I doe, and scale it with this--

Lent. Why, well said, tis done; see, we begin but now,
And are as ready to goe to Church as you.
What needes further ceremony?

Flav. Yes, a little matrimony.

Lent. I, Lady. Come *Tully* and *Terentia*;
One day shall shine on both our Nuptials;
Feare not, ile quench the fire of your Fathers heate
With my consent.

Flav. I prethee, appoint the time.

Lent. About a week hence, love.

Flav. Oh, tis too intolerable long.

Lent. Then foure daies.

Flav. Foure daies is foure times foure & twenty hours.
That's too long too.

Lent. We cannot sooner be readie.

Flav. Yes, and unreadie[291] too in a day and a halfe.

Lent. Well then two daies.

Flav. Til then weele feede on conceite; *Tully*, thanke me, but for your companie I would not tarry so long; come, *Tully*, since we shall bee married all at one time, weele goe to bed so, and he shall be maister of the Cock-pit that bids his Gossips[292] first.

[*Exeunt.*

[ACT THE FOURTH.

Scene 1.]

Enter Accutus and Graccus.

Acut. Nay quicke, *Graccus*, least our houre forestall us, ile in and deale for your disguise; tarry thou & give mine host a share of our intent; marry, charge him to keep it as secret as his Garbage. He undoes our drift [else] and cloathes the foole in sackcloath during his life.

Gra. Ile warrant thee ile manage it with as good judgement as a Constable his charge.

Acut. And I mine as a watchman his office.

Gra. Better, I hope; well about it.

[Exit [Acutus].

Enter[293] *Host. Prentices pass over the stage*.

Host. There, there my little lackey boyes, give the word as ye passe, look about to my guests there; score up at the Bar there; again, agen, my fine Mercuries; if youle live in the facultie, be rulde by instructions, you must be eyed like a Serjeant, an eare like a Belfounder, your conscience a Schoolemaister, a knee like a Courtier, a foote[294] like a Lackey, and a tongue like a Lawyere. Away, away, my brave bullies! welcome, sweete Signior, I cannot bow to thy knee, I'me as stout & as stiff as a new made knight, but if I say the word, mine Host bids the Cobler--

Gra. May I crave a word of you, mine Host?

Host. Thou shalt whisper in mine eare, I will see and say little; what I say duns[295] the mouse and welcom, my bullies.

Enter Scillicet and Getica.

Scil. By the torrid zone (sweet heart) I have thought well of you ever since I loved ye, as a man wold say, like a young dancer, out of all measure; if it please you yfaith anything I have promised you ile performe it to a haire, ere to morrow night.

Get. I wounder [*sic*] I can heare no newes of my man and my puppie.

Scil. Doe you thinke, sweet heart, to be maried by day light or by torch-light?

Get. By night is more Lady-like. Ile have a cryer to cry my puppie sure.

Scil. What thinke ye if we had an offering?

Get. That were most base yfaith.

Scil. Base, slid, I cannot tel if it were as base as a sagbut, ile be sworne tis as common as a whore, tis even as common to see a Bason at a Church doore, as a Box at a Playhouse.

Get. It greeves me not so much for my man as for my puppie; my man can shift for himself, but my poore puppie! truely I thinke I must take Phisicke even for feare, sweetheart.

Host. Tut, tut, ile warrant thee ile be as close as a bawd, ile keepe mine owne counsell, be merrie and close;[296] merrie hart lives long, let my guests take no wrong, & welcome, my bullie. [*Exit*.

Grac. There's none ment, beleeve it, sir.

Scil. Signor, by the welkin, well met, what all three so luckely?

Enter Servulus.

Ser. Gallants, saving the Ceremonie,
Stroke your haire up and admire, forsweare sacke.

Scil. Foresweare Sacke! slid, not for the spending of two farmes more, if they were come into my hands once.

Ser. I say be astonisht and forsweare sacke, for by the combustion influence of sacke five men lye breathlesse ready to be folded in the terrestiall element.

Grac. Five slaine with Sacke! ist possible?

Ser. These eyes are testators.

Scil. Nay, then tis so.

Getica. Sir, you have not heard of a puppie in your travels?

Grac. No indeede, Gentlewoman.

Ser. Five, beleeve me, Sir.

Acu. Five of one, oh devil!
What limme of him but a complete Villaine!
A tongue prophaner then Idolatrie,
His eye a beacon fixed in his place
Discovering illes, but hood-winked unto grace;
His heart a nest of vice kept by the Devill,
His good is none at all, his all is evill.

Enter[297] *Hostess.*

Hostis. Oh, the father! Gallants, yonders the most hard favoured newes walkes the streetes, seaven men going to their graves, that dyed with drinking and bisseling.[298]

Acut. Good, still, nay then I see the devill has some power over a woman more then a man. Seaven! t'will be more anon.

Get. Now I beseech *Bacchus* my puppie has not overseene[299] himself.

Scil. This is verie strange.

Hostis. And as true a report, I assure you.

Enter City-Wife[300]

Cittie wife. Out alas, where's my Gosip? Oh woman! have you not heard the newes?

Hostis. Yes, I have heard on't.

Cittie wife. Oh, woman, did your child's child ever see the like? nine men to bee buried too day, that drunk healthes last night.

Acut. Better and better, goodnes never mends so fast in the carrying: nine!

Cittie wife. They say one is your guest, **Philautus**.

Acut. And all, I dare sweare, whome ile revive againe.

Cittie wife. Well he was a propper man, yfaith.

Hostis. I, and had good skill in prick-song, yet he had a fault in his humor, as none are without (but Puritans,); he would swear like an Elephant, and stamp and stare, (God blesse us,) like a play-house book-keeper when the actors misse their entrance.

Scil. Nay, harke ye, sir, I can brooke much injurie but not that; meddle with me but not with my trade; shee is mine owne, shee's meus, tuus, suus, no man's else, I assure ye, we are sure[301] together.

Grac. Sure ye are together, sir, but is your wife your trade? You meane to live upon your wife then.

Acut. The foole has some wit,[302] though his money bee gone.

Grac. Sir, I hope ye are not offended, I assure ye I would be loath to offend the least haire of your *caput, sissiput*, or *occiput*.

Scil. *Occiput*? what meane you by *occiput*?

Grac. The former part of your head.

Scil. The former part of your head! why I hope I have not an occiput, in the former part of my head. Signior *Servulus*, what meanes he by it?

Serv. The signification of the word only amounts to this, the former part of your head.

Accut. The foole is jealious, prethee feede it.

Scil. S'lid, I cannot be so sussified; I pray you, Segnior, what meanes he by *occiput*?

Grac. No hurt, verily, onely the word signifies, and the reason is, saith *Varro*, being a great deriver from originals, it is called *occiput* for that the former part of the head looks likest the Oxe.

Scil. Likest the Oxe, by gad, if ere I come to talke with that *Varro*, ile make him show a better reason for it.

Grac. But, howsoever, it proceeded from me all in kindenes.

Scil. Sir, I accept it so, for I tell ye I am of a mollifying nature. I can strut and againe in kindnesse I can suffer a man to breake my head, and put it up without anger.

Accut. I claime that priviledge, sir, I thinke I offended you once that way.

Scil. I love ye then for it sir, yet I cannot remember that ever a Tapster broke my head, yet I call to minde I have broke many Tapsters heads.

Accut. Not as a Tapster, for I but borrow this habyt.

Scil. The fruit is knowne by the tree, by gad, I knewe by your aporn[303] ye were a gentlemen, but speciallye by your flat[304] cap.

Serv. I call to memorie, let us unite with kinde imbrace.

Cittie wife. Now well fare your harts; by my truth, tis joy to a woman to see men kinde; faith you courtiers are mad fellowes, you care not in your humors to stab man or woman that standes in your way, but in the end your kindenes appeares.

Hostis. You can resolve us, sir; we heare of great revels to be at Court shortly.

Grac. The marriage of *Lentulus* and the Orator: verie true.

Hostis. Might not a company of Wives be beholding to thee for places, that would be there without their husbands knowledge, if neede were?

Grac. A moitie of friendship that, ile place ye where ye shall sit and see all.

Cittie wife. Sit? nay, if there were but good standinges, we care not.

Acu. S'foot, *Graccus*, we tarrie too long, I feare; the houre wil overtake us, tarrie thou and invite the Guests, and Ile goe see his course mounted.

Grac. About it.

      [*Exit*[305] *Acutus*.

Hostis. Whether goes that gentleman?

Grac. About a needeful trouble; this gentleman
Hath, at the charges of his charitie,
Preparde to inter a friend of his,
Though lately entertaind a friend of yours,
Acquaintance to you all, *Philautus*; and would desire
You would with him accompany his ghost
To funerall, which will be presently on his journey.

Cittie wife. Of his charge? dyed he not able to purchase a Winding sheete?

Grac. Twere sinne to wrong the dead; you shall heare the inventorie of his pocket.

  Imprimis, brush and a Combe   o o v.d.
  Item, a looking Glasse   o o i.d.ob.
  Item, A case of Tobacco Pipes   o o iiij.d.
  Item, Tobacco, halfe an ounz   o o vj.d.
  Item, in money and golde   o o iij.d.
    Summa totalis. xix d. halfe penny.

Hostis. What was his suite worth?

Grac. His sute was colde, because not his owne, and the owner caused it to be restored as part of recompence, having lost the principall.

Re-enter[306] ***Acutus***.

Acut. What, are they readie? the Corse is on his journey hetherwards.

Grac. Tush, two womens tungs give as loud report as a campe royall of double cannons.

Enter Host, Cornutus.

Host. Tut, tut, thou art welcom; ***Cornutus*** is my neighbour, I love him as my self. Tha'st a shrowe to thy wife, gave her tongue to [*sic*] much string, but let mine Host give thee counsell, heele teach thee a remedie.

Cornu. No, no, my good Host; mum, mum, no words against my wife; shee's mine owne, one flesh, & one blood. I shall feele her hurt, her tongue is her owne, so are her hands; mum, mum, no words against your wife.

Host. Tut, tut, thou art a foole, keepe her close from the poticarie, let her taste of no licoras, twill make her long winded; no plums, nor no parseneps, no peares, nor no Popperins, sheele dreame in her sleep then; let her live vpon Hasels, give her nuts for her dyet, while a toothe's in her head, give her cheese for disgestion,[307] twil make her short winded; if that will not serve, set fire to the pan and blow her up with Gun-powder.

Cittie wife. I, I, mine Host, you are well imployed to give a man counsell against his wife; they are apt enough to ill I warrant ye.

Cornu. Mum, mum, my sweet wife, I know the world wel enough; I have an eare but I heare not, an eye but I see not, what's spoke against thee I regard not; mum, mum, I knowe the world well enough.

Cittie wife. I, and twere more seemely you were at your owne house too; your wife cannot goe abroad, but you must follow; husbands must bee fringed to their wives Petticoates. I pray you tarrie you, ile goe home.

Cor. Not so, my sweet wife, I am gone, I am vanisht; mum, mum, no anger shall stirre thee; no words, I know the world well inough.

Hostis. Twere better, by thrice deuce-ace, in a weeke every woman could awe her husband so well as she.

Gracc. Ist possible? s'foot, well I thought it had bene but a fable al this while that ***Iole*** shold make great ***Hercules*** spit on his thombes and spin, but now I see if a man were as great as ***Caesar, Julius*** or ***Augustus***, or both in one, a woman may take him downe.

Hostis. Gossip, faith ile use a little of your counsel, but my husband is so fat, I feare I shall never bring him to it.

Grac. Now, gentles, you that can, prepare a few teares to shed, for now enters a sad sceane of sorrowe.

Enter Fryer and Course.

Fryer. Man is flesh and flesh is fraile,
The strongest man at length must faile;
Man is flesh and flesh is grasse;
Consuming time, as in a glasse,
Now is up and now is downe

And is not purchast by a Crowne;
Now seede, and now we are sowen,
Now we wither, now are mowen;
Frater noster heere doth lye,
In paupertate he did die,
And now is gone his *viam longam*
That leades unto his *requiem aeternam*;
But dying needie, poore and bare,
Wanting to discharge the Fryer,
Unto his grave hee's like to passe
Having neither Dirge nor Masse:
So set forward, let him goe,
Et benedicamus Domino.

Phy. And then to *Apollo* hollo, trees, hollo.--Tapster a few more cloathes to my feete.

Omnes. Oh heavens!

Acut. Gentles, keep your places, feare nothing; in the name of God, what art thou?

Phy. My Hearse and winding-sheete! what meanes this? why, Gentles, I am a living man.

Acut. Spirit, thou ly'st; thou deludest us.

Citty wife. Conjure him, Fryer.

Fryer. *In nomine Domini* I thee charge,
Responde mihi, heere at large,
Cujum pecus, whence thou art,

Et quamobrem thou makest us start
In spiritus of the gloomy night?
Qui Venis huc us to affright,
Per trinitatem I there charge thee,
Quid tu vis hic to tell to me.

Phy. Why, Gentles, I am a living man, *Philautus*.[308] What instance shall I give ye? heare me I have sight, understanding, I know mine hostes, I see that Gentlewoman, I can feele.

Scil. Feele this Gentlewoman! s'lid if yee were ten Ghosts, ile not indure it.

Acut. Spirit, thou deludest us.

Phy. Why what should I say? will ye heare my voice, heeres not but--

Scil. Nay, that's a lye, then tis a living spirit, ile have a bout with him.

Accut. Oh sir, meddle not with shadowes. Spirit, thou lyest;
I saw thee dead, [and] so did many moe.[309]
We know ye wandring dwellers in the dark
Have power to shape you like mortallitie
To beguile the simple & deceve their soules.
Thou art a Devill.

Phy. Sweet Gent, beholde I am flesh and blood; heeres my flesh, feele it.

Cittie wife. By my troth, methinkes hee should be alive. I could finde in my heart to feele his flesh.

Grac. Trie with your Rapier, **Accutus**; if he bleede he lives.

Phy. If I bleede I die; sweet Gentlemen, draw no blood.

Accu. How shall wee knowe thou art flesh and blood then?

Grac. Take heede, **Accutus**, heele blast thee.

Phy. What instance shall I give ye? I am **Phylautus**,[310] he that must needes confesse, he was drunk in your companies last day; sweet Gentlemen, conceive me aright.

Accut. Why true, true, that we know and[311] those swilling bowels.
Death did arrest thee, many saw thee deade,
Else needles were these rites of funeralls.
And since that time, till now, no breath was knowne
Flye from you; and twentie times the houre-glasse
Hath turned his upside downe; and twenty times,
The nimble current sand hath left his upper roome.
To ly beneath, since sparke of life appeard;
In all which time my care imploide it self
To give the[e] rights of buriall: now, if you live,
Who so glad as I?

Phy. Sir, your love has showne it selfe aboundant, but the cold aire is a meanes to devorce me from your companies: mine host, let me crave passage to my chamber.

Host. Out of my dores, knave; thou enterest not my dores, I have no chalke in my house, my posts shall not be garded with a little sing song, **Si nihil attuleris, ibis, Homere, foras.**

Accut. Ha! how now man? see'st now any errors?
Nay, this is nothing; he hath but showne
A patterne of himself, what thou shalt finde
In others; search through the Globe of earth,
If there mongst twentie two thou doost find
Honester then himself ile be buried straight.
Now thinke what shame tis to be vilde,
And how vilde to be drunk: look round! where?
Nay looke up, beholde yon Christall pallace.
There sits an ubiquitarie Judge
From whom *arcana nulla abscondita*,
That see's all and at pleasure punisheth;
Thou canst not scape scot free, how cans't thou?
Why, sencelesse man in that sinne will betray
His father, brother, nay, himselfe;[312] feares not
To commit the worst of evils, secure if
Thunder-boults should drop from heaven, dreading
Nor heaven, nor hell; indeede his best state
Is worse then least, prised at highest rate.

Ser. This critique is hoarsh [*sic*], unsaverie, and reproofeful; avoyd him.

Scil. Hee speakes well, but I like not his dispraysing of drunkennes; tis Phisicke to me and it makes me to sleep like a horse with my nose in the manger. Come, sweet heart.

Hostis. Signior, *Philautus*, I pray ye a word. [*Exit.*

Acut. How now, whispering? s'foot if they should give our purpose another crosse point, where are we then? note, note.

Hostis. Heere take the key, convey yourself into the Chamber, but in any case take heede my husband see you not.

Phy. Feare not, Gentles, be thanks the guerden of your love till time give better abilitie.   [*Exit*.

Acut. Ha! nay s'foot, I must claw out another device, we must not part so, *Graccus*; prethee keepe the sceane, til I fetch more actors to fill it fuller.

Gra. But prethee, let me partake.

Acut. Not till I returne, pardon me.   [*Exit*.

Hostis. By my troth Gossip, I am halfe sick of a conceit.

Citty wife. What, woman? passion of my heart, tell me your greefs.

Hostis. I shall goe to court now, and attired like an old Darie woman, a Ruffe holland of eight groates, three inches deep of the olde cut, and a hat as far out of fashion as a close placket.

Cittie wife. Why I hope your husband is able to maintain you better, are there not nights as well as daies? does he not sleepe sometimes? has he no pockets about him, cannot you search his breeches? anything you find in his breeches is your owne.

Hostis. But may a woman doe that with safety?

Cittie wife. I, and more, why should she not? why what is his is yours, what's yours your owne.

Hostis. The best hope I have is; you knowe my Guest Mistris *Gettica*, she has pawnd her Jewels to me already, and this night I look for her Hood and her tyer, or if the worst chance, I know I can intreate her to weare my cloathes, and let me goe in her attire to Court.

Cittie wife. Or if all faile, you may hire a good suit at a Jewes, or at a broakers; tis a common thing and speacially among the common sort.

Enter Host and Constable.

Host. To search through my house! I have no Varlets, no knaves, no stewd prunes, no she fierie phagies [faces?]; my Chambers are swept, my sinkes are all scowred, the honest shall come in, the knaves shall goe by; yet will I, maister Constable, goe search through my house, I care not a sheepes skin.

Const. We are compeld to doe it, mine host; a Gentleman is robd last night, & we are to search every privy corner.

Host. Mine host is true Mettall, a man of reputation, a true *Holefernes*, he loves juice of grapes, and welcom, maister Constable.
[*Exit*.

Acut. *Graccus*, how likst thou this?

Grac. Excellent, for now must he needes fall into Constables hands, and if he have any grace, twil appear in his face, when he shall be carried through the streete in a white sheet; twill be a good penance for his fault.

Hostis. Now fortune favour that my husband find him not.

Cittie wife. Heele be horne mad & never able to indure it: why, woman, if he had but as much man in him as a Maribone, heele take the burthen uppon his own necke and never discover you.

Hostis. Alas, heere they come, lets away, Gossip.
> [*Exeunt.*

Phy. *Fortune*,[313] *my foe, why doost, &c.*

Acut. Oh fye, thats bitter prethe goe comfort him.

Grac. Faith he should be innocent by his garment; Signior, I grieve for this, but if I can help, looke for it.

Phy. I thanke ye, sir.

Const. We must contaminate our office, pray regard us as little as ye can. [*Exit.*

Accut. Me thinkes this shold put him quite out of tune now, so let him goe now to mine Host; theres he and hee, and hee,

   Theres shee, and she, ile have a bout with all:
   And critiques honneys sweetest mixt with gal.

> [*Exeunt.*

[*Scene* 2.]

Enter Host, Cornutus.

Host. Goe to, there's knaves in my house! I know of no Varlets, I have an eye has his sence, a brain that can reach, I have bene cald Polititian, my wife is my wife. I am her top, i'me her head: if mine Host say the word, the Mouse[314] shall be dun.

Corn. Not so my sweet Host, mum, mum, no words against your wife; he that meanes to live quiet, to sleep in cleane sheetes, a Pillowe under his head, his dyet drest cleanely, mum, mum, no words against his wife.

Host. Thar't a foole, thar't a foole, bee rulde by mine host, shew thy self a brave man, of the true seede of *Troy*, a gallant *Agamemnon*; tha'st a shrew to thy wife, if shee crosse thy brave humors, kicke thy heele at her huckle[315] bone.

Enter Accutus.

Acut. Gentles, most happily encountered, how good hap hath turnd two labours into one! I was addrest to both, and at once I have met both, sure I must intreate that you must not deny.

Host. Say on, my sweete bullie, mine Host will attend thee; speake roundly to the purpose, and welcome, my bullie.

Accut. Marrie thus, there are[316] great revels & shews preparde to beautifie the nuptials of *Lentulus*, and *Tully*, in which the Cittizens have the least share; now, would but you and some others that I shall collect,

Joyne hands with me in some queint jest,
Our shew shall deserve grace, and brave the rest.

Host, I have thee, brave spirit, tha'rt of the true seede of *Troy*, lets be merrie and wise, merrie hearts live long; mine Host, my brave Host, with his neighbor *Cornutus* shall bee two of the Maskers, and the Morrice shall be daunc'd.

Cor. Not so, mine Host. I dare not doe so, t'will distemper my wife, my house will be unquiet; mum, mum, I know the world, well enough.

Host. Thou shall goe, saies mine Host, merrie hearts live long; welcome, bullie! mine Host shall make one, so shall my *Cornutus*, for if I say the word the mouse shall be dun.

Enter Bos with Porters.

Porters. Save ye mine Host, heeres a parcell of Corne was directed to be delivered at your house.

Host. What ware, my little Atlas, what ware is it?

2 *Por*. I know not, but i'me sure tis as heavie as a horse and--

1 *Por*. I thinke, tis a barrel of oyle, for it spurg'd at my backe.

Bos. It was oyle, for I drew the Tap.

Grac. What, *Bos*, what mak'st thou heere?

Acc. Oh, *chara*[317] *deum soboles, magnum bovis incrementum*. *Bos*, art there, there?

Bos. As sure as you are there, Signior.

Grac. *Bos*, will ye not forsake your Cabbin?

Bos. Oh sir, he that has not a tilde house must bee glad of a thatch house. May I crave a suite of you, signior?

Grac. What suit, *Bos*?

Bos. What you please, beggars must not chuse.

Accut. *Bos* is growne misticall, hee's too dark.

Bos. I speake *Hebrew* indeede, like *Adam* and *Eve*, before they fel to spinning; not a rag.

Grac. What, naked, *Bos*?

Bos. As ye see, will ye heare my suite, signior?

Gra. Drunk, & his cloathes stoln, what theef would do it?

Bos. Any theefe, sir, but no true[318] man.

Gra. Wel, *Bos*, to obtaine a suit at my handes, and to doe some pennance for your fault, you shall heere maintaine an argument in the defence of drunkennes. Mine Host shall heere it, ile be your opponent, *Acutus* moderator: wilt thou doe it?

Host. A mad merrie grig;[319] all good spirits; wilt thou doe it, *Bos*?

Bos. Ile doo't.

Grac. Seate yee, heres my place; now, **Bos**, propound.

Bos. Drunkenness is a vertue.

Gra. Your proofe.

Bos. Good drink is full of vertue,
Now full of good drink is drunke;
Ergo, to be drunke is to be vertuous.

Grac. I deny it: good drinke is full of vice,
Drinke takes away the sences,
Man that is sencelesse is vitious;
Ergo, good drinke is full of vice.

Bos. I deny it still: good drinke makes good bloud,
Good blood needes no Barber,
Ergo, tis good to drinke good drinke.

Accu. Hee holdes ye hard, **Graccus**.

Bos. Heeres stronger proofe: drunkennes ingenders with two of the morrall vertues, and sixe of the lyberall sciences.

Gra. Let him proove that and Ile yeeld.

Host. A mad spirit, yfaith.

Bos. A drunkard is valiant and lyberall; heele outface **Mars**, brave **Hercules**, and feares not the Devill; then for the most part hee's liberal, for heele give all the cloathes off his back, though hee weepe like a Widowe all the day following; nay for the sciences, hee's a good phisitian, hee vomits himself rarelie and will giue any man else a vomit, that lookes on him (if he have not a verie good stomacke); perfect in Geomitrie, for he hangs in the aire by his own conceite, and feeles no ground; and hee's all musicall, the world turns round with him, everie face in the painted cloth, shewes like a Fairie dauncing about him, and everie spar in the house a minstrell.

Grac. Good: forward.

Bos. Then hee's a good Lawyer, for hees never without a fierie facies, *& the least* Capias *will take his* habeas Corpus:
besides, another point of a Lawyere, heele raile and rave against his dearest friends and make the world think they are enemies, when the next day theile laugh, bee fat and drunk together: and a rare Astronomer, for he has starres twinckling in his eyes in the darkest night when a wise man discernes none in the firmament, and will take great paines in the practise, for lay him on his backe in the open fields over night, and you shal be sure to finde him there in the morning. Have I sed well or shall I give you a stronger proofe? An honest man will be as good as his word: Signior *Graccus* is an honest man, *Ergo*, I must have a new suite.

Accu. The moderator concludes so, *Graccus* is overthrown so far as the damage of the suite, so away with him; come, our fire will out strip us; mine Host and you wee expect your companies; we must crave absence awhile better to furnishe our purposes: the time of day to ye.

Host. Farwel, my good bullies, mine Host has sed and the mouse is dun.

[*Exeunt*.

[ACT THE FIFTH.

Scene 1.]

Enter the dumb shew of the marriage, Lentulus, Tully, and the rest.

Enter Hostis in Getticaes apparel, Getic. in hers, & Mistris Dama.

Hostis. Come, Gossip, by my troth, I cannot keepe my hood in frame.

Cittie wife. Let me helpe ye, woman.

Get. Sir, we shall be troublesome to ye.

Gra. Oh urge not that I pray ye.

Get. I pray ye what shewe will be heere to night? I have seen the *Babones* already, the *Cittie of new Ninivie*[320] and *Julius Caesar*, acted by the Mammets.

Grac. Oh, gentlewoman, those are showes for those places they are used in; marry, heere you must expect some rare device, as *Diana* bathing herself, being discovered or occulated by *Acteon*, he was tranfigured to a hart, & werried to death with his own dogs.

Cit. W. Thats prettie in good truth; & must *Diana*, be naked?

Gra. Oh of necessitie, if it be that show.

Hostis. And *Acteon*, too? that's prettie ifaith.

Enter Caesar, Lent: Tully, Teren: Flavia.

Caes. Now, gallant Bridegroomes, and your lovely Brides,
That have ingeminate in endlesse league
Your troth-plight hearts, in your nuptial vowes
Tyed true love knots that nothing can disolve
Till death, that meager pursevant of *Jove*
That Cancels all bonds: we are to [*sic*] clowdie,
My spirit a typtoe, nothing I could chid so much
As winged time, that gins to free a passage
To his current glasse and crops our day-light,
That mistie night will summon us to rest,
Before we feele the burthen of our eylids.
The time is tedious, wants varietie;
But that I may shew what delightful raptures
Combats my soule to see this union,
And with what boundles joy I doe imbrace it,
We heere commaund all prison gates flye ope,
Freeing all prisoners (traitors all except,)
That poore mens prayers may increase our daies,
And writers circle ye with wreathes of bayes.

Grac. S'foot, *Accutus*, lets lay hold of this to free our captive.

Acu. Content; ile prosecute it.

Tul. Dread soveraigne, heaven witnesse with me
With what bended spirit I have attainde
This height of happinesse; and how unwillingly,
Till heavens decree, *Terentias* love, and your
Faire consents did meet in one to make
Me Lord thereof: nor shall it add one scruple

Of high thought to my lowly minde.
Tully is *Tully*, parentage poore, the best
An Orator, but equall with the least.

Lent. Oh no doubt, *Accutus*, be the attempt
My perill, his royall promise is past
In that behalfe. My soveraigne, this Gentlemans
Request takes hold upon your gratious promise
For the releasement of a prisoner.

Cos. My promise is irrevocable, take it;
But what is hee and the qualitie of his fault?

Acut. A gentleman, may it please your grace; his fault
Suspition, and most likly innocent.

Caes. He hath freedome, and I prethee let him be brought hither.

[Exit[321] Acut.

Perhaps in his presence we shall win some smiles,
For I have noted oft in a simple braine,
(Only striving to excell it self)
Hath corrupted language, that hath turnd
To pleasant laughter in juditious eares;
Such may this proove, for now me thinkes
Each minute, wanting sport, doth seeme as long
And teadious, as a feaver: but who doth knowe
The true condition of this *Accutus*?

Tully. My Leige, of him something my knowledge
Can discover; his spirit is free as aire,
His temper temperate, if ought's uneeven

His spleene waies downe [towards] lenitie: but how
Stird by reproofe? ah,[322] then hee's bitter and like
His name *Acute*, vice to him is a foule eye-sore
And could he stifle it in bitterest words he would,
And who so offends to him is paralell;
He will as soon reproove the Caedar state
As the lowe shrub.

Enter Acut. and Philaut.

Phy. Nay, good *Accutus*, let me not enter the presence.

Accut. Oh sir, I assure you your presence will be most acceptable in the presence at this time then a farre ritcher present. May it please your majestie, this is the man.

Caes. Let him stand forward.

Cit. W. Alas, we shal see nothing; would I were neere; now hee stands forwards.

Caes.[323] What qualities hath he, *Accutus*?

Accut. A few good ones (may it please you); he handles a comb wel, a brush better, and will drink downe a *Dutchman*, & has good skill in pricksong.

Hostis. I, ile be sworne he had, when he was my Guest.

Acut. Please it your Maiestie to commaund him?

Caes. Oh, we can no otherwise, so well be pleased.

Phy. I beseech your Maiestie, I cannot sing.

Tul. Nay, your denyall will breed but greater expectation.

Acut. I, I, please it your grace to heare? now he begins.

Phy. My love can sing no other song, but still complaines I did her, &c. I beseech your Maiestie to let me goe.

Caes. With all our heart; *Acutus*, give him libertie.

Accut. Goe and for voice sake yee shall sing Ballads in the suburbes, and if ever heereafter ye chance to purchase a suite, by what your friends shal leave ye, or the credit of your friend, be not drunk again, & give him hard words for his labour.   [*Exit*.

Caes. What, ist effected, *Graccus*?

Gra. I have wrought the foole; *Scilicet* comes alone, & his Lady keepes the women company.

Accu. Tush, weele have a room scantly furnisht with lights that shall further it.

Caes. What sound is that?

Acut. I, would ye so fain enter? ile further it: please it your Maiestie to accept what is not worth acceptance? heere are a company to Gratulate these nuptials, have prepard a show--I feare not worth the sight--if you shall deeme to give them the beholding of it.

Caes. Else should we wrong their kindnes much. ***Accutus***, be it your care to give them kindest welcome; we cannot recompence their loves without much beholdings.

Acut. Now for the cunning vizarding of them & tis done.

Hostis. Now we shall beholde the showes.

Get. ***Acteon*** and his Dogs, I pray Jupiter.

***Enter the maske and the Song**.*

Chaunt birds in everie bush,
The blackbird and the Thrush,
The chirping Nightingale,
The Mavis and Wagtaile,
The Linnet and the Larke,
Oh how they begin, harke, harke.

Scil. S'lid, there's one bird, I doe not like her voice.

***Sing againe & Exeunt**.*

Hostis. By my troth, me thought one should be my husband, I could even discerne his voice through the vizard.

Cittie wife. And truely by his head one should be mine.

Get. And surely by his eares one should be my sweet heart.

Caes. ***Accutus***,[324] you have deserved much of our love, but might we not breake the law of sport so farre as to know to whome our thankes is due, by seeing them unmaskt and the reason of their habits?

Acut. Most willingly, my Soveraigne, ile cause their returne.

Hostis. Oh excellent! now we shal see them unmaskt.   [*Exit.*

Get. In troth, I had good hope the formost had bene *Acteon*, when I saw his hornes.

Cit. wif. Sure the middlemost was my husband, see if he have not a wen in his forehead.

Enter Maskers.

Host. God blesse thee, noble *Caesar*, & all these brave bridegroomes, with their fine little dydoppers, that looke before they sleep to throw away their maiden heads: I am host of the Hobbie, *Cornut.* is my neighbour, but wele pull of his bopeeper; thou't know me by my nose, I am a mad merie grig, come to make thy grace laugh; sir *Scillicet* my guest; all true canaries, that love juce of grapes, god blesse thy Maiestie.

Acut. How now, mine Host?

Host. Ha, ha, I spie a jest. Ha, ha, *Cornutus, Cornutus*.

Acut. Nay, mine host, heeres a moate in your eye to [*sic*].

Scil. S'lid, I hope they have not serv'd me so; by the torrid y'are an asse, a flat Asse, but the best is I know who did it; twas either you or some body else; by gad, I remember it as wel as if it were done now.

Host. T[h]ou shalt answer it to my leige, ile not be so misused, ye have a wrong element, theres fire in my face, weele mount and ascend. I'me misused, the mad comrades have plaide the knaves. Justice, my brave *Caesar*.

Accut. Ile answer it, mine Host. Pardon, greate *Caesar*:
The intent was merriment, the reason this:
A true brow bends to see good things a misse,
Men turned to beasts, and such are you mine Host;
Ile show you else, you are a Goate, look here!
Now come you, this is your's, you know it, doe you not?
How old are you? are you not a Goate now?
Shall I teach you how to use a wife and keepe her
In the rank of goodnes? linke her to thy soule,
Devide not *individium*, be her and she thee,
Keepe her from the Serpent, let her not Gad
To everie Gossips congregation;
For there is blushing modestie laide out
And a free rayne to sensual turpitude
Given out at length and lybidinous acts,
Free chat, each giving counsell and sensure
Capream maritum facere, such art thou Goate.
Be not so secure. And you, my grand *Cornutus*,
Thou Ram, thou seest thy shame, a pent-house
To thy eye-browes, doost not glorie in it, doost?
Thou'lt lye in a Trucklebed, at thy wives bed feete,
And let her goe a Gossiping while thou sweepest the kitchin.
Look, she shall witnesse[325] against thee.

Corn. My wife there? I must be gone then.

Acut. Oh fye, betray not thy self so grossely.

Cor. I pray ye pardon me.

Accut. I dare not.

Cor. I sir, but afterward may come after claps. I know the world well enough.

Accut. Mischiefe of the Devill, be man, not all beast, do not lye,----both sheetes doe not.

Cit. w. I warrant this fellow has as many eies as a Lamprey, hee could never see so farre into the world else.

Accu. And thou pure asse, meere asse, thy eares become thee well, yfaith.

Scil. I think you merit to make a Musition of me, you furnish me with a good eare.

Accut. Thou deservdst it, thou't make thy self a Cucckold, be it but for company sake; thou hast long eares, and thinkest them hornes, thy onceites cuckolds thee, thou art jealious if thou seest thy wives ---- with another mans palme. And foole, thy state in that sense is the best; thou art claspt with simplicitie, (a great badge of honestie,) for the poore foole has pawnd her cloathes to redeeme thy unthriftines; be jealious no more unlesse thou weare thine eares still, for all shall be well, and you shall have your puppie againe.

Get. Shall I? by my troth, I shall be beholding to you then.

Acu. Now to ye all, be firmaments to stars,
Be stars to Firmaments, and, as you are
Splendent, so be fixed, not wandering, nor

Irregular, both keeping course together.
Shine not in pride and gorgeous attire,
When clouds doe faile the pole where thou art fixt.
Obey, cherish, honor, be kinde enough,
But let them weare no changeable stuffe;
Keepe them, as shall become your state,
Comely, and to creepe ere they goe.
Let them partake your joyes and weep with you,
Curle not the snarles that dwell upon these browes.
In all things be you kinde: of all enough,
But let them weare no changeable stuffe.

Host. Fore God a mad spirit.

Hostis. Will ye beeleeve what such a bisket brain'd fellow as this saies? he has a mouth like a double cannon, the report will be heard all ore the towne.

Cittie wife. I warrant he ranne mad for love, because no good face could indure the sight of him, and ever since he railes against women like a whot-shot.

Len. Nay, nay, we must have all friendes,
Jarring discords are no marriage musick;
Throw not Hymen in a cuckstoole; dimple
Your furrowed browes; since all but mirth was ment,
Let us not then conclude in discontent,
Say, shall we all
In friendly straine measure our paces to bed-ward?

Tul. Will *Terentia* follow?

Teren. If *Tully* be her Leader.

Host. Good bloods, good spirits, let me answer for all, none speake but mine Host; hee has his pols, and his aedypols, his times and his tricks, his quirkes, and his quilts, and his demise and dementions. God blesse thee, noble *Caesar*, and all these brave spirits! I am Host of the Hobby, *Cornutus* is my neighbour, *Graccus*, a mad spirit, *Accutus* is my friend, Sir *Scillicet* is my guest; al mad comrades of the true seede of *Troy*, that love juce of Grapes; we are all true friends, merrie harts live long, let Pipers strike up, ile daunce my cinquepace, cut aloft my brave capers, whirle about my toe, doe my tricks above ground, ile kisse my sweet hostesse, make a curtesie to thy grace; God blesse thy Maiestie and the Mouse shall be dun.

Cor. Come wife, will you dance?

Wife. Ile not daunce, I, must you come to Court to have hornes set on your head? I could have done that at home.

Host. I, I, be rulde at this time; what? for one merrie day wele find a whole moone at midsommer.

Daunce.

Caes. Gentles, wee thanke yee all, the night hath spent
His youth, and drowsie *Morpheus* bids us battell.
We will defie him still, weele keep him out
While we have power to doe it. Sound
Your loudest noise: set forward to our chamber.

Gra. Advance your light.

Caes. Good rest to all.

Omn. God give your grace God-night.

[*Exeunt*.

FINIS.

APPENDIX.

VOL. II. ***Tragedy of Sir John Van Olden Barnavelt***. In ***The Athenaeum*** of January 19, 1884, my friend, Mr. S.L. Lee, pointed out that the first performance of this remarkable play took place in August, 1619. I had thrown out the suggestion that the play was produced at Michaelmas, 1619. "I have been fortunate enough," says Mr. Lee, "to meet with passages in the State Papers that give us positive information on this point. In two letters from Thomas Locke to Carleton, the English ambassador at the Hague, I have found accounts of the circumstances under which the tragedy was first performed in London. The earlier passage runs as follows:--'The Players heere', writes Locke in London on August 14th, 1619, 'were bringing of Barnevelt vpon the stage, and had bestowed a great deale of mony to prepare all things for the purpose, but at th'instant were prohibited by my Lo: of London' (Domestic State Papers, James I., vol. cx. No. 18). The play was thus ready on August 14th, 1619, and its performance was hindered by John King, Bishop of London. The excitement that the Arminian controversy had excited in England would sufficiently account for the prohibition. But the bishop did not persist in his obstruction. On August 27th following Locke tells a different story. His words are: 'Our players haue fownd the meanes to goe through with the play of Barnevelt, and it hath had many spectators and receaued applause: yet some say that (according to the proverbe) the diuill is not so bad as he is painted, and that Barnavelt should perswade Ledenberg to make away himself (when he came to see him after he was prisoner) to prevent the discovrie of the plott, and to tell him that when they were both dead (as though he meant to do the like) they might sift it out of their ashes, was thought to be a point strayned. When Barnevelt vnderstood of Ledenberg's death he comforted himself, which before he refused to do, but when he perceaueth himself to be arested, then he hath no remedie, but with all speede biddeth his wife send to the Fr: Ambr: which she did and he spake for him, &c.' (Domestic State Papers, James I., vol. cx. No. 37). Locke is here refering to episodes occurring in the play from the third act onwards. In Act III. sc. iv. Leidenberch is visited in prison by Barnavelt, who bids him 'dye willingly, dye sodainely and bravely,' and adds, 'So will I: then let 'em sift our Actions from our ashes,'--words that Locke roughly quotes (see p. 262 of Mr. Bullen's 'Old Plays,' vol. ii.). The first performance of the tragedy we may thus assign to a day immediately preceding the 27th of August, 1619. When we remember that Barnavelt was executed on May 13th of the same year, we have in this play another striking instance of the literal interpretation given by dramatists of the day to Hamlet's definition of the purpose of playing."

I have tried hard to decipher the passages that are scored through (probably by the censor's pen) in the MS., but hitherto I have not had much success.

Vol. III.-- *The Wisdome of Doctor Dodypoll*.

The stealing of an enchanter's cup at a fairy feast by a peasant is a favourite subject of fairy mythology. See Ritson's *Fairy Tales*.

The Distracted Emperor.

William Tyndale in his ***Practyse of Prelates***, 1530, relates the wild legend of Charlemagne's dotage:--"And beyond all that, the saying is that in his old age a whore had so bewitched him with a ring and a pearl in it and I wot not what imagery graven therein, that he went a salt after her as a dog after a bitch and the dotehead was beside himself and whole out of his mind: insomuch that when the whore was dead he could not depart from the dead corpse but caused it to be embalmed and to be carried with him whithersoever he went, so that all the world wondered at him; till at the last his lords accombered with carrying her from place to place and ashamed that so old a man, so great an emperor, and such a most Christian king, on whom and on whose deeds every man's eyes were set, should dote on a dead whore, took counsel what should be the cause: and it was concluded that it must needs be by enchantment. Then they went unto the coffin, and opened it, and sought and found this ring on her finger; which one of the lords took off, and put it on his own finger. When the ring was off, he commanded to bury her, regarding her no longer. Nevertheless he cast a fantasy unto this lord, and began to dote as fast on him, so that he might never be out of sight; but where our Charles was, there must that lord also be; and what Charles did, that must he be privy unto: until that this lord, perceiving that it came because of this enchanted ring, for very pain and tediousness took and cast it into a well at Acon [Aix la Chapelle], in Dutchland. And after that the ring was in the well, the emperor could never depart from the town; but in the said place where the ring was cast, though it were a foul morass, yet he built a goodly monastery in the worship of our lady, and thither brought relics from whence he could get them, and pardons to sanctify the place, and to make it more haunted. And there he lieth, and is a saint, as right is: for he did for Christ's Vicar as much as the great Turk for Mahomet; but to save his holiness, that he might be canonised for a saint, they feign that his abiding there so continually was for the hot-baths' sake which be there." (***Works***, ed. Parker Society, ii. 265.)

Burton in the ***Anatomy of Melancholy***, Part iii., Sect. 2, Memb. 3, Subs. 5, briefly narrates the story.

In the first scene of the ***Distracted Emperor***, l. 17, for the reading of the MS. "Can propp thy mynde, fortune's shame upon thee!" we should undoubtedly substitute "Can propp thy ruynde fortunes? shame upon thee!"

Dr. Reinhold Koehler of Weimar explains once for all the enigmatical letters at the end of the play:--"The line denotes:

Nella fidelta finiro *la vita*.

For as the letters [Greeek: ph d ph n r] must be read by their Greek names, so must also the B--better written [Greek: B]--be read by its Greek name [Greek: Baeta], or by Neo-Greek pronunciation ***vita***. With this meaning the line is given in the work of Etienne Tabourot 'Les Bizarrures du Seigneur des Accords,' which is said to have appeared first in 1572 or 1582, in Chap. ii. on 'rebus par lettres.' I only know the passage by a quotation in an interesting work by Johannes Ochmann 'Zur Kentniss der Rebus,' Oppeln, 1861, p. 18. I have also found our rebus in a German novel entitled 'The Wonderful Life of the Merry Hazard,' Cosmopoli, 1706. In this book, p. 282, it is related that a priest wrote as a souvenir in Hazard's album:--

'Nella [Greek: phd]. [Greek: phnr] la [Greek: B].
As an assurance of his heart
That knows no joking
It said' ... ...

And further (p. 283):--'Hazard knew not what to make of these mere Greek letters and spent several days in fruitless thoughts, until the priest let him understand that he was only to pronounce them, then he would hear from the sounds that it was Italian and meant: Nella fidelta finiro la vita.' This is the solution of the various hypotheses that have been set up about the meaning of 'la B.'"

Vol. IV.--*Everie Woman in her Humor*.

P. 312 "*Phy*. Boy!--*Sleepe wayward thoughts*." The words "sleepe wayward thoughts" are from a song in Dowland's First Book of Songs or Airs of four parts, *1597. In Oliphant's* Musa Madrigalesca the song is given thus:--

"Sleep, wayward thoughts, and rest you with my love;
  Let not my love be with my love displeased;
Touch not, proud hands, lest you her anger move,
  But pine you with my longings long diseased.
Thus, while she sleeps, I sorrow for her sake;
So sleeps my love--and yet my love doth wake.

But, oh! the fury of my restless fear,
  The hidden anguish of my chaste desires;
The glories and the beauties that appear
  Between her brows, near Cupid's closed fires!
Sleep, dainty love, while I sigh for thy sake;
So sleeps my love,--and yet my love doth wake."

P.335. "*For I did but kisse her*."--Mr. Ebsworth kindly informs me that these words are from a song (No. 19) in The First Booke of Songs and Ayres (1601?) composed by Robert Jones. The song runs:--

"My Mistris sings no other song
But stil complains I did her wrong.

Beleeue her not, it was not so,
I did but kiss her and let her go.

And now she sweares I did, but what,
Nay, nay, I must not tell you that:
And yet I will, it is so sweete,
As teehee tahha when louers meet.

But womens words they are heedlesse,
To tell you more it is needlesse:
I ranne and caught her by the arme
And then I kist her, this was no harme.

But she alas is angrie still,
Which sheweth but a womans will:
She bites the lippe and cries fie, fie,
And kissing sweetly away she doth flie.

Yet sure her lookes bewraies content
And cunningly her bra[w]les are meant:
As louers use to play and sport,
When time and leisure is too short."

On p. 373 Philautus gives another quotation from the same song.

P. 340. "*The fryer was in the*--." Mr. Ebsworth writes:--"This song is extant among the Pepysian Ballads (the missing word is equivalent to 'Jakes'): original of 'The Friar in the Well.'"

NOTES:

[1] "The tragedy of Sir John Van Olden Barnavelt. Herdrukt naar de Vitgrave van A.H. Bullen, met een Inleidung van R. Fruin. 'sGravenhage, Martinus Nijhoff, 1884," 8vo., pp. xxxiii. 95.

[2] I fondly hoped that vol. iii. was immaculate; but on p. 21, last line, I find that *spring* has been misprinted *soring*. On p. 290, l. 3, *sewe* is a misprint for *serve*.

[3] It is curious that the next entry refers to a piece by Chettle called "The Orphanes Tragedy," a title which at once reminds us of the second plot of Yarington's play.

[4] The actor who took the part of *Truth* is to be in readiness to enter: he comes forward presently. In plays printed from play-house copies, stage-directions are frequently given in advance.

[5] *Timeless* in the sense of *untimely* occurs in Marlowe, &c.

[6] Old ed. "attended."

[7] The old form of *guests*.

[8] The word *fairing* (i.e. a present brought home from a fair) is explained by the fact that Beech was murdered on Bartholomew eve ("Tis Friday night besides and Bartholomew eve"). Bartholomew Fair was held the next day.

[9] A famous tavern in Thames Street.

[10] Proposal.

[11] Nares supposed that the expression *fear no colours* was "probably at first a military expression, to fear no enemy. So Shakespeare derives it [*Twelfth Night*, i. 5], and, though the passage is comic, it is likely to be right."

[12] "Here on" = hear one.

[13] i.e. what are you doing here so late?

[14] Old ed. "gentleman."

[15] Old ed. "ends."

[16] Mr. Rendle in his interesting account of the Bankside and the Globe Playhouse (appended to Pt. II. of Mr. Furnivall's edition of Harrison's *England*) says:--"As to the features of the locality we may note that it was intersected in all directions with streams, not shown in the map of the manor, except *Utburne*, the *Outbourne* possibly; and that bridges abounded."

[17] Use.

[18] The music between the acts.

[19] Pert youth.

[20] i.e. thread of life. (An expression borrowed from palmistry: line of life was the name for one of the lines in the hand.)

[21] Rashers.

[22] See note [105] in Vol. III.

[23] Old ed. "safely."

[24] Bushes. In I *Henry IV.*, 5, i., we have the adjective **busky**. Spenser uses the subst. **busket** (Fr. **bosquet**).

[25] I can make nothing of this word, and suspect we should read "cry."

[26] Quy. flewed (i.e. with large chaps)? Perhaps (as Mr. Fleay suggests) flocked = flecked.

[27] Old ed. "fathers."

[28] i.e. had I known. "A common exclamation of those who repented of anything unadvisedly undertaken."--Nares.

[29] 4to. "tell."

[30] Equivalent to a dissyllable (unless we read "damned").

[31] Baynard's Castle, below St. Paul's, was built by a certain Baynard who came in the train of William the Conqueror. It was rebuilt by Humphrey, Duke of Gloucester, and was finally consumed in the Great Fire of London.

[32] Perhaps this speech should be printed as verse.

[33] Own.

[34] 4to. "this."

[35] 4to. "This."

[36] 4to. "misguiseth."

[37] **White** was a term of endearment,--as in the common expression **white boy**.

[38] 4to. "ease-dropping."

[39] Dwell.

[40] Deformed, ugly (lit. branded with an iron).

[41] Cf. Middleton's *Trick to Catch the Old One*, V. 2:--

> "And ne'er start
> To be let blood *though sign be at heart*;"

on which passage Dyce remarks that "according to the directions for bleeding in old almanacs blood was to be taken from particular parts under particular planets."

[42] Is admitted to "benefit of clergy." Harrison, in his Description of England, tells us that those who "are saved by their bookes and cleargie, are burned in the left hand, vpon the brawne of the thombe with an hot iron, so that if they be apprehended againe, that marke bewraieth them to have beene arraigned of fellonie before, whereby they are sure at that time to have no mercie. I doo not read that this custome of saving by the booke is vsed anie where else then in England; neither doo I find (after much diligent inquirie) what Saxon prince ordeined that lawe" (Book II. cap. xi.). See the article *Clergie* in Cowell's *Interpreter* (1637).

[43] Brand.

[44] Therefore acted by the Queen of Bohemia's Company who at that time occupied the Cockpit.--F.G. Fleay.

[45] Some seven or eight years ago I pointed out in *Notes and Queries* that the idea of this droll incident was taken from a passage of Timaeus of Tauromenium (see Athenaeus, *Deipnosoph*., ii. 5); but others--as I afterwards learned--had anticipated my discovery.

[46] This and the following speech are marked for omission in the MS.

[47] The words "Not so, frend," are scored through.

[48] The words "*Frenshe* monster" are scored through.

[49] "Makarel" = maquerelle (a bawd).

[50] This passage illustrates 2 *Henry IV*., iv. 2:--"This Doll Tearsheet should be some *road*." See my note on Middleton's Your Five Gallants (Works, vol. iii. p. 220).

[51] Small boats with narrow sterns (Fr. pinque). Cf. Heywood's I Edward IV.:--"*Commend me to blacke* Luce, *bouncing* Bess, and lusty *Kate*, and the other pretty morsels of man's flesh. Farewell, *pink* and pinnace, flibote and carvel, *Turnbull* and *Spittal*" (Works, i. 38).

[52] Fast-sailing vessels (Span, filibote).

[53] The words "that ... husband" are scored through in the MS.

[54] This and the two following lines are marked for omission.

[55] The next word is illegible.

[56] A long barge with oars.

[57] "Misreated" = misrated? But the reading of the MS. is not plain.

[58] "Do intend" is a correction in the MS. for "have bespoeke."

[59] Old spelling of *convent*.

[60] Cautious.

[61] This speech is scored through.

[62] The reading of the MS. is not clear.

[63] Again I am doubtful about the reading of the MS.

[64] "A shewer" = ashore.

[65] Some letters are cut away in the MS. Perhaps Mildew was represented with *Judas-coloured* (i.e. red) hair; but Raphael presently describes him as "graye and hoary," and afterwards we are told that he was bald.

[66] Search, probe.

[67] The stage-direction is not marked in the MS.

[68] Track by the scent.

[69] There is no stage-direction in the old copy.

[70] This and the next three lines are marked for omission.

[71] In this soliloquy Heywood closely follows Plautus: see *Rudens*, i. 3, "Hanccine ego partem capio ob pietatem praecipuam," &c.

[72] Three cancelled lines follow in the MS.:--

"So if you ... any mercy for him,
Oh if there be left any mercy for him
Nowe in these bryny waves made cleane for heaven."

[73] This and the eight following lines appear to be marked for omission in the MS.

[74] This line is scored through in the MS.

[75] This line is scored through in the MS.

[76] The words "Some faggotts ... cloathes" are scored through in the MS.

[77] "Monthes mind" = strong desire.

[78] So the MS. But I am tempted to read, at Mr. Fleay's suggestion, "steeples."

[79] Cf. *Rudens*, ii. 1:--

"Cibum captamus e mari: sin eventus non venit,
Neque quidquam captum est piscium, salsi lautique pure,
Domum redimus clanculum, dormimus incoenati."

[80] The words "hence we may ... wretched lyfe" are scored through in the MS.

[81] In the MS. the words "whither his frend travelled" are scored through.

[82] In the MS. follow some words that have been cancelled:--"Only, for ought I can perceive all to no purpose, but understand of no such people. But what are these things that have slipt us? No countrie shall slippe me."

[83] "Salvete, fures maritimi." *Rudens*, ii. 2.

[84] Honest.

[85]   "*Trach*. Ecquem
Recalvum ac silonem senem, statutum, ventriosum,
Tortis superciliis, contracta fronte, fraudulentum,
Deorum odium atque hominum, malum, mali vitii probrique plenum,
Qui duceret mulierculas duas secum, satis venustas?

Pisc. Cum istiusmodi virtutibus operisque natus qui sit,
Eum quidem ad carnificem est aequius quam ad Venerem commeare."--*Rudens*, ii. 2.

[86] See the Introduction.

[87] In the MS. follow some cancelled words:--"Il fyrst in and see her bycause I will bee suer tis shee. Oh, *Mercury*, that I had thy winges tyde to my heeles."

[88] "Who ever lov'd," &c.--A well-known line from Marlowe's Hero and Leander.

[89] There is no stage-direction in the MS.

[90] Adulterous.--So Heywood in *The English Traveller*, iii. 1,-- "Pollute the Nuptiall bed with *Michall* [i.e. mechal] sinne." Again in Heywood's *Rape of Lucreece*, "Men call in witness of your *mechall* sin."

[91] This speech is scored through in the MS.

[92] "Whytinge mopp" = young whiting. The term was often applied to a girl. See Nares' *Glossary*.

[93] In the MS. follow two lines that have been scored through:--

"And not deteine, for feare t'bee to my cost,
Though both my kisse and all my paynes be lost."

[94] *Widgeon* (like *woodcock*) is a term for a simpleton.

[95] In the MS. follow two lines which have been so effectually scored through that I can only read an occasional word.

[96] In the MS. follows a cancelled passage:--

"*Mild* Had not thy greater fraught bin shipt with myne
We had never been oversett.

Sarl. I rather think
Had ... when fyrst the shippe began to dance
... thrown all the curst Lading over-board
Wee had still light and tight."

[97] The word *burn* is frequently used in an indelicate sense.

[98] Keys of the virginal (a musical instrument resembling a spinnet).

[99] This speech is scored through in the MS.

[100] The words "Heeres sweet stuffe!" are scored through.

[101] This line is scored through.

[102] Kill.

[103] In the left-hand margin of the MS. is a stage-direction in advance:--"Fellowes ready. Palestra, Scribonia, with Godfrey, Mildew, Sarly."

[104] Not marked in the MS.

[105] MS. "when."

[106] In the left-hand margin of the MS. is a note:--"Gib: Stage Taylor."

[107] "Too arch-pillers" = two desperate ruffians. "Pill" = ravage, plunder.

[108] "*Il a este au festin de Martin baston*, he hath had a triall in *Stafford Court*, or hath received Jacke Drums intertainment." --*Colgrave*.

[109] From this point to the entrance of Raphael the dialogue is scored through in the MS.

[110] The reading of the MS. is doubtful.

[111] "Guarded" = trimmed, ornamented.

[112] This speech is scored through in the MS.

[113] Not marked in the MS.

[114] Not marked in the MS.

[115] "Anythinge for a quiett lyfe"--a proverbial expression: the title of one of Middleton's plays.

[116] So I read at a venture. The MS. appears to give "Inseinge."

[117] Not marked in the MS. In the right-hand margin is written "clere," i.e., clear the stage for the next act.

[118] A *fisgig* was a sort of harpoon.

[119] "Poore Jhon" = inferior hake.

[120] This and the two following speeches are marked for omission in the MS.

[121] A nickname (from the apostle Peter) for a fisherman.

[122] A small box or portmanteau.

[123] Owns.

[124] This speech and the next are marked for omission.

[125] Fish-baskets.

[126] The rest of the speech is marked for omission.

[127] Bawd.

[128] i.e., **Exeunt Palestra, Scribonia, and Godfrey: manet Ashburne**.

[129] In the MS. follows some conversation which has been scored through:--

"*Fisher*. Yes, syrrahe, and thy mayster.

Clown. Then I have nothing at this tyme to do with thee.

Fisher. Marry, a good motion: farewell and bee hangde.

Clown. Wee are not so easily parted.--Is this your man?"

[130] The following passage has been scored through in the MS.:

"[*Ashb*.] Say, whats the stryfe?

Clown. Marry, who fyrst shall speake.

Fisher. Thats I.

Clown. I appeale then to the curtesy due to a stranger.

Fisher. And I to the right belonging to a ... what ere he says."

[131] The MS. is broken away.

[132] Penny.

[133] The date has been scored through in the MS.: the number after "6" has been turned into "3," but seems to have been originally "0." In the margin "1530" is given as a correction.

[134] Not marked in the MS.

[135] This dialogue between Ashburne and the Clown is closely imitated from *Rudens*, iv. 6.

[136] The words "Nowe ... scurvy tune" are scored through.

[137] Old form of *digest*.

[138] The words "will for mee" are a correction in the MS. for "at this tyme."

[139] The MS. has:--

> "Hee's now where hee's in Comons, wee ... ...
> Heare on this seate (nay hold your head up, *Jhon*,
> Lyke a goodd boy), freely discharged our selfes."

In the first line "Hee's now where hee's" has been altered to "Hee's where hee is," and the two next lines have been cancelled.

[140] The reader will remember a somewhat similar incident in the Jew of Malta, *iv. 3, and in a well-known tale of the* Arabian Nights.

[141] In the left-hand margin of the MS. is written "Fry: Jo: nod."--i.e., Friar John totters from the blow. Beneath "nod" is the word "arras," which has been scored through.

[142] i.e., I have't.

[143] The exclamation of old Hieronimo's ghost in Kyd's Spanish Tragedy. *Cf.* **Induction to** Warning for Fair Women:--

"Then, too, a filthy whining ghost
Lapt in some foul sheet, or a leather pilch,
Comes screaming like a pig half stick'd,
And cries, **Vindicta**!--Revenge, Revenge!"

[144] "**Bases**, s.pl.--A kind of embroidered mantle which hung down from the middle to about the knees, or lower, worn by knights on horseback."--*Nares*.

[145] In the right-hand margin is written "**Fact: Gibson**"--Gibson being the name of the actor who took the Factor's part.

[146] Not marked in the MS.

[147] **Quart d'ecu**--a fourth part of a crown.

[148] A quibble on the **aurum potabile** of the old pharmacists. --F.G. Fleay.

[149] In the MS. is a marginal note, "**Stagekeepers as a guard**."

[150] Sarleboyes' speeches are scored through in the MS.

[151] This speech is scored through.

[152] Mopper of a vessel.

[153] A not uncommon corruption of **Mahomet**.

[154] "Sowse" = (1) halfpenny (Fr. sou), (2) blow. In the second sense the word is not uncommonly found; in the first sense it occurs in the ballad of *The Red Squair*--

"It greivit him sair that day I trow
　With Sir John Hinrome of Schipsydehouse,
For cause we were not men enow
　He counted us not worth a *souse*."

We have this word again on p. 208, "Not a *sowse* less then a full thousand crownes."

[155] Prison.

[156] A quibble. "Points" were the tags which held up the breeches.

[157] This line is scored through.

[158] Old form of *convert*.

[159] Analytical Index to the Series of Records known as the Remembrancia (printed for the Corporation of London in 1878), pp. 215-16.

[160] See **Calendar of State Papers, Domestic**, 1611-18, p. 207.

[161] See Gilford's note on *The Devil is an Ass*, ii. 1; **Remembrancia**, p. 43; **Cal. of State Papers, Domestic**, 1611-18.

[162] Quy. "true"?

[163] Esteem, weigh.

[164] The old ed. gives: "Ile trie your courage--draw." The last word was undoubtedly intended for a stage-direction.

[165] Equivalent, as frequently, to a dissyllable.

[166] Exclamations.

[167] Vile.

[168] Not marked in the old ed.

[169] Old ed. "fate."

[170] Old ed. "brought."

[171] Old ed. "wood."--"Anno 35 Reginae (Eliz.) ... A License to *William Aber*, To Sow *Six Hundred* Acres of Ground with *Oade* ... A Patent to *Valentise Harris*, To Sow *Six Hundred* Acres of Ground with *Woade*."--Townshend's *Historical Collections*, 1680, p. 245.

[172] See my remarks in the Introduction.

[173] So the old ed. The metrical harshness may be avoided by reading "And by this sword and crownet have resign'd" (or "And by this coronet and sword resign").

[174] Owns.

[175] Old ed. "Gorges."--I suppose there is an allusion, which must not be taken too literally, to the story of Candaules and Gyges (see Herodotus, lib. i. 8).

[176] This is the unintelligible reading of the old ed.--"This action, *sure*, breeds" &c., would be hardly satisfactory.

[177] Lucian tells a story of a youth who fell in love with Praxiteles' statue of Aphrodite: see *Imagines*, Sec. 4. He tells the story more elaborately in his *Amores*.

[178] Concert.

[179] Old ed. "denie."

[180] Before this line the old ed. gives the prefix "*Val*." Perhaps a speech of Montano has dropped out.

[181] Old ed. "although no a kin."

[182] Old ed. "*light* fall soft." Probably the poet originally wrote "light," and afterwards wrote "fall" above as a correction (or "light" may have been caught by the printer's eye from the next line).

[183] *Doorkeeper* was a common term for a pander.

[184] Skin.

[185] Old ed. "crowne."--My correction restores the sense and gives a tolerable rhyme to "heare." Cf. p. 262.

"And in this Chaire, prepared for a Duke,
Sit, my bright Dutchesse."

[186] Old ed. "*Exit*."

[187] Old ed. "have her honour."

[188] In the Parliament of 1601 Sir Walter Raleigh and others vigorously denounced the exportation of ordnance. See Townshend's Historical Collections, 1680, pp. 291-5.

[189] "Letters of Mart" = letters of marque.

[190] Old ed. "now."

[191] Old ed. "when." ("Then" = than.)

[192] Old ed. "good."

[193] Old ed. "this dissemblance."

[194] See note [50].

[195] Old ed. "esteem'd."

[196] "Open ... palpable ... grosse ... mountaine." The writer had surely in his mind Prince Hal's words to Falstaff:--"These lies are like their father that begets them: **gross** as a mountain, open, palpable."

[197] Old ed. "Of Lenos mathrens." I have no doubt that my correction restores the true reading. Cf. above "**Panders** and **Parasites** sit in the places," &c.

[198] Quy. "***On***, friends, to warre"? Perhaps something has dropped out--"***Urge all*** our friends to warre."

[199] Old ed. "dishonour'd."

[200] Not marked in old ed.

[201] This speech is not very intelligible, but I can only mend it by violent changes.

[202] Old ed. "payes all."

[203] Old ed. "of this spatious play."

[204] Crack.

[205] Old ed. "sould."

[206] Old ed. "are."

[207] Old ed. "warre."

[208] Old ed. "free."

[209] Old ed. "And."

[210] Old ed. "Then."

[211] See remarks in the Introduction.

[212] Old ed. "a jemme."

[213] Quy. "creep" (for the sake of the rhyme)?

[214] Gondola.

[215] Old ed. "recover'd."

[216] "*Timelesse* lives taken away" = lives cut short by an *untimely* stroke.

[217] Old ed. "prisoned."

[218] Old ed. "playes."

[219] In *As You Like It*, Rosalind, speaking the Epilogue, justifies the novelty of the proceeding:--"It is not the fashion to see the lady the epilogue; but it is no more unhandsome than to see the lord the prologue."--Flavia is the earliest example, so far as I know, of a lady-prologue.

[220] Old ed. "Endeauours."

[221] Old ed. "smile." The emendation was suggested to me by Mr. Fleay.

[222] The old ed. gives "they are monsters *Graccus*, they call them," assigning Graccus' speech to Acutus.

[223] Old ed. "Of."

[224] The old form of *bankrupt*.

[225] *Canaries* was the name of a lively dance.

[226] A skeleton. Perhaps we should read "an atomy."

[227] Not marked in old ed.

[228] Not marked in old ed.

[229] Old ed. "Sernulas."

[230] Old ed. "Srnu."

[231] Old ed. "Here's none but only I, sing." I take the word *sing* to be a stage-direction, and the preceding words to be part of a song.

[232] "More hayre than wit"--a proverbial expression. Ray gives the proverb, "Bush natural, more hair than wit."

[233] Old ed. "Least."

[234] Old ed. "*Phy*." Scilicet is offering a second ducket to his instructor.

[235] The rest of the speech is given to "*Seru*." in the old ed.

[236] A sweet Spanish wine.

[237] Not marked in old ed.

[238] See note [63] in vol. II.

[239] Old ed. "suret."

[240] An allusion to the religious sect called *The Family of Love*.

[241] Not marked in old ed.

[242] Not marked in old ed.

[243] The old ed. gives "burbarrels." The allusion is to the *bum-rolls*,--stuffed cushions worn by women to make their petticoats

swell out. Cf. Stephen Gosson's *Pleasant Quippes*--

> "If **barreld bums** were full of ale,
> They well might serve Tom Tapsters turne."

[244] Old ed. "women."

[245] Not marked in old ed.

[246] Breeches that came below the garters.

[247] I am unable to mend this passage.

[248] Old ed. "looke."--Perhaps we should read "With him--ah, looke! looke!--the bright," &c.

[249] Old ed. "if they twang."

[250] Not marked in old ed.

[251] This is Mr. Fleay's correction for old ed.'s "Conceale."

[252] Old ed. "In on the scale."

[253] Not marked in old ed.

[254] See note [85] in vol. II.

[255] I suspect that we should read "my humour," and that the rest of the speech should be given to Flavia.

[256] The small bowl--the "Jack"--at which the players aimed in the game of bowls.

[257] Old ed. "*Scil*."

[258] Old ed. "*Sernulus*."

[259] An allusion to the *Sententiae Pueriles* of Dionysius Cato, a famous old school-book.

[260] Not marked in old ed.

[261] Old ed. "minited."

[262] The first words of a charming song printed in Bateson's *Madrigals*, 1604. Here is the song as I find it printed in the excellent collection of *Rare Poems* (1883) edited by my honoured friend, Mr. W.J. Linton:--

"Sister, awake! close not your eyes!
  The day its light discloses:
And the bright Morning doth arise
  Out of her bed of roses.

See! the clear Sun, the world's bright eye,
  In at our window peeping!
Lo, how he blusheth to espy
  Us idle wenches sleeping.

Therefore, awake, make haste, I say,
  And let us without staying,
All in our gowns of green so gay
  Into the park a-maying."

[263] "A sort of game played with cards or dice. Silence seems to have

been essential at it; whence its name. Used in later times as a kind of proverbial term for being silent."--*Nares*.

[264] Embrace.

[265] Cf. ***Titus Andronicus***, v. 1, "As true a dog as ever fought at head." In bear-bating dogs were incited by the cry ***To head, to head***! See my edition of Marlowe, iii. 241.

[266] Artery.

[267] The sword of Sir Bevis of Southampton; hence a general term for a sword.

[268] Lint applied to wounds.

[269] The mixture of muscadine and eggs was esteemed a powerful provocative.

[270] A corruption of ***Span***. "buenos noches"--good night.

[271] Old ed. "***Philantus***."

[272] Old ed. "earely."

[273] Bellafront in Pt. II. of ***The Honest Whore***, iv. 1, says--"I, though with face mask'd, could not scape the ***hem***."

[274] Old ed. "let."

[275] Old form of ***pish***.

[276] ***Guard*** = fringe. The coats of Fools were ***guarded***.

[277] "Till death us *de*part"--so the form stood in the marriage-service; now modernised to "do part."

[278] Quean.

[279] Not marked in old ed.

[280] Not marked in old ed.

[281] I have added the bracketed words; the sense requires them.

[282] A musical term.--"The running a simple strain into a great variety of shorter notes to the same modulation."--***Nares***.

[283] Not marked in old ed.

[284] Old ed. "Ye faith."

[285] Old ed. "valley."

[286] Old ed. "*Flau*."

[287] Old ed. "*Tul*."

[288] "Fortune, my foe, why doest thou frown on me?" is the first line of an old ballad.

[289] Not marked in old ed.

[290] Old ed. "Tis."

[291] "Unreadie" = undressed.

[292] To the christening.

[293] There is no stage-direction in the old ed.

[294] Old ed. "foole."

[295] "Duns the mouse"--a proverbial expression. See Dyce's Shakespeare Glossary.

[296] Old ed. "a close."

[297] Not marked in old ed.

[298] i.e. *bezzling*, tippling.

[299] "Well nigh whittled, almost drunke, somewhat *overseen*."
--*Colgrave*.

[300] Not marked in old ed.

[301] Contracted.

[302] An allusion to the proverbial expression, *Wit without money*.

[303] An old form of "apron."

[304] The citizens of London continued to wear flat caps (and encountered much ridicule in consequence) long after they were generally disused.

[305] Not marked in old ed.

[306] Not marked in old ed.

[307] Old form of *digestion*.

[308] Old ed. "Philantus."

[309] More.

[310] Old ed. "Phylantus."

[311] Quy. "and, swilling those bowels [bowls], Death did," &c.?

[312] Old ed. "him himselfe."

[313] See note [288].--In old ed. the words are given to *Grac*.

[314] See note [295].

[315] Hip-bone.

[316] Old ed. "are are."

[317] Virg. *Ecls*. iv. 1. 49. *Bovis* is of course an intentional misquotation for *Jovis*.

[318] Honest.

[319] Old ed. "prig"; but on p. 375 we have "a mad merie grig."

[320] The *City of Niniveh* and *Julius Caesar* were famous puppet-shows.

[321] Not marked in old ed.

[322] Old ed. "and."

[323] Old ed. "*Cittie Wife*."

[324] This speech is printed as verse in the old ed.

[325] Old ed. "witnesses."

www.bookjungle.com *email: sales@bookjungle.com fax: 630-214-0564 mail: Book Jungle PO Box 2226 Champaign, IL 61825*

The Codes Of Hammurabi And Moses
W. W. Davies

The discovery of the Hammurabi Code is one of the greatest achievements of archaeology, and is of paramount interest, not only to the student of the Bible, but also to all those interested in ancient history...

Religion **ISBN:** *1-59462-338-4* **Pages:** 132 *MSRP $12.95* QTY

The Theory of Moral Sentiments
Adam Smith

This work from 1749. contains original theories of conscience amd moral judgment and it is the foundation for systemof morals.

Philosophy **ISBN:** *1-59462-777-0* **Pages:** 536 *MSRP $19.95* QTY

Jessica's First Prayer
Hesba Stretton

In a screened and secluded corner of one of the many railway-bridges which span the streets of London there could be seen a few years ago, from five o'clock every morning until half past eight, a tidily set-out coffee-stall, consisting of a trestle and board, upon which stood two large tin cans, with a small fire of charcoal burning under each so as to keep the coffee boiling during the early hours of the morning when the work-people were thronging into the city on their way to their daily toil...

Childrens **ISBN:** *1-59462-373-2* **Pages:** 84 *MSRP $9.95* QTY

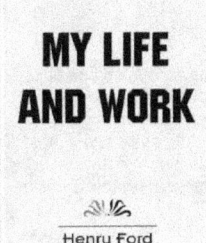

My Life and Work
Henry Ford

Henry Ford revolutionized the world with his implementation of mass production for the Model T automobile. Gain valuable business insight into his life and work with his own auto-biography... "We have only started on our development of our country we have not as yet, with all our talk of wonderful progress, done more than scratch the surface. The progress has been wonderful enough but..."

Biographies/ **ISBN:** *1-59462-198-5* **Pages:** 300 *MSRP $21.95* QTY

www.bookjungle.com *email: sales@bookjungle.com fax: 630-214-0564 mail: Book Jungle PO Box 2226 Champaign, IL 61825*

The Art of Cross-Examination
Francis Wellman

I presume it is the experience of every author, after his first book is published upon an important subject, to be almost overwhelmed with a wealth of ideas and illustrations which could readily have been included in his book, and which to his own mind, at least, seem to make a second edition inevitable. Such certainly was the case with me; and when the first edition had reached its sixth impression in five months, I rejoiced to learn that it seemed to my publishers that the book had met with a sufficiently favorable reception to justify a second and considerably enlarged edition. ..

QTY

Reference   ISBN: *1-59462-647-2*   Pages:412   *MSRP $19.95*

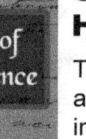

On the Duty of Civil Disobedience
Henry David Thoreau

Thoreau wrote his famous essay, On the Duty of Civil Disobedience, as a protest against an unjust but popular war and the immoral but popular institution of slave-owning. He did more than write—he declined to pay his taxes, and was hauled off to gaol in consequence. Who can say how much this refusal of his hastened the end of the war and of slavery ?

QTY

Law   ISBN: *1-59462-747-9*   Pages:48   *MSRP $7.45*

Dream Psychology Psychoanalysis for Beginners
Sigmund Freud

Sigmund Freud, born Sigismund Schlomo Freud (May 6, 1856 - September 23, 1939), was a Jewish-Austrian neurologist and psychiatrist who co-founded the psychoanalytic school of psychology. Freud is best known for his theories of the unconscious mind, especially involving the mechanism of repression; his redefinition of sexual desire as mobile and directed towards a wide variety of objects; and his therapeutic techniques, especially his understanding of transference in the therapeutic relationship and the presumed value of dreams as sources of insight into unconscious desires.

QTY

Psychology   ISBN: *1-59462-905-6*   Pages:196   *MSRP $15.45*

The Miracle of Right Thought
Orison Swett Marden

Believe with all of your heart that you will do what you were made to do. When the mind has once formed the habit of holding cheerful, happy, prosperous pictures, it will not be easy to form the opposite habit. It does not matter how improbable or how far away this realization may see, or how dark the prospects may be, if we visualize them as best we can, as vividly as possible, hold tenaciously to them and vigorously struggle to attain them, they will gradually become actualized, realized in the life. But a desire, a longing without endeavor, a yearning abandoned or held indifferently will vanish without realization.

QTY

Self Help   ISBN: *1-59462-644-8*   Pages:360   *MSRP $25.45*

www.bookjungle.com *email: sales@bookjungle.com fax: 630-214-0564 mail: Book Jungle PO Box 2226 Champaign, IL 61825*

QTY

	Title	ISBN	Price
☐	**The Rosicrucian Cosmo-Conception Mystic Christianity** *by Max Heindel*	ISBN: 1-59462-188-8	$38.95

The Rosicrucian Cosmo-conception is not dogmatic, neither does it appeal to any other authority than the reason of the student. It is: not controversial, but is: sent forth in the, hope that it may help to clear... — New Age/Religion Pages 646

☐ **Abandonment To Divine Providence** *by Jean-Pierre de Caussade* ISBN: 1-59462-228-0 $25.95
"The Rev. Jean Pierre de Caussade was one of the most remarkable spiritual writers of the Society of Jesus in France in the 18th Century. His death took place at Toulouse in 1751. His works have gone through many editions and have been republished... Inspirational/Religion Pages 400

☐ **Mental Chemistry** *by Charles Haanel* ISBN: 1-59462-192-6 $23.95
Mental Chemistry allows the change of material conditions by combining and appropriately utilizing the power of the mind. Much like applied chemistry creates something new and unique out of careful combinations of chemicals the mastery of mental chemistry... New Age Pages 354

☐ **The Letters of Robert Browning and Elizabeth Barret Barrett 1845-1846 vol II** ISBN: 1-59462-193-4 $35.95
by Robert Browning and Elizabeth Barrett Biographies Pages 596

☐ **Gleanings In Genesis (volume I)** *by Arthur W. Pink* ISBN: 1-59462-130-6 $27.45
Appropriately has Genesis been termed "the seed plot of the Bible" for in it we have, in germ form, almost all of the great doctrines which are afterwards fully developed in the books of Scripture which follow... Religion/Inspirational Pages 420

☐ **The Master Key** *by L. W. de Laurence* ISBN: 1-59462-001-6 $30.95
In no branch of human knowledge has there been a more lively increase of the spirit of research during the past few years than in the study of Psychology, Concentration and Mental Discipline. The requests for authentic lessons in Thought Control, Mental Discipline and... New Age/Business Pages 422

☐ **The Lesser Key Of Solomon Goetia** *by L. W. de Laurence* ISBN: 1-59462-092-X $9.95
This translation of the first book of the "Lernegton" which is now for the first time made accessible to students of Talismanic Magic was done, after careful collation and edition, from numerous Ancient Manuscripts in Hebrew, Latin, and French... New Age/Occult Pages 92

☐ **Rubaiyat Of Omar Khayyam** *by Edward Fitzgerald* ISBN: 1-59462-332-5 $13.95
Edward Fitzgerald, whom the world has already learned, in spite of his own efforts to remain within the shadow of anonymity, to look upon as one of the rarest poets of the century, was born at Bredfield, in Suffolk, on the 31st of March, 1809. He was the third son of John Purcell... Music Pages 172

☐ **Ancient Law** *by Henry Maine* ISBN: 1-59462-128-4 $29.95
The chief object of the following pages is to indicate some of the earliest ideas of mankind, as they are reflected in Ancient Law, and to point out the relation of those ideas to modern thought. Religiom/History Pages 452

☐ **Far-Away Stories** *by William J. Locke* ISBN: 1-59462-129-2 $19.45
"Good wine needs no bush, but a collection of mixed vintages does. And this book is just such a collection. Some of the stories I do not want to remain buried for ever in the museum files of dead magazine-numbers an author's not unpardonable vanity..." Fiction Pages 272

☐ **Life of David Crockett** *by David Crockett* ISBN: 1-59462-250-7 $27.45
"Colonel David Crockett was one of the most remarkable men of the times in which he lived. Born in humble life, but gifted with a strong will, an indomitable courage, and unremitting perseverance... Biographies/New Age Pages 424

☐ **Lip-Reading** *by Edward Nitchie* ISBN: 1-59462-206-X $25.95
Edward B. Nitchie, founder of the New York School for the Hard of Hearing, now the Nitchie School of Lip-Reading, Inc, wrote "LIP-READING Principles and Practice". The development and perfecting of this meritorious work on lip-reading was an undertaking... How-to Pages 400

☐ **A Handbook of Suggestive Therapeutics, Applied Hypnotism, Psychic Science** ISBN: 1-59462-214-0 $24.95
by Henry Munro Health/New Age/Health/Self-help Pages 376

☐ **A Doll's House: and Two Other Plays** *by Henrik Ibsen* ISBN: 1-59462-112-8 $19.95
Henrik Ibsen created this classic when in revolutionary 1848 Rome. Introducing some striking concepts in playwriting for the realist genre, this play has been studied the world over. Fiction/Classics/Plays 308

☐ **The Light of Asia** *by sir Edwin Arnold* ISBN: 1-59462-204-3 $13.95
In this poetic masterpiece, Edwin Arnold describes the life and teachings of Buddha. The man who was to become known as Buddha to the world was born as Prince Gautama of India but he rejected the worldly riches and abandoned the reigns of power when... Religion/History/Biographies Pages 170

☐ **The Complete Works of Guy de Maupassant** *by Guy de Maupassant* ISBN: 1-59462-157-8 $16.95
"For days and days, nights and nights, I had dreamed of that first kiss which was to consecrate our engagement, and I knew not on what spot I should put my lips..." Fiction/Classics Pages 240

☐ **The Art of Cross-Examination** *by Francis L. Wellman* ISBN: 1-59462-309-0 $26.95
Written by a renowned trial lawyer, Wellman imparts his experience and uses case studies to explain how to use psychology to extract desired information through questioning. How-to/Science/Reference Pages 408

☐ **Answered or Unanswered?** *by Louisa Vaughan* ISBN: 1-59462-248-5 $10.95
Miracles of Faith in China Religion Pages 112

☐ **The Edinburgh Lectures on Mental Science (1909)** *by Thomas* ISBN: 1-59462-008-3 $11.95
This book contains the substance of a course of lectures recently given by the writer in the Queen Street Hall, Edinburgh. Its purpose is to indicate the Natural Principles governing the relation between Mental Action and Material Conditions... New Age/Psychology Pages 148

☐ **Ayesha** *by H. Rider Haggard* ISBN: 1-59462-301-5 $24.95
Verily and indeed it is the unexpected that happens! Probably if there was one person upon the earth from whom the Editor of this, and of a certain previous history, did not expect to hear again... Classics Pages 380

☐ **Ayala's Angel** *by Anthony Trollope* ISBN: 1-59462-352-X $29.95
The two girls were both pretty, but Lucy who was twenty-one who supposed to be simple and comparatively unattractive, whereas Ayala was credited, as her Bombwhat romantic name might show, with poetic charm and a taste for romance. Ayala when her father died was nineteen... Fiction Pages 484

☐ **The American Commonwealth** *by James Bryce* ISBN: 1-59462-286-8 $34.45
An interpretation of American democratic political theory. It examines political mechanics and society from the perspective of Scotsman James Bryce Politics Pages 572

☐ **Stories of the Pilgrims** *by Margaret P. Pumphrey* ISBN: 1-59462-116-0 $17.95
This book explores pilgrims religious oppression in England as well as their escape to Holland and eventual crossing to America on the Mayflower, and their early days in New England... History Pages 268

www.bookjungle.com email: sales@bookjungle.com fax: 630-214-0564 mail: Book Jungle PO Box 2226 Champaign, IL 61825

QTY

The Fasting Cure *by **Sinclair Upton*** ISBN: *1-59462-222-1* **$13.95**
In the Cosmopolitan Magazine for May, 1910, and in the Contemporary Review (London) for April, 1910, I published an article dealing with my experiences in fasting. I have written a great many magazine articles, but never one which attracted so much attention... *New Age/Self Help/Health Pages 164*

Hebrew Astrology *by **Sepharial*** ISBN: *1-59462-308-2* **$13.45**
In these days of advanced thinking it is a matter of common observation that we have left many of the old landmarks behind and that we are now pressing forward to greater heights and to a wider horizon than that which represented the mind-content of our progenitors... *Astrology Pages 144*

Thought Vibration or The Law of Attraction in the Thought World ISBN: *1-59462-127-6* **$12.95**
*by **William Walker Atkinson***
Psychology/Religion Pages 144

Optimism *by **Helen Keller*** ISBN: *1-59462-108-X* **$15.95**
Helen Keller was blind, deaf, and mute since 19 months old, yet famously learned how to overcome these handicaps, communicate with the world, and spread her lectures promoting optimism. An inspiring read for everyone... *Biographies/Inspirational Pages 84*

Sara Crewe *by **Frances Burnett*** ISBN: *1-59462-360-0* **$9.45**
In the first place, Miss Minchin lived in London. Her home was a large, dull, tall one, in a large, dull square, where all the houses were alike, and all the sparrows were alike, and where all the door-knockers made the same heavy sound... *Childrens/Classic Pages 88*

The Autobiography of Benjamin Franklin *by **Benjamin Franklin*** ISBN: *1-59462-135-7* **$24.95**
The Autobiography of Benjamin Franklin has probably been more extensively read than any other American historical work, and no other book of its kind has had such ups and downs of fortune. Franklin lived for many years in England, where he was agent... *Biographies/History Pages 332*

Name	
Email	
Telephone	
Address	
City, State ZIP	

☐ Credit Card   ☐ Check / Money Order

Credit Card Number	
Expiration Date	
Signature	

Please Mail to: Book Jungle
PO Box 2226
Champaign, IL 61825
or Fax to: 630-214-0564

ORDERING INFORMATION

web: *www.bookjungle.com*
email: *sales@bookjungle.com*
fax: *630-214-0564*
mail: *Book Jungle PO Box 2226 Champaign, IL 61825*
or PayPal *to sales@bookjungle.com*

Please contact us for bulk discounts

DIRECT-ORDER TERMS

**20% Discount if You Order
Two or More Books**
Free Domestic Shipping!
Accepted: Master Card, Visa,
Discover, American Express

www.ingramcontent.com/pod-product-compliance
Lightning Source LLC
Chambersburg PA
CBHW080538230426
43663CB00015B/2630